NAPOLEON'S
INVASION
OF EGYPT

NAPOLEON'S INVASION OF EGYPT

AN EYEWITNESS HISTORY

JONATHAN NORTH

AMBERLEY

Half-title page: A French infantry corporal in Egypt.

Title page: French scholars climb and measure the sphynx.

First published 2023

Amberley Publishing
The Hill, Stroud
Gloucestershire, GL5 4EP

www.amberley-books.com

British Library Cataloguing in Publication Data.
A catalogue record for this book is available from the British Library.

ISBN 978 1 3981 1031 1 (hardback)
ISBN 978 1 3981 1032 8 (ebook)

1 2 3 4 5 6 7 8 9 10

Typeset in 10pt on 12.5pt Sabon.
Typesetting by SJmagic DESIGN SERVICES, India.
Printed in the UK.

Contents

List of
Illustrations and Maps

Illustrations

1. The expeditionary force embarks in May 1798.
2. Denon's plan of the battle of the pyramids.
3. Baron Lejeune's almost panoramic painting of the battle of the pyramids.
4. Detail from Baron Lejeune's painting. (Courtesy of Yves Martin.)
5. Detail showing French infantry storming the village during the closing moments of the battle of the pyramids. (Courtesy of Yves Martin.)
6. A Mameluke charge.
7. French cavalry fighting the Mamelukes.
8. Guérin's depiction of Napoleon pardoning the rebels of Cairo.
9. Map of the Battle of the Nile.
10. Napoleon's fleet, and his future plans, was destroyed by Nelson in Aboukir Bay.
11. The costumes of the Egyptians.
12. Denon's sketch of an Egyptian woman.
13. Two views of Egyptian villages.
14. Another Egyptian village, sketched by André Dutertre.
15. A British caricature by Gillray depicting two of the French expedition's scholars.
16. The scholars at the Institute of Egypt.
17. Sir Sidney Smith and his marines and sailors assist local forces under the Bosnian warlord Djezzar in driving back Napoleon's infantry assaults at Acre in the spring of 1799.
18. Napoleon visiting the plague house at Jaffa.
19. Some British naval officers visit a Turkish encampment.
20. Baron Lejeune's magnificent painting of the battle of Aboukir.
21. The artist's sketch of the same scene.

Maps

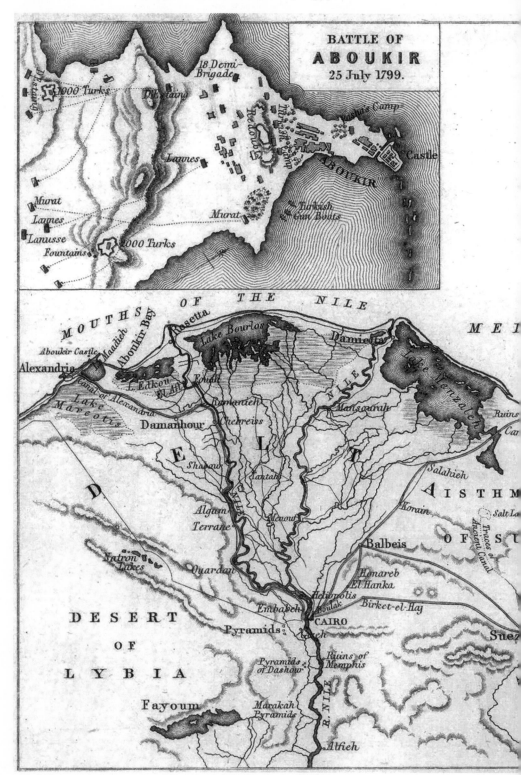

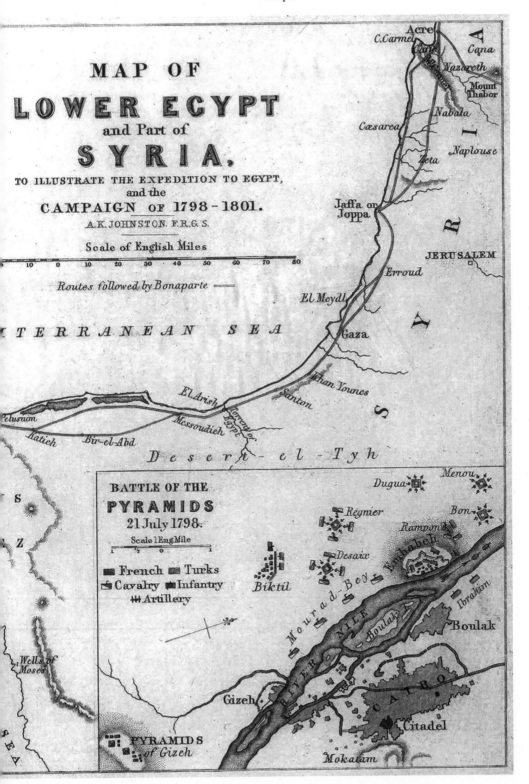

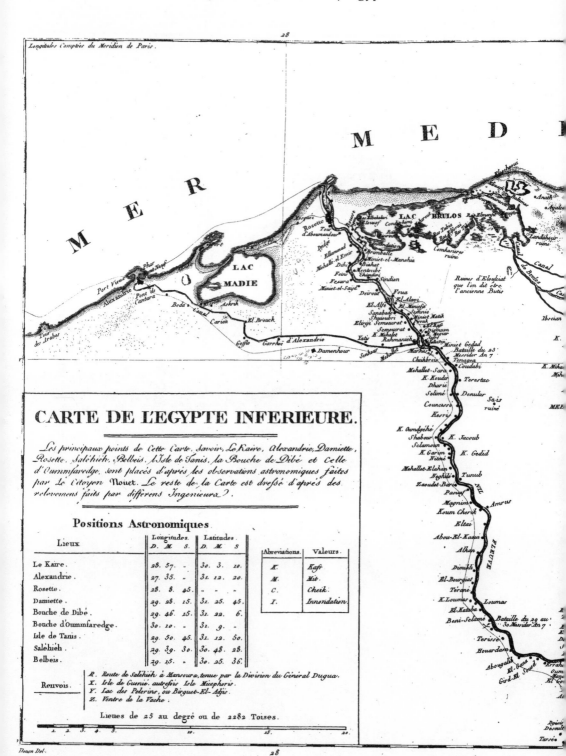

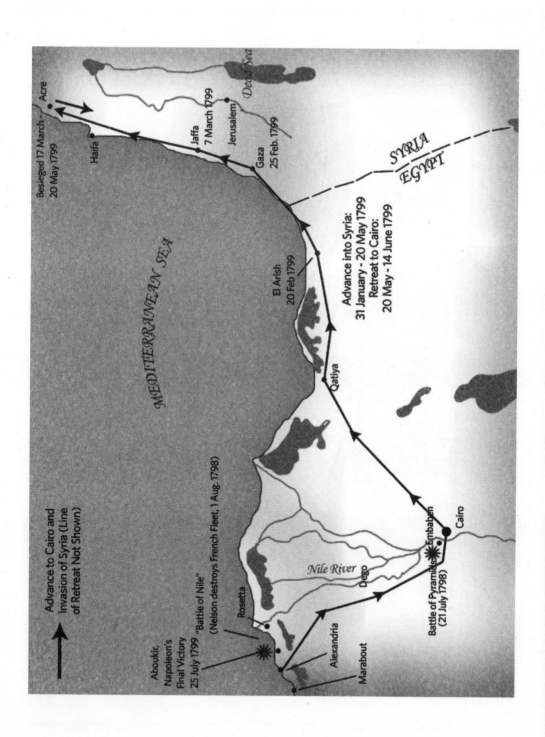

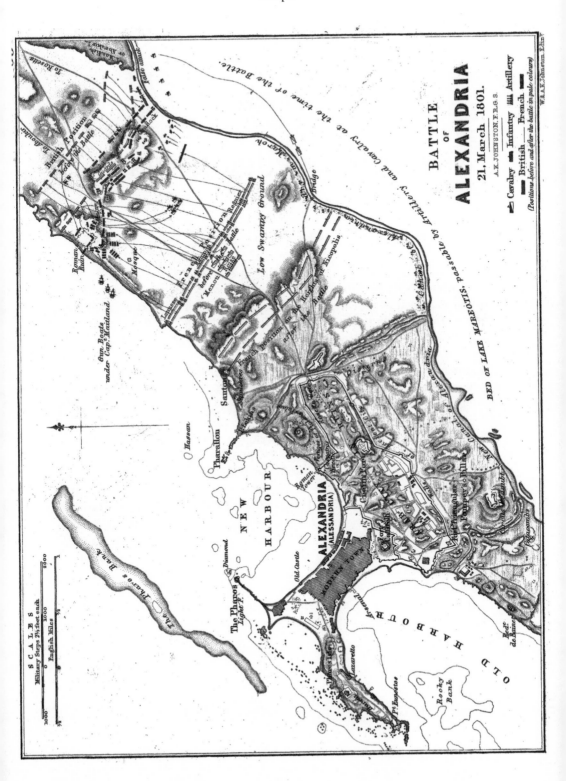

BATTLE
OF
ALEXANDRIA
21. March 1801.

A.K. JOHNSTON, F.R.G.S.

Cavalry — Infantry — Artillery
— British — French
(Positions before and after the battle in pale colours)

W & A.K.Johnston, Edin.

BED OF LAKE MAREOTIS, passable by Artillery and Cavalry at the time of the Battle.

Acknowledgements

I would like to thank Hossam Al-Abbady, Jacques-Olivier Boudon, Tom Holmberg, David Markham, Yves Martin, Alexander Mikaberidze, Jonas de Neef, Evgeniya Prusskaya, Andrew Roberts, Dr Fergus Robson, Diana Saville, Shannon Selin, Steven H. Smith, Tian Wu and Eman Vovsi for their support and inspiration, and for providing obscure material. There, too, I am grateful to Laetitia Gallet of the Société Française d'Egyptologie and, for allowing me permission to use material from François Leclerc D'Ostein's writings, to Frank Grognet of the Association Belge Napoléonienne.

I owe a debt of thanks to the staff of the British Library; the London Library; the Institute of Historical Research; the Morrab Library; the Institut Napoléon; Dr Clare Lappin of the Warburg Institute; Peter Harrington of the Anne S. K. Brown Military Collection; Peter Hicks and Chantel Prévot of the Fondation Napoleon; and the anonymous individuals who have made the Bibliothèque Nationale de France's Gallica repository such a useful resource. I would also like to thank participants at the Napoleon Series and Napoleonic Wars fora, and the La Campagne en Egypte Facebook group, and, indeed, everyone else who only hears from me when I need something. Shaun Barrington, Alex Bennett and the Amberley team have done an excellent job, as usual, and I thank them all for taking the risk.

Finally, my gratitude also goes out to my parents (Arab horse enthusiasts), and, last but not least, to Evgenia and Alexander for their spoken and unspoken support.

A Note on Money

By 1798 the French were supposed to be using the franc, but many still referred to this as the livre. 24 livres was worth 1 Louis d'or, and 6 livres was 1 écu. A livre could be subdivided into 20 sous or sols. In Egypt, the French worked in parats (1 parat being 2 centimes) or médins (1 franc to 28 médins). This is a simplification, as there were also gourdes, pataques, talaris and piastres in circulation. So too were French uniform buttons as Savary noted: 'We spent twenty-four hours at El-Burck and the locals sold us a quantity of all kinds of things, preferring to accept the soldiers' buttons as payment rather than the gold coins our men offered.' And Vertray was surprised to be presented with 'five or six tin uniform buttons which he [the tradesman] had received from my compatriots' as change.

The French found Egypt cheaper than Europe, although the exchange rate fluctuated wildly. Jean-Pierre Doguereau bought a hat for 3½ Louis which would have cost 4 Louis in France. A bath cost 2½ piastres and a nag 50. The officer of dragoons helpfully listed the cost of day-to-day items, including 'a goose for 35 parats, a chicken for 15 sols [sous], a pair of pigeons 18 sols, three eggs for 3 liards or a parat. Most difficult to obtain was meat, but when it was available it was just 6 sols for a pound of beef and 8 for mutton.' Quartermaster François was savvier and had it that a parat would buy you 'a pair of pigeons, a chicken or chick, or 12 eggs'. More troubling purchases could include a slave 'for 300 or 500 francs in our money' or a child for 250 francs.

To put all this in context, a secretary would receive 150 francs a month, and an assistant nurse 80 francs.

Introduction

Napoleon Bonaparte was a dreamer before and after he became a soldier. He began early, although much of his childhood and early adolescence was spent wandering the dreary deserts of sentimental literature and poetry before, thankfully, his imagination was rescued by that saviour of many a feckless youth, a healthy interest in history. As a schoolboy in France, he took to devouring the chronicles of empires and tales of great deeds. He turned to Plutarch and Xenophon for the lives of ancient heroes, and to Marigny on the Arabs and Tott on the Turks for descriptions of exotic lands. In bleak Autun or dull Brienne, the exploits of Alexander the Great besieged his imagination and stories from the deserts of the Mamelukes, the mountains of the Druzes or the valleys of the Kurds beyond Lebanon captivated the mind of this passionately unhappy outsider.

After school, and armed only with his ambition and the improved judgement that a love of history usually confers, the military profession claimed him before, unexpectedly, the revolution which engulfed France in 1789 changed his fate as well as that of his adopted country. Still, for all the drama around him, Napoleon could not quite set aside those dead heroes from distant lands. Indeed, his thirst for adventure would often return, most especially when ambition clamoured too loudly or glory was too quiet.

Although the revolution would be his making, glory was very quiet indeed in its early years, and drab garrisons hardly satisfied Napoleon's ambition. He was sufficiently restless in 1791 to petition Russia, offering to join General Vassily Tomara and his Corsicans in the service of the czar. Nothing came of it, but a few years later he was setting his sights on India, declaring his wish to go and wage war among the Maharajahs. Promotion following the siege of Toulon postponed such ideas but, in the summer of 1795, threatened with desk duty in Paris, Napoleon again began to dream, requesting that he be included in a mission to Constantinople to reform the

Ottoman artillery.[1] Fate again determined otherwise, and the new general of brigade was disappointed not to be following in the footsteps of Alexander and his Greek heroes. Perhaps it was just as well, for, in the following year, fame and glory finally beckoned, but in lands more familiar to Caesar than to Alexander.

In 1796, aged just twenty-six, Napoleon conquered Italy. His victories came at a critical time. France had been at war with the crowned heads of Europe and had fought all the kings' men to a stalemate by 1795. Then General Bonaparte broke the impasse by sweeping across Italy, beating the Piedmontese, the Austrians and the Neapolitans, and even, in the spring of 1797, closing the golden book on the republic of Venice. His success was such that, by the summer of 1797, the coalition against France included just moribund Portugal and truculent Britain. Portugal could easily be ignored. Britain, relentlessly hostile and busy gorging on European colonies, could not.

The French republic was happy to pause and digest its prey. It dominated the continent, establishing sister republics to replace regal rivals, although, in truth, not very much of the revolution was now crossing France's frontiers; indeed, for many, the revolution had now been reduced to little more than slogans and perpetual war. This was understandable as, following the enthusiasm of the early days, and the terror of more recent ones, the republic's government had stagnated into the Directory, an oligarchy whose ambition was global and whose greed was absolute. Paris was by now waging war for profit and, in that sense, Napoleon, the victor of Italy, was a blessing. Yet the oligarchs also acknowledged that his success came with a certain element of risk. Sensing their own unpopularity, they feared their brilliant general might turn to politics and upstage them, much as Caesar had after Gaul. It would be wise, therefore, to keep him active in the field. But how to do so against Britain, ringed as she was by protective fleets, safe from a France triumphant on land but a constant failure at sea?

That was the challenge. Fortunately, it was one which appealed to Napoleon. His long feud with Albion would last a lifetime but it had noticeably festered since a British sergeant had stuck a spontoon in his thigh at Toulon in 1793. Napoleon saw that taking the war to Britain would be difficult for a country whose navy had been ruined by war and revolution. The direct approach, seizing enough time to launch an army across the Channel, was too risky even for Napoleon. An alternative might be to coax the unhappy Irish into driving the British from Dublin and the government from Whitehall. A brave attempt had actually been made in late 1796, but General Hoche's expedition could

---

1. He wanted to lead a delegation of French technical officers including Junot, La Chasse, Livrat and Marmont. The government response was tardy and Napoleon lost interest. In early 1796 a delegation was actually sent off under Captain Camus and Antoine Pampelonne, director of the gun foundry at Lyon.

not master the Atlantic long enough to make a landing on that distant shore. Ireland, it seemed, was on the wrong side of geography.

Napoleon, as was often the case, determined to strike from a different direction. The general was still in Italy, heading to Passeriano near the Adriatic coast to sign a peace with humiliated Austria. As he set out, he imagined a cunning blow against Britain's purse, the sinews of her lonely struggle. He would use the Greek islands he had wrested from Venice as stepping stones and tip-toe across the Mediterranean to strangle the flow of wealth and goods pouring through the Middle East from British India. Napoleon would be waging his war on Britain for France, but he would also now be embarking on his own personal adventure in the east. Except this time he would be taking an army with him.

Napoleon's idea was to conquer Egypt, and in the late summer of 1797 the conqueror of Italy presented his scheme to the French government:

> The islands of Corfu, Zante and Cephalonia are of more interest to us than the whole of Italy. It is my belief that it would be better to keep these four islands [*sic*], as they are a source of such wealth and prosperity for our trade, and to return Italy to the [Austrian] emperor. The empire of the Turks crumbles with each passing day and possession of the islands allows us either to prop it up or be ready to take our share. The time is not far off when we shall see that in order to destroy England we must seize Egypt. The death of the vast Ottoman empire obliges us to prepare for measures to conserve our trade in the east.[2]

It was an imaginative idea but not an entirely original one, for French governments had periodically seen possession of Egypt as a way of hijacking the wealth flowing from India to Europe.[3] The current oligarchy could be seduced by the promise of gain, and Napoleon knew that being a prophet of profit

---

2. Written from Milan on 16 August 1797. That same day he told Talleyrand, 'It would be pointless to prop up the Turkish empire, we shall see it fall within our lifetimes. Corfu and Zante make us masters of the Adriatic and the Levant.' Talleyrand agreed, telling Napoleon, 'Nothing is more important than getting a hold over Albania, Greece, Macedonia and the other Turkish provinces in Europe and indeed all those that are on the Mediterranean, particularly Egypt which, one day, will be so very useful.' Talleyrand's view was also that 'a colony like Egypt will soon replace the West Indies when it comes to manufactures'.

3. There had been several plans since the reign of Louis XIV. The Duke de Choiseul had seen the conquest of Egypt as straightforward, having observed how badly the Ottomans had performed in the wars against Russia, and as a way of compensating France for the losses of the Seven Years War. The French got no further than taking possession of Corsica, itself a significant development. It was in late 1794 that the French government began to consider plans to seize Egypt and send troops to Suez then across the Red Sea rather than have them sail around the Cape of Good Hope.

would win Paris round, but the glory of playing a modern Alexander was more appealing to him than balance sheets and ledger books. He would therefore promote the conquest of Egypt as one guaranteeing the wealth needed by a modern empire but also one conferring the prestige of emulating an ancient one.

Meanwhile, the hero of his own romance spent much of September 1797 at Passeriano, carving up Venice and Austria but finding time to share his ideas with a small group of confidants. The liberation of Greece and Albania was certainly mentioned, but Colonel Marmont remembered how 'it was then that the Egyptian project began to form. General Bonaparte talked openly of this ancient land, his passions brimming with examples from history, and he enjoyed himself thinking up realistic and outlandish plans for the orient.' General Desaix, who had travelled overland from pretty Parma, had scarcely brushed the dust from his coat before Napoleon collared him with his enthusiasm:

> Ideas about Egypt and its resources. Project relating to it. Peace with Austria and England. Depart from Venice with 10,000 men and 8,000 Poles. Seize it, advantages, details. With five divisions, 200 guns. Concentration of the necessary equipment, qualified men. Travels of Savary, Volney, etc, communication with Greek leaders. Greek printer at Ancona.[4]

Desaix himself thought the idea a good one, but, in distant Paris, Napoleon needed his friend and patron, the lame former bishop Talleyrand, recently grown influential in the Directory's nest of vipers, to release the funds. Napoleon therefore badgered his sympathetic friend with letters, writing that 'we have to take Egypt ... we can leave from here with 25,000 men escorted by eight or ten warships or Venetian frigates, and grab it'. His only worries were how the Turks, traditionally a French ally and nominally in charge of Egypt, might react and that strategic Malta, which served as the door to Egypt, might be overlooked. Napoleon closed by reminding Talleyrand that Europe was now at their feet, although it was also clear that Asia and Africa, too, were not beyond the compass of his reach.

That December, with the peace of Campo Formio with Austria signed, Napoleon returned to Paris. The government, unnerved, hastily sent him off to command the Army of England then massing in northern France. The general obliged, enjoying his favourite pastime of organising armies, but, following a freezing tour of the Channel ports in early 1798, soon returned to inform the government that the French Channel fleet was not yet seaworthy. The Army of England would not be crossing the straits anytime soon, and Napoleon began channelling his energies into promoting his more exotic scheme for Britain's ruin.

---

4. Desaix, p. 255. Volney's real name was Chasseboeuf and he had visited Egypt in 1783. His view was that Egypt was suffering from a crisis of despotism and that Reason and Reform would transform it into a flourishing state. His academic rival, Savary, was more prone to romanticising the east.

The Directory was wise enough to see the advantages of a distant war in which victory would reflect well on them and defeat could be ignored entirely, and so it proved receptive. Few, of course, knew anything of the actual state of Egypt, with even the experts relying on the reports of travellers and merchants from a decade or so ago. What was known was that the ailing Ottoman empire thought it ruled Egypt, and still had a viceroy in Cairo, but that by the 1780s a military caste of slaves turned masters, the Mamelukes, had won autonomy. Two Mameluke warlords, the calculating Ibrahim Bey and flamboyant Mourad Bey, emerged only to divide the province, fatally weakening their rule. The former consul in Cairo, Charles Magallon, who, like all salesmen, was trained to recognise an opportunity in the weakness of others, informed the government that the Ottomans would be in no position to object should the French act[5] and that, with the Mamelukes squabbling, Egypt was ripe for the picking. Magallon had a weighty champion in the form of Talleyrand, newly appointed to the plum position of Minister of Foreign Affairs. Indeed, even before he was the Directory's expert on the lands beyond Paris, Talleyrand, the offspring of a messy copulation between power and greed, had been dreaming of capturing the Levant and dominating the trade routes to the east, thinking Egypt a more profitable colony than the expensive West Indies and Louisiana, assets which could be traded for yet more money with the Americans.

So it was that invading Egypt suited the general, the merchant and the minister, leaving only the government to provide the money. That government raised the sensible objection that the Turks might look unkindly on what was tantamount to a stab in their back, a criticism that obliged Talleyrand to turn on his silkiest charm. On 14 February 1798, as Napoleon was off inspecting Ostend in the rain, he stood before the Directors, tempting them with the economic importance of Egypt, and promising them that the Egyptians themselves, wearying of the exactions of the Mamelukes, would rise up and welcome the sons of liberty. His enthusiasm propelled him into suggesting that if Alexandria could be occupied then Cairo and Suez could be too, and that, from there, 15,000 French soldiers could even be sent across the Red Sea to aid Tipu Sultan in his war against the British in Bengal.[6] His promise of wealth

---

5. Recent reports by Jacques-Charles Dubois-Thainville and by Joseph Felix Łazowski, born in Lorraine to a Polish father and French mother, had stressed the absolute moral and military decay of the Ottoman empire.

6. Tipu had sent ambassadors, including his nephew, to Paris to request help in August 1788 but none had been forthcoming. On 14 April 1798, Napoleon had asked that Commandant Piveron be sent as special envoy to India to renew his contacts there, and a week later Napoleon sent letters to the King of Ceylon, Tipu Sultan and the Lord of Tanjaour, as well as copies of the letter with actual names and titles left blank to be completed later, asking potentates to unite against the English. Piveron only made it as far as Corfu, however.

and easy empire was persuasive, and when General Bonaparte returned to Paris with final confirmation that crossing the grey Channel was impossible, the government agreed that the invasion of Egypt would do instead. A jubilant Talleyrand immediately congratulated himself on his influence, whilst the general turned to his favourite occupation of transforming the vaguest of plans into timetables, lists of regiments and columns of figures.

On 5 March 1798 Napoleon submitted his detailed proposals for the occupation and exploitation of Egypt. With the Spanish promising to prevent British ships from entering the Mediterranean, he would embark between 20,000 and 25,000 of his best infantry, and 2,000 to 3,000 cavalry, on convoys of requisitioned transports from Toulon, Marseilles, Nice, Antibes and Corsica. This flotilla would be protected by France's Mediterranean fleet as would smaller convoys carrying the veterans of the Army of Italy from Civita-Vecchia and Genoa. Napoleon's armada would then seize Malta before landing at Alexandria and conquering Egypt.

With plans approved, and funds promised, a vanguard of officials was despatched to the southern coast to acquire those transports and purchase supplies.[7] Napoleon's divisions, regiments, battalions and squadrons were then formed up and readied to be sent to the waiting ports. Finally, in a respectful nod to Enlightenment ideals, and at Napoleon's personal behest, a select body of scholars, scientists and engineers was put on notice that they, too, would be sent overseas to study, report on and publicise France's latest conquest.

Some 40,000 men[8] would embark on this vast enterprise, placing their destiny in the hands of a man obsessed by his own. Even so, for now, the actual destination remained a mystery to the vast majority of those setting out. Egypt was a well-kept secret, and of all the sailors, soldiers and scholars ordered to ready themselves, few would guess that they were being sent on the most modern of crusades to the most ancient of lands.

---

7. Cash was only forthcoming following the 'defeat of the army of the Swiss oligarchs' and entry of the French into Bern in March 1798. General Lannes brought 3 million francs from that city's treasury to Toulon on 3 May 1798.

8. There were few women. Orders stipulated that four women were permitted for each battalion or cavalry regiment, one for each artillery company, ten for the hospitals and four for the clothing depot. Each was to be a seamstress or laundry woman. Some wives did go, however. Captain Engel's wife, Regula, went with her husband whilst General Verdier managed to have his Italian wife accompany him by dressing her as one of his aides-de-camp.

1

The Voyage

The march to the ports began and a battalion of officials under Benoît Georges de Najac was to the fore, sent on to obtain supplies and ready the fleet. Najac worked harder than Saint Louis and obtained such essentials as 2,786 axes, 576 pickaxes, 20,000 pints of vinegar and an Erard grand piano. He performed miracles when it came to logistics, but neither civic duty nor money could induce the sailors of the south, 'deaf to the nation's pleas' according to Horace Say, to volunteer for the voyage. Even after some patriotic blackmail, coercion and the activities of French press-gangs, there were hardly enough qualified seamen to man the 309 mostly inappropriate transports whilst all the ageing warships were seriously short of manpower.[1]

Those warships were another worry. Even the best of them had suffered through neglect and blockade, and whilst the fleet at Toulon boasted some first-rate ships such as the flagship, the former *Dauphin Royal*, now aptly renamed the *Orient*, the navy had been forced into making use of everything that floated, even if only just.[2] Nobody could be sure whether some of these men-of-war were still seaworthy, a question also hanging over the ancient admiral in charge, Brueys d'Aigalliers, who had joined the navy a year before Napoleon was born. Worse, Brueys was apparently being kept in ignorance as to the purpose of his command, and had had to write to Napoleon to plead for details, adding plaintively that 'it is important I know the objective of the expedition so that I can make arrangements accordingly. No one understands better than I do the importance of keeping a secret, and there is no risk in telling me.' Napoleon, however, kept in Paris by rumours

---

1. The Toulon squadron lacked 3,580 effectives in April.
2. The fleet included nine warships converted into transports, whilst the *Conquérant*, the *Guerrier* and the *Peuple Souverain* had been condemned ten years ago and the *Heureux* had not been careened since 1788.

of Austria mobilising, would insist on keeping the secret until the two met in person that May.

Napoleon lingered in Paris but his legions were rolling south. Some 26,000 infantry, 3,000 horseless[3] cavalry, 25 Balloonists under Nicolas-Jacques Conté[4] and 3,000 gunners with 181 guns would be set in motion. They were commanded by generals who had made a name for themselves in Italy, or had wanted to in Germany. The troops themselves were mostly veterans, albeit a mix of conscripts or volunteers who had rallied to the republic when the Patrie was in danger. The infantry – divided between the ponderous line regiments, which fought in dense formation, and the more mobile light, intended to act as scouts and skirmishers – included the enthusiastic young Joseph Laporte of the 69th Line, and that querulous Norman, Pierre-Jean-Baptiste Millet, of the 2nd Light. Their NCOs and junior officers and those of the cavalry had been made effective by six years of constant war and the soldiers would be commanded by brave men such as François Vigo-Roussillon of the 32nd Line; grumblers such as the former sergeant from the royal army, and now captain, Joseph-Marie Moiret of the invincible 75th and Jean-Baptiste Giraud of the 69th; quiet professionals like Charles Richardot; or flashy attention-seekers like the hussar Nicolas-Philibert Desvernois. Then, in a category of his own, was Maurice Godet, who, despite being just twenty-five, had nearly lost his nose fighting the Austrians and was already tired of war.

In the wake of these men came a smaller army of professionals including 168 medical officers and 445 civilian bureaucrats, the latter including François Bernoyer, in charge of dressing Napoleon's men yet uniformly obsessed with undressing women, and Alexandre Lacorre of a commissary which excelled in all the other kinds of corruption. Finally, on loan from the Ministry of the Interior, there came one final, gifted battalion. Napoleon had wanted his new conquest recording and studying, so 167 scientists and scholars, hoping to win laurels in the field of knowledge whilst studiously avoiding the fields of battle, would accompany the

---

3. An officer of dragoons who would embark at Genoa recalled, 'I visited all the ships in the harbour and very few of them are suitable for the transport of horses.' Some 1,230 horses would be shipped, but thousands more would be requisitioned on arrival.

4. The forty-three-year-old Conté had originally trained as a draughtsman before pursuing a passion for physics in Paris. The government assigned him to work on the experimental balloons being tested for the French army at Meudon. One experiment with hydrogen cost him the sight in his left eye following a gas explosion. In 1798 he had been at St Trou near Liege, and was ordered south on 17 March.

military and form Napoleon's Commission of the Sciences and Arts.[5] Amongst the scientists were historians, and some rather more useful orientalists, aiming to describe and explain new lands, and cartographers aiming to map them. There were draughtsmen and printers to record treasures and monuments, and mathematicians to measure them. There were anthropologists to record encounters in strange lands, and zoologists to study stranger creatures. There were botanists and miners to assess resources, and engineers, like Étienne Louis Malus and the precise Louis Thurman, to make use of them. Not far behind came men of the arts, trotting along breathlessly, with musicians, artists, secretaries and a poet (Grandmaison) making sure that French culture would be represented in this new theatre of blood and toil.

As Brueys was painfully aware, the precise location of that theatre still remained a mystery to most, with just a few staff officers privy to the details. In an initial attempt to confuse English spies, many officers initially received passports for Bordeaux, but counter orders then directed everyone south. The Rhone would funnel them to Provence, and so Lyon was soon crowded with men, horses and wagons. Lieutenant Louis Thurman trundled in on a stagecoach, the first stage in his own exciting adventure:

> There is much conjecture that the expedition being prepared at Toulon is destined for Egypt. Whatever the case may be, it will be of an original and most singular kind. ... Where we are going nobody knows as it is a closely guarded secret. In any case it looks like we will go far away, everything suggests that. As far as I am concerned I am delighted to be a part of the expedition. I need to get ready to deal with being sea sick. There will be lots of enemies to fight: the people of the country, the sea, the climate and probably the English too. But do not worry for I am young, healthy and resolute.

The next stop was Avignon and that town hosted the first fighting of the campaign when the 2nd Light fell out with the 9th Line and a wine bar was wrecked in the tumult. The skirmishing nearly made Quartermaster Charles François of the 9th miss the sight of a Rhone barge carrying a confiscated zoo from Italy northwards, and a library of 550 works and dozens of maps, including Rennell's of the Ganges delta, heading south. Grandjean kept an eye out for books. He was a civilian keen to make his fortune supplying the troops, and left his wife and child behind to take part in an 'expedition whose destination was a secret to the public'. He and his friend in the commissary, Simon de Sucy, had left Paris on 22 April and whilst halting

---

5. The famous geographer Humboldt nearly joined them in Egypt but the Swedish ship he was to travel on failed to arrive and he was diverted to Spain; from there, he preferred to head for South America.

at Avignon for a change of horses, they 'suspecting we were destined for Egypt', went scouring the bookshops for guidebooks or histories on that land only to 'find that they had nothing but Volney; they told us that those before us had taken everything there was on that subject'.[6]

Curiosity and excitement were high. Over in Italy, where more troops were massing, an anonymous officer of the 14th Dragoons, then at Monza near Milan, recalled that 'General Alexandre Berthier, in command of the Army of Italy, sent the regiment the order to hold itself ready to embark, at a moment's notice, and join an expedition the destination of which was unknown. The news was welcomed by everyone with considerable joy as, it must be said, the attractions of garrison life in little Lombard towns ruined by war was nil.'

Young Joseph Laporte of the 69th Line was just as excited:

Italy that terrestrial paradise held no interest for an 18-year-old accustomed to great events and adventure especially as I had, from an early age, acquired that yearning to encounter the different peoples of the earth, and that love of glory but also, above all, I had been seized by the notion that I should take part in an overseas expedition so that I might talk like someone who had done everything. So I was not one to regret that fine country we were now leaving.

The older, and perhaps wiser, scholar Gaspard Monge, privy to Napoleon's secret, shared these sentiments:

Right down to the last soldier, everyone is happy to be quitting an Italy where we have done our bit and to go off in search of new paths of glory, for the French military is not as others. Bread, wine and meat are not enough, it also needs glory and, whenever that is lacking, tedium follows.

Back in France, Captain Pierre-François-Jean-Baptiste Gerbaud de Malgane, a close friend of General Vial but not a confidant of Napoleon, was, like many, kept guessing:

We do not know where we are going, indeed nobody here knows that either. However, what is certain is that we will not be going too far because they have only set aside two months of supplies, so we won't be passing the straits of Gibraltar. We shall embark at the end of the month.

---

6. The secret was less secretive by the day. Indeed, Cuvier, when he reached Lyon, noted that 'our Egyptians are leaving post-haste by stagecoach'.

But on 26 April he wrote again with more, or perhaps less, information:

> We are going to go to Toulon and from there, in all likelihood, Portugal. This expedition is so shrouded in mystery that such conjecture is probably pointless. We have bought ourselves a goat.

The scientists and artists were also in motion. On 13 March the academics – some volunteers or volunteered by the chemist Claude Louis Berthollet, and some assigned by the ministry – were issued with orders to head to Lyon and, from there, to Rome. Only at Lyon were they instructed to head for the Mediterranean ports. One of the volunteers was Edouard de Villiers du Terrage, then studying civil engineering at the Ecole Polytechnique, and he recalled:

> There were rumours in Paris that there would be a new campaign but I did not have much information and merely supposed that it would be sent to distant lands, although its exact destination was still a mystery. Indeed, they let it be understood that the expedition was to be sent against England, although most doubted it even though the Directory had ordered Bonaparte to Brest. Dubois Aymé and myself, or myself and Dubois Aymé, for I cannot recall who took the initiative, were amongst those who requested that we be included.

On the morning of 19 April, quite late, as he was, after all, still a student, Terrage walked into college and was pleased to find himself nominated for inclusion. A Belgian volunteer, natural history painter Henri-Joseph Redouté, also found himself accepted:

> Although nobody knew the exact destination of the expedition, it was certain that it would be to distant lands and that it was probably going to be Egypt. Animated by a strong desire to visit a country famous for the prodigious number of historic remains, and whose name brought to mind so many grand accomplishments, I was seized by curiosity and when General Caffarelli and some others who had already enrolled suggested I accompany them I was quick to comply. I joined thirty colleagues destined to form part of a commission.

The inclusion of Raige and Belletete, interpreters from the ministry of foreign affairs, and Pierre-Amédée Jaubert and colleagues from the School of Oriental Studies, in this commission presented some clues. The engineer Hervé Charles Antoine Faye also received some hints from his friend, Duval. When Faye asked the purpose of the expedition he was told, 'Remember what they said in the papers about an expedition requiring scholars to a land that was once great, and dream, too, about fighting the nation of shopkeepers?' So he did his best to prepare, buying books on India and Egypt and trying to memorise Boyer's New Anglo-French Dictionary. The writer and conduit for Parisian gossip Antoine Vincent Arnault was informed that 'there would be an expedition to the Levant, an expedition both scientific and military in nature and one directed at Greece, Corfu more specifically'. Like many of the classically minded, he hurried to volunteer as did Etienne Geoffroy Saint-Hilaire, professor of zoology at the Museum of Natural History, who was told to proceed to Toulon. He was soon hearing that the fleet there was destined for Egypt, but merely as a first stop on the road to India. Intrigued, he and his brother were among the first to leave the capital:

> I left Paris at nine in the morning, my heart full of hope engendered by this journey. After an emotional farewell, I left my home, that wonderful place where I had experienced pure and unadulterated joy, and left behind me my good and worthy fellows, or, more properly, the kindest and best of friends. Some came with me, notably [Georges] Cuvier, my virtuous friend, to the Place de la Bastille, where I was to take the coach. My father came, too, to see off his two sons. How his sensitive soul must have suffered to see us climb up onto the stagecoach.

It took them some time to reach Toulon, and they found it full. The infantryman Jean Claude Vaxelaire was already there having come down on a barge with his regiment as far as Avignon 'then disembarking and marching on Toulon. We could see the sea before we arrived and for some of us it was our first view of the ocean.' Transports bobbed in the harbour whilst the troops squabbled in the streets over bed and breakfast, or the lack thereof. When Arnault arrived he was disappointed by the standard of accommodation and recalled that 'it was quite difficult getting billeted in Toulon. The hotels were bursting with people and so, in order to avoid sleeping in the streets, we had to accept the vilest room in the vilest hotel in the vilest part of the city. Regnauld and I shared one such hovel whilst Parceval and Denon took another larger room where we managed to smuggle in a fifth colleague.'

Henri-Joseph Redouté was also feeling unwelcome, but for different reasons:

> It was at Toulon that the soldiers began to abuse us and turned the term scholar into an insult. They blamed us for being the cause of the expedition, something they were participating in with a degree of repugnance. They accused us of being untrustworthy agents of a government that had already mistreated them and were telling themselves that everyone would seek to enrich themselves at their expense. That's when our persecution began.

Louis-Joseph Bricard, a gunner attached to the 9th Line, confirms this sense of martial unease when, upon reaching Marseilles, he found that 'some companies were destined for a secret expedition and a little later, and not without a great deal of frustration, we learned that we were to be included in their number. ... There was much talk of where we were going. Some said Sicily, others Malta and still more, believing themselves well-informed, thought it was for an invasion of Sardinia or Naples. A few said Egypt or the Indies but, amongst all these theories, nobody knew anything for sure.' Bricard sent a letter to his mother and, to calm maternal nerves, told her he was on his way to Germany.[7]

As they waited, many took the opportunity of exploring the massive fleet that would be their home for the next few months. Vaxelaire recalled how 'one day I was curious enough to go and see a warship and so set off in a sloop. When I was alongside it I saw that you have to climb some stairs, as you would in a house. As I stood looking at the sails and the decks a sailor leaned over the side and shouted down "we are selling stuff to drink here".'

Vaxelaire bought some wine for 3 sous and got a free tour of the ship. Despite smelling of sick after an unfortunate accident en route to Marseilles, Second Lieutenant Jean-Baptiste Vertray of the 9th Line also received an invitation to visit the fleet's flagship:

> The second in command of the *Elisabeth* invited me to come with him onboard the *Orient* which was anchored about a mile away. I gratefully accepted the captain's offer and my good fortune for the *Orient* was indeed the most magnificent vessel and the one armed with the most guns. No sooner had our frail rowing boat come alongside the sides of this monstrous ship, which extended above us like enormous wooden walls, than I was lost in admiration. Just climbing onboard required ascending thirty-two steps.[8]

These jaunts were rudely interrupted by the arrival of Napoleon. Quitting the capital after watching a performance of *Macbeth*, the general reached Toulon early on the morning of 9 May. He amused himself by immediately carrying out a series of surprise inspections and his first victims were the 18th, 32nd and 75th Line. Lieutenant Laval of the 18th Line recalled how 'Bonaparte had those officers and non-commissioned officers present at

---

7. Many family members left behind were in ignorance as to where their relatives had been sent. Corancez's father told a friend, 'He has left for Toulon to go who knows where, to do who knows what and to return who knows when.'

8. Bernoyer also went for dinner on the ship and noted, 'There were three thousand people onboard. They showed us down to the galley where dinner was served. There was a good spread but we were so tightly packed that we could scarcely lift the food to our mouths.'

Toulon form a circle around him and he talked at us, telling us that we were going to a country from where no soldier would return to France without bringing with him the means to purchase four or five acres of land. "You know that I tell you the truth, just as I did in Italy. Count on my word."[9]

The promise of land went down well. Captain Pierre de Pelleport of the same regiment noted how the men 'cheered him for more than a quarter of an hour' whilst Lieutenant Jean-Baptiste Giraud watched the general 'walk slowly before the ranks with his hands behind his back, examining everything carefully from weapons to uniforms'. According to François Vigo-Roussillon of the 32nd Line, he then hinted they were going somewhere hot:

> He told us that we were going to fight a nameless enemy but that there would be deserts to cross, difficulties to endure but that our expedition would be a death blow to England. He added that each soldier would receive four or five acres. When he mentioned England the soldiers cheered, delighted that they would be fighting the eternal foe.

The army seemed keen to be off. Gerbaud was ready and jotted down, 'I have cut my hair short, purchased some coloured shirts and a large number of books and await the sea and this long voyage! How happy I am that I shall experience a campaign under the command of this new Alexander!'

André Peyrusse, an assistant paymaster, was, however, keeping a ledger of the risks:

> The greatest secrecy surrounds our destination and nearly 50,000 men have abandoned themselves to the caprice of the waves, voluntarily risking all at sea purely in order to follow in the wake of a general who has always led them to victory. Before we reach that promised rose, there are a fair number of thorns to brave first.

Grumpy Moiret of the 75th had already dismissed attempts at guessing the purpose of the armada, writing that 'such preparations inevitably gave rise to conjecture among our soldiers, and each thought himself sufficiently astute, or felt sufficiently capable of playing politics, to guess the purpose of the expedition', but Napoleon's arrival motivated him to add a significant disclaimer, namely that 'the confidence the army had in its general left us in no doubt as to the success of the enterprise, whatever it might be going'.

---

9. Sulkowski, Napoleon's aide-de-camp, confirms this promise: 'He reminded them of what he had done for them in Italy, the booty they had acquired, and he promised them the same again in this new campaign, also promising each man four acres.'

Over in Genoa, an officer of dragoons also saw how news they would be led by Napoleon conferred confidence on the assembled men: 'Without knowing exactly where we are going, we do not doubt that we shall win further laurels for General Bonaparte is at our head. We joked and drank to future victories until well into the night.'[10]

Further south, Desaix's division, idle at Civitavecchia near Rome, waited for word. Desaix took the opportunity to say his farewells:

> Yes, I, like you, think it an extravagance, a whim, to leave the most delightful country, where friendship and discretion have achieved perfection, in order to venture into hideous deserts, endure a horrendous climate, see men who are quite barbarous and women who have been so reduced by humiliation and despair. ... But when you see the great names attached to this expedition it is clear they are renowned for their exploits. Would you have wanted me to be less energetic, less tough and to have remained idle at the rear? Could I have listened to their names being passed from mouth to mouth and rendered famous, their native towns rejoicing in having produced them, their regions congratulating themselves on creating them, whilst I was forgotten? I confess that it is ambition which drives me. A noble ambition, that which would have me exposed to the greatest danger and risk glory in order to obtain more.[11]

In Provence danger and glory were still subordinate to curiosity. Now Napoleon had arrived and the troops were ready to leave, the intensity of speculation reached new heights. Jean-Gabriel de Niello-Sargy on the staff saw how Napoleon was always surrounded by those clamouring to know the object of the expedition: 'Some thought it was Portugal, Brazil or England; others said Ireland, Sardinia or the Crimea. Egypt was not forgotten and the sailors were particularly obstinate in saying it was so. The staff were soon convinced that the goal of the expedition was Egypt.'

Gerbaud seems to have been taken into someone's confidence and confided:

> The mystery has been revealed and lots of people know where we are going. It seems we are first to head for Malta and occupy it if we arrive in sufficient force. We shall then sail to Alexandria at the mouth of the Nile and take it before marching on Cairo and fortifying it. We shall then see if we have the means to get to Hindustan and reaching

---

10. General Kléber would have disagreed. He had a poorer opinion of Napoleon's skill. His diary contains the note 'Bonaparte obtained his fame in combat against the house of Austria, but all their generals are imbeciles'.
11. *Carnet de la Sabretache*, 1936, p. 294.

Bengal shall be our crowning achievement. How happy I am to be part of such an expedition! That's a great thing to be able to say. I was with the army in Italy and this one might be just as glorious. Do not tell mother about my voyage, persuade her that we are just going to Malta.[12]

Malta and Bengal would have to wait, as first came the arduous task of getting tens of thousands of men onboard and settled in for their Mediterranean voyage. Bernoyer found it easy enough:

On 18 May, at six in the morning, the drums summoned us for a review by the commander-in-chief in the Place d'Armes. Then we proceeded to board, all as happy as though leaving for a wedding. This boded well for our expedition. At noon I had my baggage loaded onboard the *Patriote*, a fine transport and the largest in the convoy.

Napoleon had more baggage. He embarked on the even larger *Orient*, and established his headquarters there,[13] bringing his staff and his campaign library onboard. This latter included Madame Daubenton's racy *Zélie dans le Désert*, as well as more worthy tomes. In a sign that, in those days at least, publishers could make money from Napoleon's Egyptian campaign, Horace Say, tasked with purchasing the books, spent 25,000 francs on 550 items from Charles Pougens' bookshop.

Napoleon and his library were soon comfortably quartered on his flagship and Grandjean, dismayed when a case carrying white wine had fallen open and drenched him, perked up when offered a place on the same ship. However, he found his situation rather more spartan:

We were horribly placed on the *Orient*, squeezed in, if I may use the expression, like anchovies in a barrel. Imagine if you can, a ship containing 2,000 infantry, 1,000 crew and 200 more from the administration of the commission of the arts. Bonaparte had a cabin to himself so he had a sleeping space, a dinning chamber and a salon.

---

12. He was better informed than many. Jean Claude Vaxelaire recalled, 'We did not know where we were going, some said England, some of the better informed said that we were going into the rising sun whilst England was in the direction of the sunset. There was a general of brigade on our ship and he was none the wiser.'
13. Bricard described it as being an enormous chateau made out of planks and so big that you could be forgiven for thinking that you were on land.

Contrary winds meant that departure was not immediate, which suited Lieutenant François Leclerc D'Ostein as he was able to continue a liaison with 'an amiable person' in Toulon. Then, on 14 May, the *Junon*, *Diane* and *Alceste* frigates were sent out to scout for enemy ships. The French knew that Nelson's squadron of three warships and four frigates had slipped past the Spanish and entered the Mediterranean. Happily, the French frigates returned to report the Royal Navy was still nowhere to be seen and, on 19 May, as Josephine Bonaparte clambered up to gladly wave everyone off from a balcony, the French armada finally set sail. Bernoyer was for once almost lost for words:

> All the ships had run up the national flag and they extended a vast distance. Everyone was up on deck to take in a sight the like of which had never been seen before in the Mediterranean. It was an immense fleet sailing majestically on the sea and all the regimental bands were playing those precious airs which always accompanied our glory and urged us to victory.

Jean-Gabriel de Niello-Sargy also felt a surge of pride, remarking how 'not since the crusades had there been such an imposing fleet in the Mediterranean'. The scribe Arnault marvelled at how 'thousands of men were so joyful and enthusiastic and confident of success'. Lieutenant Laval agreed, writing, 'Whatever our destination might be, and nobody knew for sure, we were all quite happy and we could hear "Vive La République" from all the ships.' Antoine Galland, a printer assigned to the expedition and a passenger on the *Sensible*, was of a sensitive disposition, and his goodbye to France came tinged with regret as he confided that 'nobody can be unaffected when quitting their country, their mistress, relatives or friends when travelling to a distant and unknown land'. Giraud, a 'humble lieutenant', was also affected, but chose philosophy for consolation, limiting himself to the saying that 'a soldier always knows when he is to leave, he just never knows when he is coming back'.

This fleet's departure was more complicated, however. Enlarged by the ships from Genoa, but not yet by Desaix's convoy idling in Civitavecchia, it was an impressive mass but badly coordinated and, in the scrum to get out of the harbour, it was a miracle that only the *Carrère* briefly ran aground, especially given the contrary winds. Indeed, a laconic comrade of Vertray was moved to remark:

> The sea is an English one, captain, and it seems as though the Supreme Being does not want us to leave. If Nelson, who is just off over there, knew about our difficulties getting out he would have no trouble getting at Toulon. Brueys is unlucky and if this continues we shan't get very far.

Nelson was, thankfully, some way off, only reaching Toulon on 4 June[14] and so mercifully out of earshot of Napoleon's regimental bands playing the March on England for the diversion of passengers and crew. François Vigo-Roussillon had actually thought they would be marching on England, or at least sailing to it, but the fleet's direction soon convinced him otherwise:

> I embarked on 15 May and joined the colonel on the *Mercure*, a warship of seventy-four guns. We headed towards Sicily, being surprised to see that we were turning eastwards for, after what we had been told at Toulon, we expected that we would head for Gibraltar and from there move against England or the English colonies.

Even as the fleet sailed to the east of Corsica's rocky coast, there were some still convinced the expedition was destined for the Atlantic as General Kléber, in charge of one of the expedition's divisions, notes:

> There are fewer than forty people in the entire expedition who know what route we are taking to where; Blanquet spoke out against Egypt as he wanted to go to the Crimea, others were for Greece, others Sicily and still more for Portugal, even though we were now going in the wrong direction.[15]

That forty was an underestimate for Captain Thévenard of the *Aquilon*, his tongue loosened by extra rations of rum, was soon informing his dinner guests:

> Sardinia is not worth the trouble of such a major expedition; Sicily cannot be our destination given that the Treaty of Campo-Formio spares it, as well as Naples, from any hostilities on our part; Crimea is only accessible through the Dardanelles and, the Turks being at peace with Russia, they will not allow us passage through the straits. So, I have shown you that the expedition cannot be for Sardinia, Naples, Sicily or the Crimea, still less for dealing with the corsairs of Tunis, Algiers or Tripoli. Indeed, the only destination possible is Egypt.

---

14. Nelson was hampered by conflicting orders and the weather, indeed his squadron had been scattered by strong winds and driven towards Sardinia on 17 May.
15. This is odd as Etienne Geoffroy Saint-Hilaire states that 'the generals are being quite open that we are going to the Indies. This is what General Kléber told my brother yesterday as they dined.' He either misheard, or Kléber was bluffing. At least the staff were up to date. Jean-Gabriel de Niello-Sargy, among the diners, was soon writing that 'amongst the staff, no one doubted that our goal was Egypt'.

For André Peyrusse, assistant paymaster, the journey was more traumatic than the destination. As a true Frenchman, he was already complaining about the catering:

> What bothers me the most, and that which requires me to maintain a severe fast, is the stink of the stagnant water they give us to drink and the unhygienic cook who smokes and chews his tobacco and allows it to fall into the cooking pots and casseroles.[16]

Gaspard Monge, setting off later from Italy, seems to have had a better cook. 'If I continue like this,' he told his worried wife, 'I shall be as fat as a monk. I eat from morning to evening but I drink little, for the water is so bad. I sleep through the night but also sometimes during the day, especially when it is hot.'[17]

The young veteran Joseph Laporte also complained about the water:

> For more than a month we would live off naval rations, viz hardtack, bacon, salted meat, smoked fish. What troubled us the most was the lack of fresh water.

The salt water all around them was also causing problems. Colonel Marie Laugier on the *Peuple Souverain* had quickly seen the sea's effect on the landlubbers, watching how 'the ocean was rough and was a real challenge to our men and sailors, many suffering grievously from seasickness'. Lieutenant Pierre Louis Cailleux was not immune:

> It took us a few hours but we now found ourselves in the open sea. The waves were rather high and we were pitched from left to right. It was rather frightening as we had not yet got our sea legs. We were as pale as death and suffering so much. There was no need for violins to make us dance or doctors to make us vomit.

François Leclerc D'Ostein 'paid his tribute to Sir Neptune' early on, 'joining those who spent the day lying down and not wishing to see any

---

16. Attempts were also made to address the unhygienic conditions, for the risk of fever was great. Orders were issued that hammocks and sheets should be aired, hands and feet should be washed as often as possible, even in sea water, and shirts changed 'every eight days'.
17. Bernoyer had actually brought a cook with him to ensure edible food: 'We decided that each one of us should contribute 50 francs each so we could hire a cook to take care of feeding us during the voyage. Judging by the amount of supplies, we were in for a treat.'

food', while Second Lieutenant Jean-Baptiste Vertray saw many more laid low:

> The effects of the breeze, which had been felt in harbour and now made the ship seem like a plaything, soon led to many feeling indisposed. The shouting and jesting from the soldiers subsided and none of the brave men, who had survived the bloody campaigns of 1792, of the Sambre-et-Meuse and of Italy, were immune to a sickness which sent even the most robust amongst us running.[18]

Antoine Galland, evidently unaffected himself, thought it all quite amusing:

> It was a strange sight on those first days of our voyage. Especially when the sea was rough. Then the poor passengers, both men and women, run out and throw up like drunkards, all of them as pale as death.

Monge would place his trust in Dr Vandermoinde's patented remedy for seasickness whilst General Augustin Belliard would rely on his brand of noxious tobacco. Once the sea, and stomachs, settled, however, the expedition found itself drifting into a routine. Pierre-Laurent-Marie Théviôtte of the Engineers describes a typical day at sea:

> Life on board was very monotonous. I rose at five or six in the morning. I read until nine. Then it was lunch, which was quite substantial. We dined at four and went to bed at 11. Night in our stifling and airless quarters was normally anything but quiet. The superior officers and the captains slept in the battery of 36-pounders and above the powder magazine. The other officers slept in a cabin, some in hammocks some in bunk-beds.[19]

François Leclerc D'Ostein benefitted from his father's rank as general to enjoy private quarters:

> We were on the ship the *Tonnant* where they gave my father a tiny corner to hide in and where I too was quartered. It was all very amusing when, that night and for the first time, I had to climb up to

---

18. Vertray, p. 12. Jean-Baptiste Guillot of the 25th Line was badly affected, telling his mother, 'I suffered a great deal during the two months of our voyage. Throughout that time I was seasick almost constantly and was even bringing up blood.'
19. Rations were nominally issued at seven for lunch, dinner at eleven and supper at half-past six. This being a French army, cheese was provided every fourth day and there was three-quarters of a pint of wine to drink.

my suspended bed. It was difficult to get into, which made us all laugh, but, eventually, I slept very well in it.

Joseph Laporte, with the ordinary soldiers of the 69th, was less impressed, remarking that 'our new quarters did not seem very comfortable ones at first glance. We were strung up in canvas hammocks and tossed and twisted the whole night, sometimes your head was up, sometimes it was down, so you can tell how glad we were to see the dawn.'

Antoine Galland on the *Sensible* also had trouble with hammocks:

I had barely slept the previous nights but that night managed to get off until the wife of a soldier, thrown against my hammock by the rolling of the ship, and grabbing at the ropes to steady herself, knocked me out of my crib, and I fell into the midst of the slumbering soldiers.

Henri-Joseph Redouté on the *Diane* was still suffering from a persecution complex:

After we had embarked our mistreatment continued. The army officers and those of the navy treated us with contempt. We were not given quarters or bedding and only eventually were we given simple hammocks to hang under the deck. Mine was covered with the bloodstains of a midshipman who had recently been killed.

Etienne Geoffroy Saint-Hilaire on the *Alceste* was also feeling short-changed:

We were given a little cubbyhole, six feet by six. I managed to divide it so it had two storeys. I went on top, using a hammock whilst my brother preferred the deck and lay his mattress out on it.[20]

Still, Saint-Hilaire found he had good company in General Reynier, a man who shared his interest in natural history, and he soon began to enjoy himself:

When I wake up I go to the bridge in order to find out whether anything occurred the night before and to learn about the ways of the sea and the different parts of the ship. We lunch and then spend some time at leisure. I work in bed. We dine at four and after dinner I enjoy

---

20. And poor Coquebert de Montbret on the *Tonnant* was also feeling neglected: 'The ship was so crowded with soldiers that we had no idea at first where we might go. We spent the first night on the gun deck. I lay on the deck on my coat. The same on the second night, but at least with some fresh air. It was only after that that we were given a place to hang my hammock. I am in what they commonly call the lion's ditch, the place where they keep the ropes.'

taking part in the very interesting conversations. As the day closes, I play cards with General Reynier, General Manscourt and the wife of the commissary. All my time passes in such pursuits that I can hardly say that I am bored. As for food, I have nothing to complain about. There is lots of it and many interesting delicacies. A day does not go past without us having pastries and, even better, we have fresh bread.[21]

General Belliard would also enjoy himself:

This evening I had generals Veaux and Mireur over for dinner as well as the colonel of the 21st Light. What a party. Bordeaux wine, Champagne, Frontignan, no expense spared. We drank to the health of the republic, and remembered our friends.

As, of course, would Bernoyer:

There were 400 of us, military as well as civilian. We knew most of these from Italy and so we had good company. There was an extra ration of wine and brandy for the more junior ones who shared quarters with the ordinary soldiers. As for me, I had only had a few cups of tea to drink. The evening was spent in various amusements. There was dancing, fencing, music and, above all, listening to the tales told by the soldiers.

Laugier saw some of the dancing:

In order to amuse us, whenever time permitted, they would have the sailors dance and the sight of them doing so joyfully and with much skill was quite entertaining.[22]

Pierre Dominique Martin, a maths lecturer at the engineering school, says that some infantry went even further, putting on a play for their officers in which 'a French soldier delivers a slave from an old Turk's harem and

---

21. General Belliard would have been jealous. On 25 June he noted, 'We started on the hardtack today as we have no bread. It is difficult to bite, especially for those with bad teeth.' His comment would have found favour with Monge: 'Our bakery caught fire so we had to throw it into the sea. We will be on hardtack for the rest of the voyage. That would not be so bad if my teeth were in good shape, for the hardtack is good, but it will take me two hours to eat my ration.'
22. General Dugua also noted that 'whenever the weather permitted they would have the sailors dance and the sight of their good humour and skill in this art amused us greatly'.

she, out of gratitude, marries the French soldier'.[23] The diminutive engineer Hervé Charles Antoine Faye, on the *Timoleon*, spent his days chasing fleas and lice, playing cards, strolling on the deck and reading Volney on Egypt. But he too was dreaming of the orient, and tired of the rank smell of rotten fish and human waste onboard, wondering aloud, 'When shall we lie on soft Asian cushions, breathing the scent of roses and indulging in sorbets?'

Assistant Paymaster André Peyrusse was probably dreaming of harems and cushions when he mused:

> Unlike you, I do not have the presence of the charming sex, in short there are no women here. Such privations will not last, and we shall see whether the Circassian and Georgian ladies, who they say are pretty, merit their reputation.

Antoine François Ernest Coquebert de Montbret, the impressionable young naturalist from Hamburg, and a passenger on the *Tonnant*, was also growing impatient, although for different reasons:

> Nine days of this voyage has exhausted my patience. Do not think, dear parents, that I am alone to think thus. All my companions think the same and suffer cruelly from boredom and being kept idle. We do not lack for books, many of the officers and others gladly lend theirs out, but one cannot read all day! Chess, dice, etc, kill time, but it all becomes so insipid.

More exciting pursuits were on the horizon. The republic's warriors soon turned to gambling their fortunes away in games of chance. Denon saw how 'the greedy ones sold their equipment to lay bets, others gambled and lost in a quarter of an hour more than they would make in their entire lifetime. Once the money was gone, out came the watches and I saw six or eight bet on a roll of the dice.' Bernoyer, naturally, was one of the winners: 'The table was covered in so much gold, such that it seemed as though we had returned from conquering Peru. I gambled a gold Louis and won three.' Still, Captain Blanquet, concerned about the erosion of discipline, felt it timely to issue a stern warning: 'I have been informed that a number of officers and, following their example, many soldiers, have recently been giving themselves over to games which can only lead to excess and to disturb the harmony which exists onboard. It is my duty to remind you that all forms of gambling are prohibited.' He added that any money found on gambling tables would be confiscated for the profit of the crew.

---

23. Many of the French were looking forward to liberating a harem. Old Monge told his wife that 'where we are going there will be harems available to us. If you could hear what our frustrated youth are planning there you would laugh for a quarter of an hour.'

Meanwhile, that greater gamble, sending an army across the sea whilst Nelson's squadron was at large, proceeded apace. Once a small convoy joined from Corsica, the fleet was strung out for 12 miles. Arnault was amazed that the ships kept together:

> The convoy was spread out during the course of the day but, as evening approached, a signal was given and the transports grouped themselves around the warships like pupils around a teacher, sheep around a shepherd or chicks around a hen. Some of the transports were deliberately slow as their captains were being forced to serve against their will and hoped to steal away during the night. They were not allowed and the shepherd would send one of his dogs to catch the stray sheep.[24]

One stray flock was the Italian convoy coming out of Civitavecchia carrying Desaix's division. The troopships there had been kept waiting in port until word came that the Toulon fleet was at sea and the morose Maurice Godet of the 21st Light had spent his final day ashore saddened by having to sell his horse for a vile price. General Belliard also noted that 'the troops began to embark at noon, and the hussars of the 7th were so attached to their horses that those who had to leave theirs behind them burst into tears.' Not all the hussars were upset, however, with trooper Alexandre Ladrix writing to his parents:

> I hope you are not too worried about our expedition, and we think we are not going so very far as we have embarked 100 horses. So that has calmed our fears. I am not too worried about it. I could easily have switched to another unit that was not going, and could have settled in amongst some friends there, but I don't think you would have been too happy and so I shall see where destiny leads me.

Destiny sent them off on 26 May, and the convoy also contained clues as to what was in store in the form of some intriguing passengers. Belliard on the fair *Josephine* saw them climb aboard the *Courageuse*:

> I don't yet know where [we are going], but it is likely Egypt. At least that is what all the precautions suggest. Arab interpreters and printers, with Arabic characters and printing presses, have been brought onboard. Monge is working on learning the language and that can't be

---

24. The image of the hen was repeated by General Belliard: 'The squadron fell back today to watch its chicks (the transports) catch up and, as a good hen would, to prevent any of those messing about behind from falling into the clutches of a fox.'

because we are bound for England. Perhaps we shall take Malta and the money we need and then go further afield.[25]

As the fleet sailed away, Major Charles Antoine Morand of the 88th Line also guessed that the destination was to be somewhere exotic:

The curtain of mystery was lifted a little by the way in which Desaix hunted through libraries for all the books and charts relating to Egypt, Syria and Persia, and how he sought information from Syrians and Egyptians who were studying at the Office of Propaganda and who would accompany the expedition. The theory which is most likely is that the Directory, seeing that it is not the right time for a descent on England itself, dreamed up the idea of sending an army to India via Asia or the Red Sea. ... Such a project seems fanciful to those who know that, in order to reach India, one has to go through vast, hot and sterile regions, or even deserts, inhabited by ferocious people.

Ferocious people were closer than Morand thought, however, and Captain Guiraud of the *Cisalpine* reported seeing Nelson's ships, one dismasted, off nearby Saint-Pierre. Nerves calmed a little when it was Malta, rather than Nelson, that first hove into the view, but, kept waiting, idling off the islands of the knights until Napoleon and Brueys' fleet arrived, the tension returned to the convoy as Savary recorded: 'Everyone was worried about the fleet, we looked out for it but could not see it. Anxious, we lost appetite. ... That evening we spied several large ships bearing down on us from Gozo. They turned out to be Maltese.'[26] Belliard felt the situation more ridiculous than troubling, confessing in his diary, 'I hesitate to think what the Grand Master and the knights of Malta think of us when they have seen us cruising about for the last three days.'

All doubts disappeared in the breeze when a large fleet, with 'as many ships as there are hairs on your head' as one lookout put it to Belliard, was sighted on 9 June:

They shot up to the birds' nest and raised their telescopes. It was the squadron. It already seemed as though we could make out the *Orient*, that mobile fortress, gloriously carrying the conqueror of Italy. No sooner had General Bonaparte arrived than General Desaix went to see him. Preparations were made to attack the island and take water

---

25. A printing press had also been loaded onboard the fleet in Toulon. It was supposed to have Arabic fonts but only Greek ones had made it in time. The printing press was directed by Marcel, who brought his wife with him.
26. A warship, the *Religion de Malte*, or Order of Malta, as well as a frigate and a corvette.

by whatever means. So it seems that now the little man[27] is here we shall have no peace.

Godet confirms the relief that this rendezvous must have created in both flotillas:

A feeling of electric joy swept through the convoy at this sight as it was clear that this was the Toulon squadron, along, it was supposed, with those from Marseilles and Genoa. These had been much talked about as we discussed our mysterious destination and the capricious seas. Meanwhile the ships drew closer and that afternoon the squadron reached the convoy and I think it superfluous to add that relief took the place of worry throughout the convoy. The reunion of all the convoys, the protection of the fleet and the presence of Bonaparte made us feel secure and the sight of the sea covered with warships and transports, containing the expeditionary force, offered a magnificent spectacle as far as the eye could see.

Malta was also a magnificent spectacle and an impregnable-looking one. This island fortress, strategically placed to dominate shipping routes across the Mediterranean, and lusted after by France, Britain, Naples and Russia, was home to the once-great Knights of the Order. There had been ample time for the knights to prepare for unwelcome visitors[28] but the order was not what it had once been and Ferdinand von Hompesch, the gouty Grand Master, only had 1,500 men to man the islands' extensive walls. Still, those walls were a wonder of the world, and General Belliard worried that 'it is possible it will resist, just as when the Turks tried to take it with an army of 100,000 men in 1565'. Godet was also anxious about having 'to use force against the masters of this rock which their predecessors had rendered famous by their fierce resistance against the Ottomans'.[29]

Napoleon, who had heard from spies that resistance would be rather less than fierce, was still concerned that Nelson might catch the French

---

27. Regarding Napoleon's height, François-Etienne Sanglé-Ferrière, a midshipman of the *Dubois*, 'saw General Bonaparte for the first time. I was struck by his severe and imposing expression. Although rather short, the aura of glory which surrounded him made him seem taller.'

28. François Philippe de Schönau de Saasen, representing the knights at the conference at Rastadt, had written to the Grand Master, von Hompesch, that 'a major expedition is being fitted out in Toulon for Malta and Egypt. You will certainly be attacked.'

29. André Peyrusse also knew his history: 'One should not forget the great siege of 1567 when 60,000 Turks were forced to abandon the siege and retire after six months and the loss of two-thirds of their men.'

between his guns and those of Valletta. He therefore moved quickly and, after making his demands, sought to persuade the knights to capitulate by launching Desaix against the south-east, Vaubois to the north near Valletta, Baraguey d'Hilliers further north and Reynier against Gozo. Gozo fought back and Vertray was on the receiving end of Maltese fire:

> It was three in the afternoon of 10 June when our unit set off. I was in one of the first four boats being rowed and it contained our colonel and General Reynier. The closer we got, the more intense the enemy fire became. However, they could not stop us, indeed we only had one man killed and another wounded, and soon we were disembarking on the rocky shore. Our enthusiasm overcame such obstacles, and the enemy ceased fire but switched to rolling huge boulders down upon us.[30]

Gunner Bricard watched as the troops landed:

> The enemy opened fire as our brave soldiers approached but they, rowing hard, covered the distance and landed on the beach. Then, bayonets fixed, they charged the Maltese who promptly fled to safety. We seized their redoubts and although a few small forts wanted to continue resistance they were forced to cede and so, after just one hour, we were masters of the island.[31]

Gozo had fallen but Valletta, with 910 guns, still held out. The French advanced, although Belliard found this prelude to a war in the desert hard going: 'For the last two days we have been running around this blasted island which consists of nothing more than scalding rocks beneath a burning sun which pursues you everywhere for there is not one tree to provide any shade.' Saint-Hilaire seemed more concerned that his sunburn gave him 'the face of a moor' whilst Grandjean innocently complained that 'there are few countries where the heat bears down with more force than on this island'.

Experience would soon teach them otherwise, but for now, with the French closing in, von Hompesch summoned just enough energy to order a suspension of arms. Napoleon sent Junot and Dolomieu, a mineralogist and a former knight of the order, to tell the Maltese that 'I will give them generous terms, I will buy the island from them and pay them whatever they want for it.' The French emissaries arrived just as the Grand Master was sitting down to his soup so he sent his

---

30. Niello-Sargy was with another detachment attacking Gozo, or Calipso as it was also known, rowing ashore with 'Reynier, Fugier, Louis Bonaparte, the engineer captains Sabatier and Geoffroy and a company of grenadiers of the 35th Line'.
31. The enemy resistance had been token. Saint-Hilaire noted how the next day 'the commandant of the fort and six other knights came over the following day for a friendly luncheon with the general, my brother and myself. They were all French.'

secretary, Doublet, back to the *Orient* to see Napoleon. The general welcomed them in his cabin and, according to Doublet, addressed his visitors thus:

> It is a good job you came, Messieurs, as I was about to subject the town to some rather rough treatment. But I see you are not well and are cold (we were wearing coats of black taffeta) so perhaps a little punch will warm you.

After pouring the drinks, Napoleon then called for a pen and, in less than half an hour, drafted terms of surrender which called for the Order to relinquish control of Malta, Gozo and Cumin and to transfer authority to the French Republic.[32] When presented with these terms, the Grand Master briefly hesitated between cowardice and shame, before opting for both and surrendering at three that morning. He received a chivalrous compensation of 600,000 francs, half of which he kept after paying his debts, and scurried away to exile as French flags were raised over the battlements.[33]

The islands had fallen easily, too easily perhaps, although their capture would ruin relations with the Russian czar, who indulged a paternal affection for the order, and the king of Naples, who, just as unrealistically, claimed the islands, along with Jerusalem, as his own. This would lead to declarations of war from both these powers but, on this day of victory, such concerns could be brushed aside as easily as Malta's dust could be brushed off Napoleon's finest uniform as he made his triumphal entry. The short-sighted Monge could not fail to miss the drama:

> The general, in dress uniform, accompanied by his staff, went ashore and slept in Malta. The ships and warships were flying our flag. He climbed into a longboat and with two sloops on either side, carrying his foot Guides and mounted Guides, and accompanied by music, left for the port as the ships fired a salute. It took a while to cover the distance, because we were six miles from the port.

Napoleon's army was also glad to be coming ashore, François Leclerc D'Ostein remarking that 'it is a joy that you can only appreciate when you have been cooped up behind planks for so long' but puzzling over the 'corrupt Arabic' of the locals and their tendency to hide their women behind screened balconies, which he thought 'quite Turkish'. The more serious-minded, including Étienne Louis Malus, captain of Engineers, were

---

32. To sweeten this bitter pill, Napoleon promised a pension to those knights of French origin. Much of the meeting was taken up arguing over the value of this with the knights asking for 1,000 francs and Napoleon offering 600.
33. Hompesch seems to have spent the money rather quickly and passed his retirement, in poverty, in Montpellier. He died and was buried there in 1805.

puzzled by the ease of their success. Malus applied a soldierly logic and concluded that 'their government had become flabby after so long a peace and had neither the energy to control the populace nor sufficient troops to withstand an active and enterprising enemy'. The garrison behind such feeble resistance was now dissolved, Laval watching as 'the troops of the Grand Master were disbanded but the soldiers were allowed to take service with us. Some seventy knights were embarked even though most of them had fought against us in Condé's army[34] and allowed into our units and retaining their rank.' Some 358 men from the Grand Master's guard agreed to follow the French,[35] and, in addition, 500 Turkish slaves were freed from the galleys and prisons. Laugier saw his ship, the leaky *Peuple Souverain*, 'receive about sixty and they worked hard and enthusiastically, telling us that they would always wish to serve France. They ate pork and drank wine, saying that the time of superstition was over.'

Napoleon also liberated the Grand Master's Chinese porcelain and, on 13 June, had the treasure of Saint John nationalised. Denon spotted a number of works by Calabrese but the gold and silver was mostly melted down for the army. The troops were also taking what they needed. Quartermaster Charles François saw that some of his men had pinched 'an enormous lump of silver, a bell some three feet high and in the same metal, and a rather rare Chinese carpet'.

With energy devoted to these rites of conquest, there was little time for sightseeing. One anonymous officer had time to note that the locals used dried horse manure as fuel rather than the scarce wood. Most, including Joseph Marie Moiret, thought Malta 'a detestable place, and I could not believe there was a worse place in the world. We shall see how wrong I was.' Few were sorry to leave, and indeed there was a general sigh of relief when Napoleon, leaving a garrison and the sick behind,[36] ordered the men to embark. On 19 June the odyssey continued and the *Spartiate* lead the fleet away from Malta in the direction of Greece. At this turn eastwards, the sigh of relief turned into expressions of astonishment, as Godet noted:

---

34. Condé's army was a royalist force of emigrants. Laval notes that the Maltese (although many were Roman, having deserted Papal service) were formed into a legion when they reached Egypt, the Legion Maltaise. The officer of dragoons would lambast the soldierly qualities of these 1,500 foreigners: 'The Maltese will form a legion under Citizen MacSheedy [*sic*] but I doubt he will be able to do much with them for they are all, without exception, robbers and lazy cowards.' MacSheehy would soon agree and in May 1799 he was writing to Dugua begging that 'you have me leave this unit, for it can only dishonour anyone who commands it and compromise our plans through cowardice or treason'.

35. Dugua reviewed the guard of the Grand Master: 'The soldiers of this unit are married peasants, most of them short and rather ugly. They are mostly barefoot.'

36. Some 178 with fever, 75 wounded and 65 with venereal disease.

Our surprise was great for nobody knew where we were going save the handful in on the secret. We had been unconvinced that our destination was the Levant, even though there had been rumours, and the surprise attack and occupation of Malta, coupled with the proximity of Sicily, had led us to believe that this latter target was our goal.

More were being let in on the secret and the admirals and the staff were now told their destination was to be Alexandria. Bernoyer, still fantasising over his seduction of a nun in a Maltese convent, was taken aback, writing, 'So, we must go and conquer Egypt in the name of the republic. The fact that we were destined for Egypt hit me like a thunder bolt.' As the news swept the decks, some, including young Niello-Sargy, felt excitement rather than awe. He saw himself involved in an event of vast historical import: 'Rumours were circulating among the European courts that the Ottoman empire was about to fold and that speed was essential if any of the remnants were to be seized.'

A few officers restrained their emotions and prepared, at least intellectually, for what was to come. Théviôtte was among them:

I spent my time reading those authors who visited Africa, and Egypt in particular, in order to banish those moments when one could see nothing but sea and sky. Whilst nothing official has been announced, the destination of our voyage cannot now be mistaken. I am therefore spending as much time as I can reading books which look at Egypt, its topography, soil, climate, customs, historical origins and diseases, etc.

The soldiers, however, continued to fritter their time away. Godet turned from his own books to watch them at play:

Our voyage continued in the same direction and the sea was so calm that each ship disgorged a crowd of swimmers. They were splashing about happily when suddenly a school of rather large fish swam up. We were told they dolphins and we watched how they swam in amongst our swimmers. The speed with which our men shot back to their ships had to be seen to be believed and no orders were required.

Some actual predators were also cruising close by and, as the fleet passed Crete, Quartermaster Charles François heard rumours that the French were being hunted by a reinforced squadron of the Royal Navy:

The officers on our ship told us that whilst we were in Malta an English fleet under Saint Vincent had positioned itself off Crete whilst Nelson, commanding the Mediterranean fleet, was looking for us between Genoa and Naples with thirteen ships. They said that as he had not found us he had gone for Egypt.

Nelson had indeed shot ahead and was already to the north-west of Alexandria. The French themselves were not so very far from the Egyptian shore, and the passengers began to ready themselves for their invasion. The studious Théviôtte noted how 'they have started work on some proclamations to elucidate the people of Egypt. They are looking for the Arabic characters.' These high-sounding texts, given local colour by the Orientalist Venture de Paradis, were designed to win friends and allies. Should they fail – and they probably would, given the poor quality of the Arabic and the inability of the French to convey their revolutionary concepts in any meaningful way – bullets would have to do. Alexandre Lacorre of the commissary, sent onboard the *Orient* to collect supplies, saw how munitions were being issued en masse, and sensed that 'something significant was afoot'. Quartermaster François recalled that it was on the morning of 28 June that he received orders to distribute sixty cartridges to each man.

Then, two days later, land was sighted. It was Egypt. Only now did General Belliard, enveloped in the smoke of his pungent tobacco, realise that Egypt had been their destination. Joseph Laporte also seemed surprised:

At dawn on 30 June we could make out a headland and some said it was Egypt. The fleet was brought together and sailed in formation, and we could soon make out things a bit better. The next day we could clearly see the Egyptian shore and it became clear we were going there as we were given orders to prepare to land and be ready for action.

Godet and the transports went to take up a position 'about three miles to the west of Alexandria, before the Marabout tower'. Jean-Pierre Doguereau also saw the Arab tower, which he thought, understandably, was a mosque, whilst Quartermaster François recalled seeing 'the Arab tower on the African coast' and added that 'before long we were able to pick out the minarets of the city of Alexandria'.[37] There was considerable excitement. Lieutenant Giraud watched as 'everyone raced for the deck, glad to finally have the chance to escape our floating prison'. Laporte and his comrades were also rejoicing:

Everyone on our ships was overjoyed as we had been onboard for nearly two months and had had to do without, especially as regards water, and, with the exception of when at Malta, had only had biscuits and salted meat to eat.

Bernoyer, however, was rather glum, seeing nothing to stimulate his interest or his wide array of passions:

---

37. The tower was 20 miles, or 36 kilometres, south-west of Alexandria.

Our eyes hungrily devoured this country, so famous for the marvels it contained, and its grand and ancient monuments, and who knows what else. I stared hard to try and discern something, anything, which might give a clue as to why it had a great reputation, but could see nothing save a vast stretch of sand.

Denon, too, shows that the aspect of the barren shore came as a shock to some, and recalled those hasty promises of land made that May to the troops gathering at Toulon:

There was not a tree, not a house. A tragedy of nature or, rather, an absence of nature and in its place silence and death. The soldiers were not silent and one of them, pointing at the desert, turned to his comrade and said 'look, there are the four acres of land they promised you'.

2

Landing

The sun shone brightly on the morning of 1 July but dark clouds were not far away. Bad news came from the French frigate *Junon*. It had sailed ahead of the herd, reconnoitring Alexandria and seeking out the consul, Jean André Magallon, nephew of the former consul then in Paris, along with his deputy, Carlo Rosetti, and their interpreter, Damien or Damianos Brasevich, for intelligence on the expedition's likely reception. Denon was on the *Junon* and the intelligence was worrying: '14 English ships had just quit Alexandria and they were saying that they were hunting us in order to bring us to battle.' These bearers of bad tidings were immediately ushered over to Napoleon and the anchored fleet bobbing off the coast.

Nelson had indeed just quit Alexandria, sailing off to what the French assumed was Alexandretta. The one-eyed admiral could return at any moment, but, to make things worse, Magallon's party also made it clear that Alexandria was readying to resist. The port belonged to Mourad, the leading Mameluke bey, but the Ottoman authorities, nominally Egypt's imperial masters, also claimed some authority in Egypt's best harbour, and both powers, buoyed by popular hostility to the invading unbelievers, had united to bar French entry. This again raised the spectre of Nelson catching the French and their transports in the open sea, although Denon observed that Napoleon was keeping calm as he listened to this report, which 'did not change the expression on the general's face, and he repeated what they had told him and then ordered the disembarkation'.

Speed would again be essential. Napoleon's plan had been to enter Alexandria whilst also occupying the coast from the port to the delta. The British threat and Alexandria's likely resistance forced him into finding any suitable landing place near the port and Captain Motard hurried off on the *Amoureuse* to find one. There looked to be an abundance of choice to the engineer Girez as 'the entire coast seemed flat and sandy just like the coast between Gravelines and Calais'. Motard, however, opted for the bay of Ajami just to the east of Marabout, and some 12 miles to the west of Alexandria.

The fleet was reluctant to approach too closely because, as Théviôtte heard, the naval officers' 'charts are insufficient'. Still, by around eleven o'clock that morning, with the *Franklin* leading the way, the French ships had come in as close as they could without encountering any of the feared sandbanks and reefs. The impatient soldiers were then loaded into small boats and barges and sent off across miles of agitated sea to the waiting sands. Desaix was supposed to land first but his pilot hit a sandbank and so it was 1,500 of General Menou's infantry, crammed into 250 boats, who had the honour of being the first to land in Africa, a fact old Menou, leading the way in the barge of the *Sérieuse*, was happy to recall:

> The sea was exceptionally rough but we pushed through it and my boat was the first to land on the coast of Africa at a point to the east of the Marabout tower. No enemy on the shore. I had the vanguard landed. A few boats overturned but nobody drowned. I had the tricolour raised on the tower of Marabout.

The eighteen-year-old Laporte of Menou's 69th Line followed his commander ashore but saw that in fact some horsemen had appeared to dispute the landing:

> In the two hours it took for us to reach land we watched a number of riders leaping around on the beach ... the boats were rowed to the shore and a mass of cavalry showed itself and seemed ready to wade into the sea to oppose the landing. A few rounds of artillery saw them off and some 2,000 or 3,000 of our men came towards the beach and, seeing the water was only a few paces deep, began to wade ashore.

Next in were some of Bon's division, with the haughty Jean-Pierre Doguereau among them:

> The sea was rough and we were drenched by the waves whilst most of the soldiers were also laid low by seasickness caused by the rolling of the boats on the water. We were also concerned that we might strike some of the reefs that were dotted along a shore that was still something of a mystery to us. We had set off towards the beach by the Marabout headland at around six but it was only after eight that evening that we landed on the African shore some nine miles to the west of Alexandria. We did not have to fire a shot.

Kléber's division was also landing. Amongst them was Chasseur Pierre Millet, a phlegmatic Norman in the 2nd Light, and he described his part in the conquest:

> The commander-in-chief ordered us to start the landing and all the barges were lowered into the water. The sea was so rough, much more than it had ever been before. Bouts of seasickness began again. Nevertheless, we did manage to land, taking the time from noon to eight in the evening to cover the three miles between where we were anchored and the beach just because the sea was so rough.

One of his officers, Lieutenant Pierre Louis Cailleux, confirmed that the waves seemed against them:

> The squadron anchored off the port and we began to disembark in the most horrible conditions. The sea was so rough that it felt as though the barges would be overturned at any moment. We only made it ashore the following morning, nine miles from Alexandria.

François Leclerc D'Ostein recalled:

> The sea was rough. I got into the second barge with my general and we waited behind the galley we had seized at Malta and which was supposed to protect us as we went in. We waited there for three hours. Throughout that time I suffered terribly and I was shrieking like a martyr. I had never had it so bad in the voyage thus far, doubtless because we were in a small barge the movement of which caused me to suffer.

General Kléber, looking for orders, found that Napoleon had actually transferred to that Maltese galley: 'I left the *Franklin* and went to the galley Bonaparte had embarked on earlier, it was a tricky jump from the boat to the galley.' The two generals then seem to have switched to a smaller boat and landed in Egypt just after midnight. Étienne Louis Malus, a captain of Engineers, sent in search of orders by Desaix, was with them:

> He [Napoleon] had been onboard a galley which had changed position several times during the course of the day. It was night and the sea was rather rough. We had passed backwards and forwards through the fleet in the hope of receiving information on his whereabouts when I took the decision to make for the shore to see if he hadn't landed. I came across some seven or eight barges off Marabout and they were being rowed towards the land. I followed them. One of them had the commander-in-chief onboard. It was midnight. I did not speak to him until after we had landed. He seemed astonished that the division had not yet arrived and vented his frustration.

Bernard MacSheehy, a twenty-five-year-old Dubliner exiled to Napoleon's staff, nevertheless saw that an army of sorts was gathering in the dunes:

> When we got onshore we found generals Menou, Kléber, Bon and Reynier already there, the three former with their divisions, the latter with just a few of his men about him. So he was left to secure the landing beach whilst the others marched off in three columns for Alexandria.

Napoleon, calmer after a quick nap in the sand, had indeed marshalled 4,000 infantry and, ignoring the lack of artillery, led his men off towards Alexandria whilst more troops and equipment came ashore. Godet was amongst those to have been delayed and he arrived to see the beach 'covered in troops and supplies that had been landed and were still being landed. The gun barrels were proving difficult to bring ashore as were the limbers whilst the caissons had to be taken apart and then put back together onshore, taking care to guard against the risk of an explosion. The horses, which had been cooped up in prison for thirty-six days, now swam ashore in the wake of the longboats. It was most curious to watch them come ashore and they seemed astonished to finally have something solid beneath their hooves.'[1]

Nicolas-Philibert Desvernois of the hussars had problems getting his men and horses ashore:

> It was my regiment's turn. We were to disembark in the midst of these rough seas. The barges could not get in close enough. Officers and hussars jumped into the water, we swam, we trod water, we sometimes went under. But we finally made it. Fortunately, the sea calmed that evening and we were able to land guns and horses. Unfortunately, though, nobody had remembered to issue us with any rations.[2]

Rations were not an issue for Louis Thurman as he 'spent that first evening sat on the sand. We had a pleasant meal consisting of a leg of lamb, poultry and ships' biscuit, all washed down with wine and water.' They may have

---

1. Savary also remarked on the fate of the horses: 'The disembarkation took place in a rough sea. They had rigged sails in the boats and it took a quarter of an hour to reach the shore and one and a quarter hours for the boats to return to the ships. The horses caused problems. They were held down in the boats and then made to swim.'
2. The expedition had brought 1,200 horses with it, but only 700 of these were for the cavalry. Most of them would soon succumb to the rigours of the climate. They were replaced by local breeds but the French saddles were too big and heavy for them, leading to further losses.

come from the supplies Desaix's aide-de-camp, Savary, had noticed on the shore and which included 'wine, biscuit and vegetables ... abandoned on the beach as there were no means of transporting them'.

Still, the landing was no picnic and, indeed, was growing more dangerous by the hour, as Alexandre Lacorre noted:

> During the day a few Frenchmen who wished to bathe took themselves away from the rest of us. They were massacred or seized by the Arabs. From that point onwards we knew who our enemy was.

Citizen Grandjean of the commissary also witnessed horsemen harassing the new arrivals:

> The troops were barely ashore when the Arabs began to assemble in large numbers. These horsemen were so agile, and their horses such good mounts, indeed the best in the world, that they could suddenly fall on our troops, seize a man from the ranks and make off with him in a flash.[3]

By now Napoleon and a few thousand men were on their way to Alexandria to deal with other, less mobile, enemies. Their first march on African soil was a tough one as Laporte recalled:

> The night had been cool and there was plenty of dew but as soon as the sun rose high enough the heat became excessive and then got worse as we marched 12 deadly miles across the moving sands of the desert. There was no water or shelter and we suffered greatly from thirst, particularly as we were in no way acclimatised.

The march was at least mercifully short. Louis Thurman was amongst the first to spy their objective, the ancient walls of Alexandria:

> It was five in the morning. I, along with Poitevin and T was then ordered to reconnoitre Alexandria and we left the columns pushing forward on foot, clutching sabres and with pistols in our belts. Advancing like this we were soon before the walls of the city and could see that they were in really bad condition, as were the ancient towers, for they looked like they were on the point of collapse.

---

3. Some were kidnapped. Quartermaster François heard that a few Arabs offered to return some French stragglers they had captured for sheep or goats, and that thirty-seven men were liberated this way.

François Leclerc D'Ostein saw the enemy artillery was firing too high to affect them but Bernard MacSheehy, the Dubliner, witnessed one of the earliest casualties of Napoleon's war in the east:

> The commander-in-chief sent me forward to reconnoitre the position's situation and strength and I advanced alone to within pistol-shot of the walls. I had barely begun to survey the walls with my telescope when I heard horrible screaming from some women and children crowding the ramparts. At the same time some volleys of shot were directed against me and a soldier some 30 or 40 paces behind me was shot in the left shoulder and fell down.

General Davout summoned the governor, Seid-Mohammed-el-Koraim, but Captain Joseph Sulkowski,[4] a Polish officer on the staff, was dubious they would capitulate so easily:

> It would be wrong to underestimate the obstacles that this mass of barbarians could place in our way as, whilst not impregnable, their defences were impressive enough, for each gate had artillery and the walls and towers bristled with defenders. And the dull Turk is always a worthy opponent when he defends a position, for he is too ignorant to be afraid of that which might befall him. He thinks a prayer can protect him as much as a city wall.

Another officer, glancing through his telescope, spied 'an immense mass of women and the elderly screaming down abuse at us from beneath their black banners of death' on the nearby hill of Mamfeis. Inevitably, then, the negotiations proved short-lived and fruitless. The expeditionary force would have to storm the city. So, at nine that morning, the French advanced. Lieutenant Laval of Bon's division still thought it would be plain sailing:

> A crowd of Arabs or Turks, inhabitants of that town, waited for us on the ramparts of the old city wall. We surrounded the place, and fired a few shots against this old wall which, however, was already in ruins and unlikely to bar our progress.

---

4. Sulkowski had fled to Paris in 1793, staying at the Hotel de Moscovie, whilst waiting to see if he could be employed in the army. After being sent on mission to Constantinople, he joined the army destined for Italy in May 1796, joining Napoleon's staff that October. He was married to the daughter of Venture de Paradis, the expert on Oriental languages.

However, François Vigo-Roussillon, in Bon's 32nd Line, saw there were casualties:

> Alexandria was defended by some Turkish Janissaries, the crews of some ships from the same nation and a number of Arabs. We had no artillery but as the city was poorly defended and the walls were in a bad state, we launched an assault right away. The 32nd had the honour of leading the column against the old wall. I was amongst the first to reach the walls and stretched out a hand to steady the second in command of the unit, Monsieur Mas. Just then a Turk, who I had not seen opened fire and killed Mas right next to me.[5]

Laporte, in Menou's division, was also startled to find that 'when our troops reached the ramparts, the enemy, who had remained out of sight, then appeared in great numbers and rained a large number of rocks down onto us as well as shooting at us, which caused many to be knocked over although we had few wounded'. Despite such resistance, Kléber's men also surged forwards, as Chasseur Millet recounts:

> The front of the column led the way and began to scale the walls which, on account of the debris at the foot of them, was easy enough, even though they were high. No sooner had those leading got up than they helped those behind them and we were thus able to enter the town. The sappers broke the gates down with their axes. The divisions on the left as well as our men came into the town to be met by fire from the houses but we broke through to the square which is by the sea.

Captain Pelleport had also seen how the sappers of the 4th Line had smashed the Rosetta Gate, thus creating a way in for Bon's division, and soon the French were swarming through the streets. The citadel still held out, as did isolated pockets of defenders and some of the populace, and Laporte could see how 'the Ottomans and the troops of the Grand Seigneur as well as those inhabitants ... were hidden in the gardens and behind the rubble and we lost a few men before they were charged with the bayonet and forced to flee'. Indeed, Laporte was on the receiving end of some pot-shots as they pushed through the streets: 'We were showered with stones and shot at, without us being able to see from where, but we could tell there were not

---

5. Godet would remark that resistance had been stiff: 'The fall of Alexandria had caused more casualties than expected even though it had only been defended by its inhabitants. They saw coming against them the descendants of the ancient Crusaders and expected either death or slavery. Thus they defended themselves with desperation.'

many enemy soldiers but mostly those inhabitants who were incited to resist by the enemies of France or, because they were Muslim, out of fanaticism.'

Chasseur Millet also came under fire:

> We thought the city had surrendered so we were surprised that as we were passing a mosque (a place where they say their prayers) we were shot at. The general who was with us gave the order that the doors be forced in and that no quarter be shown to those inside. Men, women, children, all were killed by our bayonets. However, humanity is stronger than vengeance and we then called off the killing, sparing a third of those inside.

Adjutant[6] Pierre Boyer's account to his parents suggests a little less humanity, however:

> Our soldiers rush the ramparts and climb them in the face of an obstinate enemy. Many generals are wounded, including Kléber,[7] and we lose nearly 150 men, but courage finally overwhelms the Turks and, we push them back from their positions. They place themselves in the hands of God and their Prophet, and take refuge in their mosques. Men, women, old, young, babies at the breast, all are massacred. Only after a few hours of this do our troops cease and tranquillity is restored.

With this example deterring them, and Napoleon's promise to keep the fort's commander, Koraim, as governor encouraging them, the city surrendered and buried its dead. Napoleon then had a proclamation nailed up across the city.[8] It emphasised clemency to the bemused locals whilst also explaining the invasion to them, informing them that the French had come to release the people of Egypt from the tyranny of the Mamelukes. Godet was puzzled

---

6. The armies of the French republic included ranks designated as adjudant-commandant (staff colonel) and adjudant-général. For the sake of simplicity we have used adjutant for both.

7. He was in pain for some time afterwards, complaining on 17 September: 'The migraines are still not over, and the stabbing pain obliges me to shut myself away in my room.'

8. It is a colourful piece of text: 'In the name of the French Republic, founded on the principles of liberty and equality, the commander-in-chief Bonaparte, Emir of the French troops, wishes it to be known to the people of Egypt that the beys which govern the land of the Egyptians have, for some time, acted with disdain and hostility towards the French nation, oppressing its merchants through all kinds of exactions and usurpations, but that now the hour of punishment is come.'

by the text and the elaborate justifications for a war of colonisation. 'The Mamelukes?' he queried. 'But who on earth are these Mamelukes? That was the question asked by those confused by such an announcement. We hardly knew ourselves what these people or their princes had done to harm anyone, especially as we had never heard of them.'

With the port in French hands, and despite the awkward presence of an Ottoman warship, Idris Bey's the *Reale*, the transports were able to offload much-needed food and equipment on the quaysides. It was easy going until the *Patriote* ran aground on 4 July. The strong north-easterly wind had driven this transport, laden with engineering and ballooning equipment, and Bernoyer's baggage, against the reefs and she was lost. Only Bernoyer's possessions made it out, as he himself relates:

> There was a light breeze which carried us along quite nicely, but the pilot failed to spot a rock and the boat hit it with a loud bang and ground to a terrible halt. You can imagine we thought we were all done for and were going to die. Fortunately, we floundered against a rock, the boat resting on one side for more than an hour when a galley arrived and we evacuated the boat with our luggage.

Following this, the warships naturally hesitated off the coast, doubtful as to whether ships of their size could enter the harbour. Still, the port was crowded enough without them as Pierre Jaubert, purser of the fleet, confirms:

> I came ashore with the admiral and went to headquarters on the other side of the town. There, all was movement and bustle of the kind that had long been lacking. Our men were disembarking, others were preparing to cross the desert to Rosetta. The generals, the soldiers, the Turks, the Arabs, the camels, all made for such contrasting scenes of the revolution that was about to change the face of this country. In the midst of all this chaos was the commander-in-chief, overseeing the march of the soldiers, policing the city, taking precautions against the plague, planning new fortifications, coordinating the navy with the army, sending out proclamations to the Arab tribes.

Still Jaubert found time enough to dismiss the place as 'a mere heap of ruins and where you can see a paltry hovel of mud and straw propping itself against the magnificent remains of a granite column'. Godet was also unimpressed. He had entered 'through the gate which had been blown in by our sappers. Then I came in to the open area which lay between the port and the city and found it contained a rubbish dump on which some twenty or so individuals of both sexes, all of whom were almost naked, competed for objects with as many goats and dogs. These people sheltered in some miserable tents and, in the midst of incredible dust and heat, were tearing strips of cloth into rags.'

Alexandre Lacorre was also shocked by the city and its people:

The way it is built, its general ugliness, and the rather sinister atmosphere struck me at once, but the menacing and sinister glances of its people only increased my aversion to the place. At every step I saw misery on the faces of the crowd. Thin and dusky faces, women swathed in rags so that just their noses were visible, street dogs who seemed to be summoning death through their bitter howling, everything was most displeasing. That was when my far from favourable idea of what Egypt was began and indeed this grew more pronounced when I saw we were surrounded by deserts.

The city, 'twice as big as Caen' according to Faye, was a disappointment and André Peyrusse considered it to be 'just a mass of Jews, Greeks, Turks and Egyptians in a ruined or badly built city. There are no real monuments here other than the baths of Cleopatra and her ruined obelisk. Our scholars are more taken with Pompey's column a few miles from here.'

Those scholars were glad to have something to do to banish memories of a difficult voyage and difficult and delayed arrival. It had, for example, taken Jean-Baptiste Prosper Jollois, on the frigate *Montenotte*, 'five hours to get ashore despite the shouting, the encouragement, the begging and the threats of the poor captain who just could not get his people to exert themselves'. Worse, by the time they had landed there was no room at the inn. The botanist Coquebert was luckier than most:

I am lodged in the abandoned house of the English consul [George Baldwin], the consul having left three months ago. I share two small rooms with Ripault, Villiers (a pleasant young man from the polytechnic) and Pourlier, the antiquary. I have a mattress on the floor. For the last two days I have been dining with eight or ten young fellows at the Dutch consul's [Consul Valin's]. He has made his table available to us and we all bring something with us. Some contribute chicken, others pigeon, vegetable, salad and so on. This is how we manage to get ourselves quite a feast, one perhaps even better than the top brass. We drink some excellent Cyprus wine that the Venetian ships sell in the harbour.

Charles Norry was evidently less fortunate:

We sought out quarters in Alexandria in the houses of the Europeans as the Turks were not obliged to do anything for us. There were so few houses and so many of us that we were ten or twelve per room. It was excessively hot and our food was bad. For the first few days the markets had nothing to offer and little was issued by way of rations, excepting some rotten biscuit and meat that was going off. Then the water in the wells was dirty and tasted bad, and the mosquitoes which devoured us day and night. All this made our first month horrible.

The printer Antoine Galland even sounded nostalgic for the ship he had just left:

I found accommodation in the house of the Venetian consul and spent the first night on some straw and then, after that, on some damp matting, being devoured by lice, fleas and bugs. Those who still had hammocks were the lucky ones.[9]

Bernoyer had survived his shipwreck, but so too had his sense of grievance and, from the Hotel de la Régance, where he slept on the floor in his coat, he began one of the first of many rants:

As I waited I cursed a thousand times the one who had brought us to such a country. I found out that our government had tricked us by sending an army into the lands of the Grand Seigneur without declaring war, and with no reason for declaring war. Bonaparte had won too much influence in France through his victories, and he was an inconvenience, not to say an obstacle, to those who reigned in France. In order to keep power these latter sought to rid themselves of the one man they feared.

Jollois, a civil engineer with the scholars, heard some of his colleagues expressing similar opinions:

Citizen Dolomieu was angry and displayed his discontent at the way in which a group of young men had been tricked into leaving their hearths, their relatives, their friends by promises of marvels and wonders, only to be abandoned.

Jollois noted that this sense of disappointment was becoming nearly universal amongst the soldiers too, adding, 'We entered the French camp where the soldiers were still eating their biscuit and, on the whole, most were happy to be on land although many were unimpressed by the country's resources and already wanted to leave.'

---

9. The residence of the Venetian consul was where the French established their printing press. Two Arab presses (one from Rome) and one French press ran out 4,000 more copies of Napoleon's proclamation. A smaller press, managed by Marc-Aurel, was soon sent south to Cairo.

They were soon to leave, but only for Cairo. General Kléber was left to manage the port, and to pacify the scholars, whilst Napoleon's attention switched to waging war on the Mamelukes. In order to reach the Nile and then Cairo, at least according to D'Anville's flawed map of 1765, he had two options. These were described by Sulkowski as

> one route along the coast which in five hours would bring you to Aboukir and its castle, harbour and fresh water spring ... from there there was a way down to Rosetta, some eight hours' distant for infantry. The other cut straight across the desert only reaching the Nile after 48 miles at Ramanieh passing through Damanhour, quite a sizable town for Egypt, before it did so. This route was shorter.[10]

The latter was also considerably more difficult, given that it ran through an arid desert and badlands haunted by hostile Bedouins. Napoleon was keen to strike quickly, before the Mamelukes could organise, so whilst Dugua, who had replaced the injured Kléber, took his division and his teenage son off along the easier path to Rosetta, Napoleon prepared the bulk of the French expeditionary force for the ordeal of the sands. The commissariat was burdened with supplying everyone's needs, and managed to hire 1,000 camels, but canteens for water were scarcer and food for so many men was hard to come by, or unsuitable, as Vigo-Roussillon noted:

> The squadron and transports landed supplies consisting of livestock, salted meat and some Provencal wine and brandy. This was distributed and supposed to last a few days. They also issued biscuits and some dried vegetables but, lacking pots and water in which to cook this food, it proved useless. In any case salted meat, Provencal wine and brandy are not the best stuff to give soldiers marching across a waterless desert during an Egyptian July.[11]

---

10. The lowly infantryman Laporte agreed and adds the distance to Damanhour: 'There were two routes from Alexandria. One towards the branch of the Nile which passes through Rosetta and from there on to Cairo, the other through Damanhour reached after a march of 24 miles of arid desert.' Contemporary measurements gave the Damanhour route as 19 Leagues and 25 Leagues via Rosetta.

11. Chasseur Millet did not get any of the wine but confirms that 'we were just issued with a pound of biscuit for three days'.

3

Desert

On 7 July Jacques Miot caught sight of Napoleon riding out of
Alexandria. The general, or Emir of the French, was in good spirits,
'his head wrapped in a handkerchief and he tapped shoulder of General
Berthier several times, telling him "well, Berthier, here we are at last".'
Behind him came his army, or rather military caravan, which Théviôtte
delighted in describing:

> There were generals mounted on richly harnessed French horses and
> riding alongside hideous camels carrying huge loads, donkeys and
> mules charged with water, and goats and sheep herded by soldiers
> who would kill them in the desert. Many of the French officers were
> mounted on mules. I saw 5,000 or 6,000 Frenchmen far from their
> homeland, transplanted to foreign climes and burnt by the oppressive
> heat; but they were all so patient and good-humoured just as if they
> were in the plains of Flanders.[1]

The good humour would only last as long as the unfortunate sheep. Godet
was among the first to lose patience:

> Imagine the position of the French army as it waited at Alexandria
> having arrived expecting to find itself in the most fortunate country
> in the world, but only to find itself in the midst of nothing but sand,

---

1. One of the camels belonged to the Irishman Bernard MacSheehy: 'I am indebted
   to the energy and good sense of my servant for the camel which I am now
   loading with two goat-skin bags, one for water, one for vinegar. This camel
   shall also carry a part of my baggage and that of my comrades, and five days of
   provisions consisting of biscuits procured from the ships.'

ruins and dust. Panting in the sun and overcome with fatigue we suffered in the excessive heat without any fountain to quench our thirst or any trees to provide shade in which we could escape this scourge. What sad reflexions weighed upon us. But we had started so we had to continue and we thus consoled ourselves that no doubt the interior of the country more closely resembled that promised and this hope, combined with necessity, that imperious mistress, encouraged everyone to hope things would improve.

There was indeed water ahead, just not much of it and that in the first well at El-Beydah was almost undrinkable. Besides, according to Belliard, it was only sufficient for 1,000 or 1,200 men. Then it was gone, as Quartermaster François found to his horror:

> The water ran out within five minutes. The soldiers had thrown themselves at it in such a way that a number were suffocated whilst others were crushed by the crowd. More than thirty men died at these wells and many of those who could not get at the water killed themselves.[2]

Sulkowski noted that once the existing water had gone 'it took several hours of work to get some fresh water out, and even then it was mostly mud. Each man of the division was issued with half a glass'. His plaintive 'what a start' summed up the chaos. Savary on the staff agreed: 'There was anger when they saw the wells. Morale plummeted and the soldiers began to curse and complain ... It took the sappers an hour to clear the well and for some water to trickle in. It was yellow and brackish, muddy really, but even so they began to fight to get at it. We were obliged to post sentries and organise the distribution. We made soup out of it, burning brush for want of wood. Others drank it, gulping down this foul liquid. Knoreng opened a bottle of wine as we began to die of thirst.'[3]

---

2. Vertray was saddened to see 'the men collapse on the right and the left, dying of thirst, panting. I saw men begging their comrades as they fought to get at that brackish sludge, and I saw others collapse and die following this atrocious torture.' Godet's men lacked canteens or the means to store water. His commander, Belliard, noted in his diary that the dearth of water 'caused considerable suffering amongst the soldiers who had had nothing to drink since Alexandria'.
3. Captain Garbé of the engineers was the one tasked with restoring the flow of water at the destroyed wells of El-Beydah. He remembered 'taking the sappers and working for four hours but only managing to obtain a small quantity of brackish water which was, however, soon gulped down. It was consumed and we had to wait for two more hours before the water was replenished.'

Poor Laval in the infantry could only dream of wine as he tried the water:

> We had not found any water since leaving Alexandria but there were
> four wells here. We had four divisions making nearly 9,000 men and
> each division was allocated a well. They were drunk dry and whatever
> remained was impossible to stomach. I was extremely thirsty and was
> obliged to squeeze some mud through my handkerchief in order to
> obtain something with which to quench my thirst.[4]

At the next well at Berket there was so little water that even the lucky ones
had to spoon it into their cups. Things were getting desperate as the more
fortunate made money on the suffering of the thirsty. Jean-Baptiste Vertray
was asked to pay 12 francs for two bottles whilst young Louis Thurman was
ready to offer even more:

> I would have given ten years of my life for a glass of water. I was not
> the only one to think so but many were taking huge gulps of brandy to
> quench their thirst. Temporary refreshment was soon followed by regret.

In addition to thirst, Godet was also concerned about food and he was
relieved that at least at Berket, 'the inhabitants had organised a little market
outside the gates and there were eggs, chicken, pigeons, geese and little
breads (of the kind they eat here), all supervised by an inhabitant who spoke
some Italian. We paid for everything exactly.'[5]

Poultry was welcome for what paltry rations had been issued were gone
within a matter of days, as the republican Count Sulkowski noted:

> By the 5th there was a real lack of food as, despite the soldiers being
> issued with supplies for three days, they had, as usual, consumed
> everything at once or thrown it away. There was no bread to be had
> and the soldiers had only just reached a well when Desaix received the
> order to push on. We had to leave without obtaining anything.[6]

---

4. Godet used a muslin cloth to serve as a filter.
5. Savary confirmed that 'in the twenty-four hours we were based in Berket the
   villagers sold us a quantity of things and preferred that the men pay with their
   buttons rather than with the coin we were offering them'. Bernoyer heard how 'a
   soldier had offered a woman some coins for two chickens, but she had preferred
   to take the lens from a telescope'.
6. François Durand, a musician in the 75th Line, was 'quadruple tired' and having
   spent the night undressed now found himself 'absolutely devoured by insects'. He
   had just enough energy to complain of the dearth of food, recalling that 'the rations
   were really meagre, each soldier got three little buns the size of a six Franc coin'.

Pierre Boyer saw some of the consequences:

> The soldier, loaded with provisions, is soon overcome by the heat and
> the burden he carries in less than an hour, throws everything away
> without thought of tomorrow. Thirst torments him, and hunger, for he
> has not a piece of bread. So, it was in this scene of woe that we saw
> several soldiers die of thirst, of hunger and from the heat, whilst others,
> witness to the suffering of their comrades, blew out their own brains.[7]

Under such circumstances, the mood turned very sour. Vigo-Roussillon was
looking for someone to blame:

> Lives could have been saved if each soldier had only been issued with
> a canteen in which to conserve water. The commander-in-chief who
> knew where we were destined and who knew what to expect, was
> responsible for this lapse. If he was concerned that such equipment
> would give our destination away, he could have had them secretly
> loaded and stored, only handing them out, with water, at Alexandria.[8]

The strain on the officer corps was immense and many of them were trying
to set a good example, as Théviôtte of the Engineers noted:

> The soldiers make off with lots of poultry, pigeons, melons, some rice,
> lentils and beans, and some of the local bread, dough cooked to the size of
> a six Franc coin. The officers have more to complain of than the soldiers as
> they cannot obtain food by pillage and they are overwhelmed by having to
> deal with all manner of details. For the last eight days I have been sleeping
> in my coat on the sand. I get up at two and drag myself through the day's
> heat, reduced to eating meat without bread and some imperfect melons.

Godet also mused on the injustice of rank:

> As for we officers, we could not pillage. So I spent twelve days without
> anything to eat other than melons and watermelons. Only on one

---

7. It was worse for the dismounted cavalry. Desvernois noted that 'the hussars of my
   regiment were obliged to carry their saddles and harnessing as well as the rest of
   their equipment'. The officer of dragoons noted that 'those soldiers who carried their
   saddles were promised that they would be the first to be mounted'. He adds that they
   'made a bundle of their saddle, bridle and helmet and carried it on their heads'.
8. Vertray was a little luckier, finding water in Al-Qaryah: 'I have never drunk so
   much water, and so greedily. It was as though we had become sponges that could
   never be saturated. The water was so sweet I could not get enough and I emptied
   the steel cup I had purchased in Marseilles twenty times.'

occasion did I find some bread. At Chobrakhit I saw a woman on a roof and signalled to her that I needed bread. I threw a coin to her and she brought me two loaves. I asked if there was more but she said, 'la, la, mafich'. Such a small amount would not go far.

Joseph Marie Moiret agreed that, in such circumstances, the officers' lot was an unhappy one:

The officers were suffering enormously, for the ordinary soldiers could obtain food through pillage and violence, leaving nothing for the officers to purchase. We were too polite to sit at the table of our subordinates, so, whilst the soldiers ate pigeons, chickens and other birds, the officers were reduced to eating some disgusting and insufficient beans. We had never suffered so badly, exhausted after marching over burning sands, we were deprived of wine and bread and other fortifying foods whilst surrounded by an enemy ever ready to ambush us, thus depriving us of sleep and rest too.

MacSheehy was soon telling a friend that 'on the fleet we regretted France. In Egypt, I fear, we shall come to regret the fleet.'[9] Jean-Baptiste Guillot of the 25th Line also found himself prey to negativity, complaining that he did 'not have a bit of bread to eat nor a drop of water to quench my thirst, indeed I had nothing by way of comfort except damning and cursing this vile trade of war for a hundred times each day'. Louis Gay was already nostalgic for France, telling his parents:

If we have the good fortune to soon return to France, I shall ask to be discharged regardless of the cost. I can no longer endure this damned business. Always risking my life and at every hour of the day. For the rest, I think I have done my bit, let everyone do a little. I am no longer greedy for glory. I was once, I confess, because it was a requirement. Now my only desire is to spend my life peacefully with you. This is the sole object of my ambition. Some hopes of a promotion are held out to me but I will have none of it. I have seen service in Europe, but I have no desire to see it in Africa and in a country as hot as this one.[10]

---

9. Poor MacSheehy was soon asking to be relieved because 'six months in the most horrible country in the world has destroyed my health and my physical and moral strength'.

10. A consignment of complaining letters was intercepted by the Royal Navy on 7 August 1798. The British, rather uncharitably, published them and even included a letter from Napoleon to his brother Joseph in which the general, referring to his wife, confesses that 'as for myself, I suffer much from domestic troubles'.

François Leturcq was also having doubts, telling his father:

> I will not pretend to deny that it is a great advantage to me, already
> a veteran, to be taking part in such an important and instructive an
> expedition. However, having seen the country as it really is, and having
> been through a great deal of privations and suffering, I am not too
> sure, were it to begin again, that I would want to undertake it.

If morale was low amongst the officers, that of the soldiers had collapsed.
Niello-Sargy, on a staff always sensitive to hints of insubordination, saw
that 'the soldiers were nearly at the point of refusing to march'. Worse, some
were making the point by suicide: 'I saw soldiers finish themselves off before
the commander-in-chief, declaring "this is your fault".'[11]

As the murmuring continued, General Belliard confessed in his diary
that 'the army is, on the whole, discontent and the officers careless as they
let their soldiers run amok through the villages we march through, taking
whatever it is they need. Still the soldiers are not happy and entire brigades
are making it known. The commander-in-chief gave them a stern harangue
and nobody said a word.'

Jean-Baptiste Prosper Jollois heard about the harangue and how one
regiment had shouted back, obliging Napoleon to tell them, 'We are in this
fucking country and will stay here. Six months from now I hope to have
left and I shall take those who have most distinguished themselves with me.'

The muttering continued. An anonymous officer of the 32nd Line noted
that 'every evening our soldiers talked politics, debated or complained.
"Why have we been sent here?" they said. "The Directory has deported us!"
Others turned on the scholars, saying that they had tricked the general to
come so they could pillage the ruins. For the soldiers the scholars were the
reason behind the expedition and the full weight of their ill-humour was
directed at them. When the Bedouins approached the soldiers would form
square and shout "scholars and donkeys to the centre".'[12]

---

11. An episode repeated by Captain Rozis who recalled that 'we had several men
    blow their brains out in the presence of the general, telling him first "you are to
    blame".'
12. Chanut, p. 29. Bernoyer's explanation for this was that 'there has always been a
    kind of antipathy between the soldiers and the employees of the administration.
    Here, however, there is real hatred of the scholars. The soldiers accuse them of being
    the cause of the expedition to Egypt, their motive being, apparently, curiosity and
    the pursuit of knowledge. This caprice obliges the soldiers to expose themselves to
    numerous dangers daily, and all the fatigues associated with this difficult land. So,
    wherever the scholars find themselves, they have to run the gauntlet of the soldiers'
    mistrust. Despite Bonaparte's efforts to maintain discipline, there are complaints
    coming in every day about the insubordination of the soldiery.'

The Bedouins seemed to be everywhere and would ride along the columns 'like sharks following ships'. This was significant for these ferocious nomads stopped the French from living off the land, as Godet noted:

> It was impossible to stray beyond our outposts as there was a risk that one would be captured by the Bedouins who infested the region and who, mounted on excellent little horses, could swoop down and massacre or carry off into the desert anyone who went 20 paces beyond our lines. They killed two carabiniers of the 1st Battalion and a drummer, making off with his drum.

Gerbaud had time to note that the Arabs 'are mounted on fast horses and have high saddles and large iron stirrups. They wear white and carry a musket, sword and pistols.' Gunner Bricard, however, was less afraid of their weapons than their reputation:

> Several men were seized by the Arabs as these wretches continuously swirled around our column and massacred anyone who wandered too far off. Indeed, after using them to satisfy their criminal passion in a way in which, in any other country, nature would revolt, they would torture them to death with a thousand cruelties.[13]

As the main body struggled through the desert, those sent off down the coast to Rosetta also found themselves in trouble. Chasseur Millet of the 2nd Light recorded a spate of suicides as there was 'no bread, no water in this desert which burns our feet. Overcome with fatigue, hunger and thirst, despair was such that several soldiers blew out their brains.' Fortunately, the white minarets of Rosetta could soon be seen and this trading station and pretty Nile port proved a welcome relief, except for Joseph Moiret who complained that 'the Jews sold us some foul wine at an exaggerated price'. Others, however, were more fortunate and Lieutenant Pierre Louis Cailleux rejoiced in 'the immense groves of date trees, and the superb gardens full of lemon and orange trees with their superb scent'. Laugier of the staff also found Rosetta something of an oasis: 'We made our entrance at noon. The town seemed quite pretty. The inhabitants watched from their doorsteps and all the shops were open. You cannot imagine such confidence, such trust. This was the first nice thing to have happened to us since reaching Egypt. The view of the Nile from here is quite charming and did us much good.'

---

13. François-Michel Lucet thought the Arabs 'cowardly, barbarous and ill-disciplined. Anyone who had the misfortune to fall into their hands fell victim to their ferocity.' One twelve-year-old daughter of a dragoon was spared, however. She was married to Abou Kourah of the Bakaryeh tribe and was still alive in 1830.

Meanwhile, the main body reached Damanhour where the first generals to arrive were greeted by a mufti carrying a platter of bread, honey and cheese. Quartermaster François, however, found the place considerably less welcoming, recalling that 'as we entered the town we were shot at and as we always carried our weapons handy we returned fire. The firing became intense. A few of the inhabitants were seized and killed. ... This severity dissuaded the others from any further disobedience and they brought out food which we paid for. They had bread flat as pancakes, lentils, pigeons and chickens.'[14] With their stomachs full, the troops began to sing the Marseillaise as they marched back out into the desert.

It was then that they had first sight of the enemy, the cavalry of the Mameluke warlords who controlled Egypt. It turned out to be just a few enemy scouts under Mohammed-el-Elfi sent on ahead of the Mameluke main body. Godet recorded this development: 'That afternoon a detachment made up from different regiments of cavalry was sent out on reconnaissance. It encountered a body of Mamelukes perhaps 250-men strong and they came to blows, with our men eventually returning to camp. They brought back some wounded along with amazing tales of the ability and bravery of these new foes.'[15]

Savary, who had spent the night sleeping on a rug in a bathhouse in the same room as the Pole he calls Sabronoski (Sulkowski), confirms this account, noting that 'as we came out of the town we were attacked by some Mamelukes. The two guns with the Guides saw them off. They retreated less quickly than Austrians, taking their time to do so.'

Sulkowski himself was unimpressed, but tempered his optimism with a soldier's reasoning:

> Those in favour of the expedition as well as all the soldiers themselves, thought that just a handful of Europeans could take on this undisciplined horde which would flee at the sound of artillery, whilst the locals thought that these men represented the pinnacle of valour and the most redoubtable set of men the Turks had. For those of us who had fought them, it is difficult to give a precise opinion, for much will depend on the weather, the ground and the circumstances.

General Belliard was glad this first skirmish had gone so well:

> The enemy approached and drew close, leaping about on horseback and skirmishing by firing some carbine shots whilst we were being issued our meat ration. ... We had two wounded but this little action,

---

14. A chicken cost 20 parats, a pound of rice 3 parats.
15. The Mameluke vanguard was under the command of Osman-el-Bardisi, whilst the main body was still being organised outside Cairo.

which was little more than a tease, was good for the morale of the men. The soldier could see what we were up against and that the enemy had no idea regarding tactics and that he had nothing to fear from men who had never waged war. In truth, I have never seen men so badly organised [as the enemy]. They chase each other around chaotically and without listening to their officers.

Godet agreed with his superior:

During this encounter we learned a great deal about their tactics and, however brave they were as individuals, the way they fought did little to trouble us. They threw themselves forward at great speed, making as if to fall on the square but, arriving at a certain distance they suddenly reined their horses in, wheeling around and firing a carbine shot at us over their shoulder. In order to deal with such a threat, all that was required was to maintain order and not show fear.[16]

After this little skirmish, morale was raised still further when the soldiers caught sight of the majestic, refreshing Nile. Vertray and his men were delighted to see the river at Ramanieh, and he celebrated by going for a swim. Savary saw he had company as when 'we reached Ramanieh the soldiers threw themselves into the water and began to drink like animals. In a flash, the entire division was in the river.' Desvernois the hussar 'took my horse to drink. I did the same, then found some hay and barley for my horse Constant, a magnificent Norman mount, strong, sturdy and whom I greatly valued.' Only then did he 'go for a bathe in the Nile and stayed there for two hours, washing and refreshing myself. Coming out of the river I felt ever so hungry but I had nothing to eat.'

The infantryman Laval also found that drinking water did not wash away his hunger, but he found temporary relief in strange fruit:

Having nothing to eat, and not knowing the language of the country, you can imagine the situation I and my comrades found ourselves in. We owed our existence to watermelons which we found beside the Nile. You can imagine the surprise of the entire army which had been promised a rich and fertile country in the general's proclamation. He spoke of gold and silver, but we would have just been happy to find some bread.[17]

---

16. Sulkowski soon agreed, recording that 'it was the third skirmish we had with them in three days and it had an excellent effect on the soldiers as they saw how their enemy's valour failed before discipline and coolness'.
17. Admiral Jean-Baptiste Perrée of the Nile flotilla would agree. He wrote, 'We were six days without anything to eat but watermelons, watermelons for our dinner and watermelons for our dessert.'

Napoleon must have heard the complaint for he came amongst Moiret's invincible but dissatisfied 75th, 'chatting familiarly with the soldiers as they openly expressed their discontent and their misery. In order to console them and to give them courage, he did not spare his promises. In a few days, he said, when we reach the capital of Egypt, you will have plenty, white bread, good meat, excellent wine, sugar, mocha coffee.' Bernoyer must have heard the same promise about the bread for he quipped that 'we should have replied that it was completely unnecessary to bring us to Africa for bread, as Europe is full of the stuff'.

Ramanieh provided some food but the soldiers supplemented their diet by shooting all the town's pigeons and then by stealing. Appetites were satisfied and Major of Engineers Jean-François Detroye watched as the soldiers settled down:

> Some were employed plucking the poultry or skinning the sheep they had stolen, whilst others queued for rations. A few hours later and there were birds cooking on the ends of ramrods and soup was boiling in all kinds of pots and pans. Then they turned to their other need and straw and blankets were laid out and the soldiers fell asleep in their clothes.

After sharing some of its plenty, the Nile also brought relief in the form of a French Nile flotilla. On 11 July the aptly named gunships *Victoire* and *Esperance*, ably supported by the *Sans Quartier*, escorting barges with ammunition and biscuit, arrived as did Dugua's division which also now rejoined the main body. Battle seemed imminent for the Mamelukes had also sent some gunboats on ahead of their sizable army. This mass had formed under the Prophet's Banner and, like an agitated sea, was now advancing from Cairo and Boulak.

It was the Mameluke vanguard, sent forwards by the scar-faced Mourad, that first tested Napoleon's resolve with a reconnaissance in force. The two sides met on 13 July at Chebreiss (also known as Shubrakhit or Chobrakhit). The morning began fresh and cool, and Napoleon again had the Marseillaise played, which, according to Vertray, had 'the usual effect on the men'. The French were advancing in square formations, like the ancients in their phalanxes, to protect themselves from cavalry. Pelleport noted how 'each division was ordered to form squares six men deep and with any civilians and the baggage in the centre. The grenadiers formed the reserve and the artillery was placed in the intervals between battalions. Then the squares were placed in order to offer mutual protection.' The French had expected a cavalry charge but the Mamelukes surprised everyone by seizing the initiative on the river, their Greek-manned gunboats sinking some French boats and their infantry butchering those who made it to the bank.[18] The engineer

---

18. The French gunboats opened up on the enemy between the villages of Miniet-Salameh and Chebreiss; six of their smaller boats were sunk by Mameluke artillery and the enemy flotilla.

Detroye saw how 'the enemy fire was intense and accurate and their first discharge sank the boat containing the engineers, the crew and the officers barely managing to escape. Some other boats quickly succumbed to the same fate despite the efforts of our xebec, and the galley was abandoned.' This first naval setback was not fatal, for the French soon recovered their composure, 'blowing up the enemy's flagship, which exploded with a horrific bang'.

By then the army was also in action. The squares had continued forwards, Sulkowski watching as 'Desaix's [division] occupied the village, Reynier's was on the right, Bon's on the left. Vial and Dugua protected Reynier's right whilst between Bon and the Nile there were a few hundred men more.' Now the Mameluke cavalry responded and Desvernois marvelled at 'such a magnificent sight. The desert beneath the blue sky and, before us, beautiful Arab chargers richly harnessed and leaping, pirouetting and caracoling beneath warlike riders in armour enriched with jewels and gold ... it was such a novel sight for the soldiers on account of its splendour.'

It was a novel but also dangerous sight. Godet was pacing around inside his square when 'a corps of around 8,000 mounted soldiers, amongst whom we could see many unarmed slaves, swarmed over the plain. Some advanced to trade shots with the squares but they were soon driven back. One of them, dressed magnificently and riding an excellent horse, galloped at close range along our line, seemingly conducting a reconnaissance which might proceed their attack.'

Jean-Pierre Doguereau, commanding Bon's artillery, also watched as some of the Mamelukes opted for valour over discretion and rode forwards:

> They were rearing up on their horses when, doubtless to encourage the others, a few of the bolder ones came forward and charged our skirmishers. Death was the reward for their audacity. It was a superb sight, watching this brilliant army wheeling around before our battalions, their bright armour, their saddles, their harnessing embellished with gold and silver, all brilliantly shining in the sun. They came forwards a few times but our guns and the discipline of our squares made them less keen to attack us.

Godet also had the impression that the magnificent Mamelukes were hesitating before their strange adversaries:

> The Mamelukes came before us as a body of cavalry, numerous, armed with excellent carbines and mounted on the continent's best horses. Their curved sabres, decorated with silver, are fine, well made and often very valuable. There is no cavalry which is more agile, better armed or better mounted; even so, few of them dared to hurl themselves against our infantry and those that did seemed to be doing so to bait us into moving. However brave and tough they were, they were also prudent.

Joseph Laporte was glad to see the horsemen discomforted by French artillery, observing how 'the enemy was within half a cannon-shot range when the commander-in-chief had the artillery fire and it was so well aimed that each shot told and the howitzers especially sowed disorder in the enemy ranks'. Still, the mass of riders continued towards them, with the 'Mamelukes being so well received by one side of the square so that they thought to try another or the rear, directing their charge accordingly only to be met even more warmly'. Laval agreed, suggesting that despite 'their soldiers being the finest cavalry in the world' they could not 'endure a few rounds of artillery and they were also unaccustomed to see soldiers formed up in squares. We had four, each division forming one. They thought that the French soldiers were joined together.' The French artillery, firing grapeshot, canisters packed with shot, was proving just as devastating for the Mamelukes as it had for countless squadrons of cavalry on the battlefields of Europe. The squares, too, proved their worth. However, Sulkowski admitted that the novel technique of advancing in that formation was a test of endurance, for 'a long march squashed together like that was a kind of torture for everyone involved'. Miot, whose imagination compared the enemy to the army of Darius, also saw that waiting in the ranks required patience and observed that when a square brought down riders 'some soldiers then quit our ranks, running over to their victim as a hunter would to his prey; this proved a successful tactic, and the reward for such audacity was the pillaging of the fallen Mameluke'.

The Mameluke tactics were not working, and Bon's division now advanced into the plain to drive them back. The horsemen made a final effort, and one of Mourad's officers, incensed by the prospect of defeat, sought to lead by example. François Vigo-Roussillon marvelled at his temerity:

A Mameluke officer approached our square and shouted out in Italian 'if, amongst you Frenchmen, there is anyone brave enough, I await you'. Our cavalry was in no state to take up this challenge and he followed us, insulting us, wheeling about. We fired a few rounds at him but a sergeant of voltigeurs was lucky enough to send him flying with a lucky shot.

The first battle was over. Adjutant Pierre Boyer felt it had been an anti-climax:

This rabble, for I can scarce call them soldiers, have no idea about tactics and know nothing about war save the blood that is spilt in it. They first appeared before our army on 13 July and from dawn on that very day showed themselves and then straggled round and round our troops like so many cattle, sometimes galloping and sometimes trotting past in bands of 10, 50 or 100. Before long they made a ridiculous but intriguing attempt to get at us but, finding unexpected resistance, they spent the day keeping us standing beneath the burning sun. Had we been a little more enterprising on that day then I think we would have swept them away but General Bonaparte was cautious so that he could test the enemy and see their manner of waging war.[19]

But, whatever the result, Chasseur Millet and his fellow infantrymen were exhausted:

> That evening we lay down to rest without bothering to ask which of us was to cook for we had no bread, no meat, no wood, no pot and it had been like that for ten days. We just had melons and Nile water, although they found some rotten biscuits in a barge on the Nile and these were issued to us.

It was left to General Zajaczek, a man with 'all the qualities of an honest man but none of those of a general', to pursue the enemy and he followed the retreating Mamelukes that hot and dusty Bastille Day, their path to Menouf marked by vultures feeding off the dead horses. Victory had not brought plenty for the French and, at Abou-Nochabeh, Gerbaud saw a 'frightful amount of pillaging in the village. Women screaming and crying. Cruelty of our situation – having to see the soldiers dying of hunger and fatigue and then witness a crowd of women begging for our protection.'

Sulkowski noted the effect of such thievery on the locals and concluded that the French were having to teach them the hard lesson that 'it is better to sacrifice some of one's belongings than to be exposed to the full ravages of war'. Some of the locals were, however, flourishing under their new masters. At Menouf the villagers were soon back and charging exorbitant prices, and Łazowski was taken aback by this unexpected entrepreneurial streak, writing to his superior that 'the pay the soldiers receive is insufficient for even a part of his needs, the villagers are selling things to us at twenty times the price the locals pay and I do not have to tell you, general, that if we wish to rein in the indiscipline of the troops, which is frightful, then we should acknowledge that they have cause'.

Within a matter of days, however, the French army had more pressing concerns. The main body of Mamelukes under Ibrahim Bey and Mourad Bey, with 6,000 horsemen and 10,000 servants and foot soldiers, had positioned themselves to bar the French advance to Cairo. The French would have to beat them to enter the capital and so, after a brief rest at Wardan, Napoleon's men again marched off to battle.

On Saturday 21 July Laugier trotted out to scout the enemy:

---

19. MacSheehy of Dublin put it more succinctly as 'they are men perfectly well-mounted and well-armed who come to be massacred'.

It was early and as the division was setting out, General Murat, accompanied by just one dragoon, expressed a wish to ride out to meet the enemy. I agreed to go with him and we went to within cannon shot of the Mameluke camp. We could clearly make out their tents and saw that they were mounting up and forming ranks.

François, in Reynier's division, also saw that another battle was due:

Desaix's division was a little in advance, followed by Reynier's. At dawn we saw a body of Mamelukes, perhaps 6,000 men. They fell back slowly and soon we were before their main body. At six the sun came up and before us were the pyramids. The army halted. It was then that Bonaparte motioned towards them and told us 'soldiers, you shall fight the masters of Egypt and, as you do so, remember that forty centuries look down upon you!' We shouted long live the republic, long live Bonaparte.

Laporte was caught up in the enthusiasm:

When the sun rose above the horizon we saw the pyramids of Gizah before us and we spontaneously halted to admire this, our very first sight of them. 'Soldiers', declared Bonaparte to a group of men close by, 'you shall today fight for control of Egypt; recall that from the heights of those monuments forty centuries look down upon you'. These memorable words were appreciated by the victors of Lodi, Arcole, Castiglione and Rivoli and, after a pause, the French army advanced so it was one and a half miles from the village of Embabeh [Imbaba] where the enemy was.

Pelleport heard Napoleon's epic speech but failed to feel the hand of history on his shoulder, snidely remarking that 'in order to stimulate our courage he rode along the front of each division, gesturing to the pyramids and shouting "40 centuries look down upon you!". He might have been speaking Greek for all our comrades understood his rhetoric, but, in any case, they applauded out of habit.'

Napoleon, who outnumbered his enemy, and thought that he could exploit the distrust between Mourad Bey and Ibrahim Bey, again deployed his troops into squares. He had Desaix and Reynier on the French right, whilst Dugua was in the centre with Vial and Bon close to the banks of the Nile, shuffling towards the village of Embabeh, occupied by the Mameluke infantry and their artillery. Sulkowski saw that the dust kicked up by so many troops was proving a torture, but, through it, Vertray's experienced eye caught sight of an enemy ranged below the pyramids:

The Mamelukes lined up along the Nile covering Gizah and masking some pieces of artillery. Their tents were still erect for they had no doubt of victory. There were three times as many and they greeted us with their trilling, but we had seen them once already and knew not to show our fear.

The squares helped bolster morale and Godet, amongst the 21st Light, checked behind his wall of infantry to see 'the donkeys and the scholars as well as the administrative staff and the cavalry, whether mounted or not, in the centre of the square whilst the artillery was at each corner. Each square was ten or twelve ranks deep.'[20]

Desaix's division, halted in the gardens of the village of Bechtil, where the men were busy pillaging grapes, was not quite ready when the attack came. The men scrambled to get into their defensive formations and, despite a donkey thrashing about, managed to just in time for Laporte saw the enemy had begun this battle of the Pyramids with a tremendous charge of mounted warriors:

At the sight of our five little squares the Mamelukes swarmed out in great numbers from behind some earthworks, where there were 2,000 infantry and thirty-seven guns, and began to divide up into groups which then began to bear down on Desaix's and Reynier's divisions. When they drew within range, two of these masses charged forward with extraordinary impetuosity. One went for the right-hand corner of Desaix's division, the other the left side of Reynier's.

The riders, charging into the wind, sand, dust and smoke, swept forwards and General Belliard, putting some order into Desaix's ranks, watched them approach:

We saw the enemy drawn up before the village of Embabeh. No sooner had we established ourselves in position and rested the men a little than the Mamelukes mounted their horses and came forwards to do battle. They rode like lightening and arrived like thunder. Their first target was the divisions formed on our right. They charged with a rare impetuosity and bravery. Our soldiers, once they had got over their fright, met them with much coolness.

Laporte confirms the initial bout of nerves before this splendid host:

The French were a little intimidated by the sight of this cavalry but recalled that they were 150 miles from Alexandria and 2,400 from their homeland, with no prospect of any support other than their own

---

20. Most scholars had, as we have seen, remained in Alexandria. Monge, Berthollet and a handful of others had, however, accompanied the army south.

courage, and no possibility to retreat and so knew that they would either have to be victorious or die in the attempt.

Vertray and the men in Reynier's division had no intention of dying:

In the blink of an eye we formed square six-ranks deep ready for the coming shock. The order to fire came when the cloud of cavalry was almost upon us. Our firing by ranks was so effective that the charge broke and swirled around our battalions. The Mamelukes lost a large number of men including quite a few officers. It mattered little, they launched another furious charge although this time they left even more men scattered across the ground. ... The soldiers fired so calmly that not a shot went to waste for they only pulled the trigger when the cavalry was almost upon them. The number of corpses around us was enormous and many of them caught fire.[21]

François in the 9th Line also saw the French wait until they could see the whites of the enemy's eyes:

We were ordered to stand still. We could barely breathe. Colonel Marmont told us not to open fire until his command. The Mamelukes were nearly upon us. The order was given. It was a massacre. Even so the enemy's sabres struck out at the bayonets of the men in the first rank and chaos ensued. Horses and riders flung themselves against us, others turned away. Some of the Mamelukes had their clothes set on fire by wadding from our muskets. I stood by our standard and could see how the Mamelukes who had been wounded or burned were now slashing at the legs of our first rank. I never saw men who were braver or more determined.

Godet confirms the effect of such deadly musketry:

They came at great speed against Reynier's division but it remained firm and met them with a well-aimed discharge and so they then turned against us only to be received the same way. The first three ranks, having fired a volley, presented their bayonets and created a wall of iron from behind which the other ranks continued to fire. The battle was

---

21. Laporte confirms that the French fire was devastating: 'The Mamelukes were received with the calmness and bravery that characterises the true soldier and the fire from our squares was so accurate and effective that the ground before us where the Mamelukes had charged was instantly covered with dead or wounded men and horses.' Niello-Sagy adds that the French 'opened up at ten paces, and brought 200 crashing down; canister did the rest'.

soon over. The ground was covered with the dead and wounded and a few brave men who had come to die on our bayonets. The charge had been pressed home but they were probably astonished by the resistance they met and some of them, perhaps having lost control of their horses, found themselves to our rear.

But the French did not get things all their own way. François Vigo-Roussillon saw some of the enemy cavalry break through the French ranks:

General Reynier's division, to our right, was the first to be attacked. Even though the soldiers were veterans, gaps were created in the ranks by the flailing of falling horses brought down at point-blank range just as they were launched at our men by their riders. Some twenty-five Mamelukes seized the opportunity of this gap to force their way in but they were all killed or taken.

The musician François Durand of the 75th under Dugua saw a similar incident, and watched as such temerity was addressed:

A dozen of them broke in to the square of General Bon having fought their way through the rampart of bayonets, the wall of muskets, but they did not succeed as they were cut down and their chivalry was finished off. Shouting Allah was the last thing they did.

The dismounted dragoon Merme was just as appalled by this Mameluke fury:

They were so angry that I saw some of them attempt to force their horses to leap onto us in an attempt to break our ranks. Others who had lost their mounts or been wounded crept up to the legs of our soldiers in an attempt to bite or stab them. They were bayoneted or struck down.

Belliard showed a more professional respect for such valour:

I have never seen, in all the years I have been at war, a charge pushed forwards with such determination and which cost those charging so many casualties. The space in front of the squares was covered with enemy dead, whole rows of them. That day was most exhausting but the soldiers did not complain. Fortunately, we were commanding veterans, otherwise there would be no more Frenchmen in Egypt.

Meanwhile, Bon's division, over by the Nile, was being raked by the Mameluke gunboats and artillery and suffered more than most. Jean-Pierre Doguereau, an artilleryman himself, watched as 'their guns in the earthworks, supported by those on their boats on the Nile, opened up and hit our flank. For a moment there was shock. Files of five or six men were knocked down with one shot and the troops, drawn up in such dense formations, suffered greatly.'

Bon's men countered by advancing in column, and emerging through clouds of dust and smoke to storm the village, drive out the Mameluke's Albanian and Cretan infantry and bayonet the gunners. The loss of the village threatened the Mameluke rear and the Mameluke army began to tear itself apart. With the battle turning into a triumph, France's own cavalrymen grew bolder and the hussar Desvernois quit the safety of the French squares to ride out and meet, in chivalric combat, an Egyptian rival:

As the battle drew to a close, a tall Mameluke bey, boasting a long and luxurious white beard, rode out from their ranks and, as he passed the ranks of General Bon's men, fired some pistol shots in order to provoke the French infantry. Seeing this, anger seized me and I spurred my Arab stallion forward, shooting past General Bon's square and drawing close to this audacious bey. Shot was falling all around us but we ignored it. I fired my pistol and his horse went down. He shook himself loose and crawled towards me. Seeing him do so I thought he was coming to implore mercy. To show him he had nothing to fear I tucked my sabre away and opened my arms wide. But I had not counted on my enemy. He continued forwards, defiantly. I turned my horse to avoid the man's sabre but this slight movement played into my enemy's hands as he was able to come under my horse, and, quick as a serpent, seize the reins with his left hand and deliver a blow with his sabre with the right. My horse took the force of this, but I was able to hack at his hands and land two or three blows to his head. Wounded quite badly, he went down only to try again. I was tired of this game, so I threw myself onto him and staved in his head. I heard the infantry shout victory and a few of the soldiers rushed over and finished the man off with their musket butts as he was still not quite dead. I allowed them to take his turban and 500 gold coins whilst I kept his weapons and harness for myself.

The victory of the hussar reflected the more general success of the French as Napoleon's men advanced. François-Michel Lucet summed the day up:

Arriving at the heights of Cairo we were attacked by the enemy who were camped on the left bank. After a number of charges for four hours we won the battle. The enemy lost a large number of men and horses, many of them drowning in the Nile.

François Vigo-Roussillon explains the drowning:

Major Duranteau, who commanded us, ordered us to advance on the village of Embabeh on the left flank of the enemy camp. We took it and thus found ourselves in charge of the only exit from the camp. The Mamelukes attempted to force us out and, before long, the entrance into the village was cluttered with the bodies of dead men, horses and camels. As this barrier formed the carnage was horrendous for both sides showed no quarter. As we took Embabeh the rest of the division struck the enemy camp from the front and we were now witness to a horrendous spectacle. A body of 4,000 men, mostly cavalry, found itself trapped and fired at from all sides. If they tried to force a way out they were beaten back by bayonet charges and so they were reduced to either letting themselves be killed or saving themselves by throwing themselves into the Nile. Most were shot as they made a swim for it.[22]

As does Jean-Baptiste Guillot of the 25th Line:

In about three quarters of an hour they lost 3,000 dead whilst the rest, not being able to flee, plunged into the Nile, which is as wide as the Rhone, and were consequently drowned or shot as they swam.

Even Doguereau had brought up his guns to add to the slaughter:

There was a dreadful massacre. Many of them threw themselves into the Nile and we spent some time firing canister at the thousands of bobbing heads seen in the water.

Whilst thousands were killed, very few were taken prisoner. Godet counted just a handful:

They brought in four Mamelukes who had been taken by the 3rd Battalion. These were the only prisoners from the battle of the Pyramids that I saw. They were well-dressed, reasonably good-looking and as white as a European.

An entry in Gerbaud's diary also confirms this lack of prisoners:

Some twenty prisoners taken. Horror on the battlefield. Fury of our soldiers. How skilled they are at robbing those they come across. Some found enormous sums. Many horses taken and sold at once. Wonderful weapons found on the Mamelukes, including swords, pistols, muskets,

---

22. Laval confirms the massacre: 'They could not escape because as they tried to swim they were shot at and hit and they sank. However, those who had time to mount their horses tried to get away towards Upper Egypt. But of 12,000 only around 4,000 escaped and the rest drowned.'

axes, maces. Horses richly harnessed and the men even more richly dressed.[23]

Miot agrees that there were rich pickings:

The battlefield had transformed into a market place and one could find whatever one wanted. The soldiers called out the price of whatever it was they were selling ... such confusion, what a scene. It was noisy chaos amidst the silence of death. Some were eating, some were drinking and others put on turbans still wet with blood.

At Embabeh he was amazed to see 'our soldiers busy fishing with rods at the end of which were hooks or claws designed to attach themselves to the bodies of the Mamelukes who had drowned. There were large numbers of them. The heat had caused the bodies of the dead men and horses to swell up so that they all looked like giants. My horse shook and refused to pass between the bodies.'

François also saw that many of the survivors had made their fortunes:

Many soldiers found that the Mamelukes were wearing belts which contained between 600 and 1,500 Marabouts, gold coins which were valued at 6 livres 9 sous. As for me, I acquired a superb scimitar with a silver and gold handle, a pair of pistols again decorated in silver, three cashmere turbans and a belt containing 460 gold coins. This day probably enriched two-thirds of the soldiers in Desaix's and Reynier's division, anyway they were the ones to first bear the brunt of the terrible cavalry charges.[24]

---

23. Bernoyer agrees that there was little quarter: 'I saw quite a few of the unfortunates hesitate on the brink of their doom, hoping that the soldiers would show some compassion, but they were deaf to all feeling and intent only on carnage.'

24. Moiret adds that 'our soldiers amused themselves by fishing out the dead bodies of the Mamelukes who had drowned in the Nile. They found 300 or 400 pieces of gold on some of them, which paid them handsomely for the trouble they had in getting the bodies out of the water.' François Leclerc D'Ostein thought 'there was not a Mameluke on whom our soldiers did not find 300 or 400 Louis'. General Dupuis commented that 'there is not a single soldier who has not gained 100 gold Louis; I do not exaggerate, many have as much as 500'. Laugier noted of the 32nd Line that 'it included men who would stop at nothing to get hold of money; they took a great deal off the Mamelukes at the battle of the pyramids and were soon betting 12 Louis or more on a card'.

There was little booty left for the locals. Indeed Detroye, on the French Nile flotilla, watched the corpses floating past, 'some white, some black and some green and blue ones which had putrefied. I counted 160. These corpses, all swollen and rotten, looked unpleasant and gave off such an unpleasant stink.' He adds that 'the locals were trying to strip them of whatever clothes still remained'.

The surviving Mamelukes had made off and the French, too busy with their booty, or exhausted by the fight, did not really pursue, as an officer of dragoons confirms:

> Our cavalry remained inside the squares, firing volleys just as if they were infantrymen, until the Mamelukes of Mourad, having launched several unsuccessful attacks, turned tail and fled into the desert. We were given permission to pursue them and we set off but only managed to sabre a few as they were well mounted and their horses were much faster.

The battle was over. General Belliard thought that 'this was the most exhausting day we have ever had, although the soldiers do not complain' and adds that it cost 'the Mamelukes 1,000 dead or wounded and thirty or forty pieces of artillery'. Ibrahim Bey had fled for Syria whilst Mourad Bey, as befitted a lover of chess, removed himself to Upper Egypt, where he was to be pursued by General Desaix. The French had suffered comparatively lightly and Napoleon admitted to twenty dead when writing of his victory to Paris, although General Bon's division alone reported eighteen men dead, including an officer, whilst the officers of the 9th Line counted 'seven dead and eleven wounded by swords'. François Leclerc D'Ostein made a sober, and credible, estimate of 'fifty dead and 120 wounded'.

Still, with the desert behind them and their enemies at their feet, there was reason to be cheerful for the survivors. Especially as Cairo now lay at their mercy.

4

Cairo and Disaster

With the elite Mameluke warriors swept away to the fringes of what had once been their empire, and slowly pursued by a French detachment sent up to Belbeis, Cairo belonged to Napoleon. The city's authorities recognised their helplessness and, on 22 July, Malus watched as 'a deputation from Cairo arrived and invited the general to take possession. To accomplish this he sent in General Dupuis and I accompanied him. There were five of us and we first reached Boulaq where we were met by some elders who greeted us politely and then prayed before us. A detachment of the 32nd joined us that evening.'[1]

Malus and Dupuis and his staff, along with their infantry escort, then 'entered the city with a military band. We headed for the palace of Mourad Bey. We encountered nobody on our route. ... The following morning, on the pretext of looking for suitable quarters for headquarters, we searched the houses of the beys. The jewellery and the horses were gone.'

Dupuis duly took possession of a capital in which there had been some disorder, and some houses burnt down, but the republic's tricolour was soon hoisted above Saladin's old citadel where trophies captured from crusaders were still on display. Following in the wake of their vanguard, the modern crusaders then crossed the Nile and entered Cairo on 24 July. The army could not really expect to be welcomed, indeed, according to an Italian[2] Vertray met, Ibrahim Bey had completely prejudiced the citizens against the

---

1. An anonymous officer of the 32nd Line saw how his unit was selected for the honour: 'I recall how our regiment had performed at the battle of the pyramids and its bravery was recognised when it was tasked with being the first unit to enter the capital of Egypt.'
2. François must have found the same man, an Italian who served him coffee mixed with goats' milk and brandy.

irreligious French, those 'infidels and enemies of the Prophet who had come to Egypt to pillage and massacre and to rape women and destroy the religion of the Prophet'.[3] The reception was therefore bound to be a cool one, and Lieutenant Laval found it bordered on open hostility:

> We entered Cairo and the population was filled with consternation. They knew what a Mameluke entailed but not what it was to be under French rule. In addition, the death of so many Mamelukes, most of whom were married to women in this city, greatly affected them and turned them against us as we had been the cause of their loss.

However, Hussar Desvernois felt the conquering heroes were greeted warmly enough, especially the horsemen:

> A great number of inhabitants crowded around us, astonished to see that it was our smiling young soldiers who had vanquished their former tyrants. They seemed most impressed by our cavalry and our sappers, who had such fine beards, whilst the infantry were treated with some indifference, something which reflected the Turks' disdain for the common folk who serve them as foot soldiers.

Quartermaster François also registered curiosity, and surprise, as the occupied met the occupiers:

> These men of all colours and all classes looked upon us with astonishment as we marched in. Bonaparte was smiling. Our strange clothes, so different from what is worn in the East; the ostentation of those worn by our generals (apart from Bonaparte); the simplicity of our weapons; our natural openness and our smiling faces, contrasting with what the Turks had been led to expect; all this generated real surprise amongst this rather simple people.

The officer of dragoons and his sixty mounted companions was rather amused when the crowd 'boldly gathered around us. Our helmets shining in the sun, our heavy cloth tunics, our leather breeches tucked into high boots, all contrasted markedly with their loose white linen, their clothes being much more suitable to the climate.'

However, Bernoyer, who trooped in a day later, felt that whatever the reaction to the French entry had been, it had soon given way to indifference:

---

3. Ibrahim exaggerated, if only a little, when he described the French as having 'nails a foot long, enormous mouths, ferocious eyes. They are savages who are possessed by the devil and who fight chained to one another.'

We never saw, as we would back home, crowds of people come out to satisfy their curiosity. Everything was quiet, and there was the usual traffic. The shops were open and the shopkeepers, as well as the craftsmen, were busy at work, and continued being so and ignored us as we marched past.

As Bernoyer nursed his disappointment, the bulk of the army settled down in and around the capital, and stocked up in those shops. Cairo offered the delights of strong Arabian coffee, sugar and white bread, although Quartermaster François, just outside the city, had to make do with 'some very black bread, rice and mutton. The Turks flooded our camp in order to sell us bread, poultry, eggs, dates and so forth. Plenty of them tried talking to us but we could not understand a thing.' The officer of dragoons also seems to have been left out, bewailing the 'lack of wine and brandy whilst the garrisons of Rosetta and Alexandria received a distribution of those three times a week'.[4]

Still, most appetites were satisfied, and the irritations of peace were soon replacing the disasters of war, allowing the occupiers to indulge in some tourism. Abdurrhaman, a local chronicler, watched them wandering about:

They walked through the streets without weapons and without bothering anyone. They laughed with the people and bought what they needed, paying an exorbitant price, for example they would pay 6 francs a chicken and 10 sols an egg, paying what they would pay in their own country!

Vertray had put his strolling to good use and, as ever, jotted down a precise description of France's latest conquest: 'I walked around the city with a friend in order to get to know it better and to find out about the local customs, and I found it has 300,000 inhabitants and 300 mosques. Our soldiers went around as they would in a garrison town in France.' Doguereau, however, thought there were 400,000 people 'of the dirtiest and most hideous kind' and he was soon fulminating against the badly built houses and having to 'breathe the stench and smoke from the dirty Turkish cooking', although another officer had it that this was the 'stench of rotten mummies' hanging over the city. Godet was just as dismissive in his own pedantic way:

Cairo was the long-awaited city but it did not meet our expectations. It had narrow, twisting streets and the houses were so close to each other that one could shake hands by leaning out from the wooden grills they have as windows. There are ghosts of whom only the eyes can be seen and from which they can be recognised as women, piles of rubbish

---

4. Some French officers obtained wine, but it was 'only a few bottles of bad Cypriot plonk obtained from the western or eastern Christians'.

and rotting animals drying in the sun, lots of ruins, four-fifths of the population nearly naked, a few palaces to contrast with the public misery, an awful stench, water only for sale, tremendous heat, many people with one eye and many who are blind, others gravely wear their long beards. That's Cairo.

François, too, registered his disappointment early:

On entering Cairo, one is struck by the misery. The city is populated by the unfortunate and those who fill the streets were either covered in hideous rags or were in a state of revolting nudity. Everything we saw or heard indicated it was in a state of slavery. The people were afraid. They spoke of nothing but want, robbery, murder. There is no security for life or property. A man's blood is spilt as easily as that of a cow.

Gerbaud was also unimpressed by a city which was so 'vast, although viewed from the citadel it seems smaller than Paris',[5] whilst General Damas went as far to tell General Kléber that

We have arrived at last in this place which we so eagerly desired. Yet, how different it is to what our cool and dispassionate imaginations had led us to expect. This horrendous sh**hole of a city is inhabited by a set of wretches who are so lazy that they do nothing but squat before their filthy slums smoking, drinking coffee, eating watermelons and sipping water.

Still, General Dupuis, fresh from hunting Mameluke jewellery, was, despite a veil of cynicism, soon hinting at hopes for a better life for his new subjects:

Here we celebrate all the feast days of the Prophet, tricking the Egyptians by feigning attachment to their religion, a faith in which Bonaparte and the rest of us believe in as much as we believe in that of the fugitive [Pope] Pius. Anyway, here we have come to replace wretches who scarcely let the people keep the shirts on their backs and if things can be well-managed here, then we shall see some changes.[6]

---

5. Chasseur Pierre Millet also tried to compare it to French cities: 'The city of Cairo is the second largest in the Ottoman empire and is bigger than Lyon and has more people than Paris.'

6. Dupuis would later write, 'We have got rid of the rascals who stripped the people of everything but their shirts and, having made contributions fairer, we see changes for the better. The temper of the inhabitants is calming. Our way of doing things seem strange to them but, little by little, we are civilising them even if we have to be strict as we have to make them fear us by doling out punishments from time to time.'

Napoleon always sought to manage things well, and he turned to forming a government of locals to add a layer of velvet to his mailed fist. He tried to impress and compromise those notables who had not fled, and win back those who had, and he tried even harder to undermine religious opposition to the rule of infidels, aware that resistance would flow from every mosque if he did not act quickly. Sheikh Sayyid Khalil El-Bekri, keeper of the holy rug, was the initial target of this Napoleonic charm offensive, and the general gifted him an ermine cloak and listened carefully to his advice. He also flattered representatives of the provinces of Egypt by having them participate in government[7] and retained local middlemen to tax and govern his new subjects. To police them he would send Mustapha Agha-Tchourbadji and 325 militia, mostly Greeks, into the streets of a Cairo which, in imitation of distant Paris, was divided into arrondissements. The most conspicuous step in ruling Egypt was, however, the creation of a central Divan, an assembly of nine local notables, intended to help weigh new laws and bear a share of responsibility for their unpopularity. The notables included sheikhs Abdullah al-Sharqawi, Shams Al-Din Al-Sadat and the aforementioned El-Bekri of the holy rug, but Pierre Boyer could never sweep his thoughts under a carpet, holy or otherwise, and was outspoken in his criticism of this new government:

> Yesterday I went to see the Divan which Bonaparte has established. It consists of nine individuals. And what a sight! I was introduced to nine bearded automatons dressed in long robes and turbans and whose posture and appearance put me in mind of the twelve wooden apostles in my grandfather's little cabinet. I can say nothing about their talent, qualifications, knowledge, intelligence and so on, for that is always a blank page in Turkey. Nowhere is there to be found such deplorable ignorance as can be found throughout this country.

To further improve understanding between rulers and ruled, Napoleon also organised celebrations that August to mark the anniversary of the birth of the Prophet. There were fireworks, but Napoleon caused more sparks by declaring himself the protector of all religions, promising a new mosque to the faithful.

It was not clear whether anyone believed him but, even if bread, circuses and religion helped secure the country, Napoleon knew that it was armed force that made all the difference. Reynier and Lasalle's cavalry had already been sent off after fugitive Mamelukes, through the scorching deserts to

---

7. Provincial divans, working with military governments, would serve to administer the colony and carry out the directives issued by the central body. French military administration included overseeing security, health and sanitation, roads and bridges and irrigation and food supply.

Belbeis. They found the land there more fertile, and explored the caravan routes towards Syria, finding traces of Saladin's castle at Salheyeh. A restless Napoleon soon followed them and it was there that the French cavalry encountered Ibrahim Bey's Mamelukes. The battle lasted ten minutes. Morand saw that the French cavalry were initially out of their depth against such expert horsemen:

> Our cavalry, impatient for an opportunity to shine, saw their chance, and the possibility of rich booty. They would now learn some of the differences between the horsemen of Europe and those of Asia. They charged forwards along with the staff, even General Caffarelli took part despite his wooden leg. The battle was a tough one for the Mamelukes are amongst the bravest and most capable cavalry in the universe. We were equal in valour but there were fewer of us and our mounts were not as good. This skirmish would have ended badly had not the 3rd Dragoons then arrived, drawing up in line and opening fire on the Mamelukes, forcing them to retreat.

Laugier was also thankful for the dragoons, noting that 'the 3rd and 15th Dragoons arrived just in time to rescue them and did so by firing their carbines as swords are useless against the armoured Mamelukes'.[8]

The consequences for the French were, according to Niello-Sargy, 'fifty wounded and some twenty men killed'. Quartermaster François expressed some admiration for the enemy's prowess at maiming and, as he did so, revealed some of his own strange pastimes:

> After the battle of Salheyeh I saw a number of our dead cavalrymen. We observed that many had had their heads cut right off, others nearly so. Arms, fingers sliced clean off as well as legs detached from bodies. Amongst the corpses I saw a chasseur of the 22nd cut from his left shoulder to his kidneys. You can see how effective the Mameluke swords were. I have on a number of occasions cut a goat, a sheep or a dog in two with a single blow from one, not by striking down but by thrusting it into the kidneys.[9]

---

8. Detroye was amazed to see how agile the Mamelukes were, writing that 'a Frenchman just struck by a carbine shot would find himself struck by a scimitar from the same hand an instant later'.

9. Ladrix proved to his distant mother and father that not all blows were fatal, writing, 'I am well and my health is, as usual, fine. I have been spared by the fighting, although I was dangerously wounded one time by some blows from a lance and a sabre, they counted fifteen wounds on my body and my head, but I survived, thank God.'

The French turned to head back towards Cairo, their morale raised still further by the capture of some wild boar. Then Captain Loyer, General Kléber's aide-de-camp, ruined everything. He rode in and informed Napoleon that his fleet had been destroyed by Nelson at Aboukir Bay, that the French ships had nearly all been sunk, burnt or captured. That Brueys was dead. That contact with France was lost. Quartermaster François saw the effect of these awful tidings:

> On 14 August General Bonaparte left Salheyeh with the rest of the army in order to return to Cairo and only Reynier's division remained at Salheyeh. The 2nd Battalion of the 9th Line was by Koraim and the battalion of the 85th at Belbeis, and, warned of Bonaparte's proximity, we were under arms. These two battalions provided an escort for an aide-de-camp of General Kléber, the governor of Alexandria. He brought a letter from Admiral Gantheaume to General Bonaparte informing him of the battle of Aboukir in which our fleet had fought that of the British under Admiral Nelson. Bonaparte received the letter at the village of Courina where we, the 2nd Battalion of the 9th Line, were drawn up. Bonaparte was not far away. We saw him, his arms behind his back, listening to what the aide-de-camp was saying and keeping calm throughout. News soon got around. Bonaparte, passing before us, informed Major Grandjean. The coolness, the calmness of the general-in-chief, and his ability to inspire, made us believe in a glorious outcome and chased doleful thoughts from our imagination. He had apparently told the messenger, 'Well, either we shall die here, or burst forth like the ancients!'

The army had forgotten about the French fleet during the harsh march on Cairo. After the successful, if chaotic, landing and the fall of Alexandria, Admiral Brueys, hounded by the fear of Nelson's inevitable return, had weighed his options. Napoleon had hoped he would enter Alexandria, but Brueys was less sure and was concerned that the approaches to the port, as well as the harbour itself, were insufficiently deep for his bigger ships. Some of the shallower Venetian frigates had been sent to test the waters but the grounding of the *Patriote* on 4 July persuaded the already pessimistic admiral that Alexandria was not really suitable for his leviathans.

Brueys had to look elsewhere for a sanctuary. Some of his subordinates were pressing him to sail at once for the safety of Corfu, indeed Jaubert, purser to the fleet, heard that 'the common opinion was that no sooner had everything been landed than we would leave for Corfu where we would join with the ships from Malta, Toulon and Ancona and thus be ready to face anything'. Admiral Blanquet du Chayla was an outspoken advocate of this plan but his faction was overruled and, at dawn on 5 July, the captains were ordered to follow Brueys to the bay of Béquier, or Aboukir, a few miles down the coast. Captain Thévenard on the

Aquilon shrugged and 'wrapped myself in the cloak of philosophy, seeking to reassure myself those in command knew better than I what we were about'. Brueys was convinced he had few options and, faced with struggling to enter Alexandria or starving to death at Corfu, opted for the least-worst alternative of Aboukir.[10] His choice of that shallow bay at least sheltered the ships from the summer squalls, and, to shield them from Nelson, the French thought to position a forty-gun battery on the little island off the bay's western tongue. Indeed, General Kléber would send over the engineer Jean Étienne Casimir Poitevin to prepare the fort at Aboukir for a garrison of ninety men and to determine a suitable position for those vital guns.

Gantheaume 'along with many other officers in a host of little boats piloted by locals' was left to continue sounding the roads off Alexandria, whilst Brueys and the fleet sailed off to their bay. The *Salamine* was first to enter, guiding the bigger vessels into position as 'inexact information, incorrect charts and information from pilots who were not sure or who contradicted each other' still plagued the French. Their fleet was surprised to find some of General Dugua's men already established in the semi-ruined fort. Colonel Laugier of the staff was among them:

> After having crossed an immense desert we were overjoyed to see a building which, from far off, seemed huge and superb. It was the fort of Aboukir. Up close, and inside, it seemed more like a farmhouse. There were eighteen guns without limbers. ... We spent that night camped and with only biscuit and foul water.[11]

Some firewood came from Corfu but the foul drinking water would remain a problem, and the fleet would belatedly discover that the wells by the fort could only supply half of what was needed. Still, at two in the afternoon of 7 July, the fleet began to moor, positioning itself in a line pointing west but still some distance from the shore. It took several days to form the line,

---

10. Napoleon, who needed the fleet to remain close, would later claim that he wanted it to leave for Corfu. He had asked on 3 July whether the fleet could enter Alexandria or whether it could defend itself in Aboukir, only adding that if it could not then it should head for Corfu. An explicit order, dated 30 July, directing the fleet to either enter Alexandria or take on rice and water and leave for the Greek island did not reach Brueys as the messenger, Captain Julien, escorted by men of the 75th Line, was ambushed and killed at the village of Alqam. This is confirmed by Captain Morier of the 75th who accompanied General Lanusse when he was sent to raze the village to the ground in revenge.

11. The engineer Schouani noted that 'there is a village of 100 men and there are poultry, goats, sheep, a few horses and donkeys. The inhabitants eagerly sell bread, chicken, etc, to the soldiers.'

according to Captain Jean-Pierre Etienne on the *Heureux*, and even then the ships were too far apart, a fault which Brueys, beset by dysentery and migraines, did not correct even whilst constantly fiddling with the sequence of ships.[12]

Not everyone had doubts, indeed some of his subordinates thought the position a good one. Jaubert wrote that 'we are now [8 July] moored in such a manner as to bid defiance to a force more than double our own'. Brueys' idea was that, should the English arrive, his under-crewed fleet would fight them at anchor, trusting to the firepower of half his 1,216 guns and the battery on the island to keep them at bay. Blanquet du Chayla objected to this static tactic, advocating a battle of manoeuvre should Nelson appear. Brueys responded that 'it has been decided that we shall fight at anchor as the crews are understrength and this would prevent us from manoeuvring and firing at the same time'.[13] Of greater concern to Captain Léonce Trullet was that no proper soundings of the bay were being taken[14] and that no frigates were being sent out to keep watch for enemy ships.

Whilst the acrimony in the cabins continued, the hapless crews were kept busy, despatching detachments in ever wider circles to gather in supplies and water, or sending flat-bottomed barges down the Nile to Rosetta for spiced rice, tobacco and mutton. In the cool of the evening the crews trained, repaired their vessels and passed the time complaining about the lack of decent food and wine, and their arrears of pay.[15] This grumbling routine was interrupted on 20 July when the British frigate the *Terpsichore* came to spy on the bay, but such ominous signs were soon forgotten when news of Napoleon's entry into Cairo reached the fleet. Brueys marked this victory with an awkward pronouncement which ended with the resounding

---

12. On 9 July Brueys wrote, 'I have not heard of the English, perhaps they have gone to Syria or, more likely, having fewer than fourteen ships, and thus not being superior in numbers, they have thought better of taking us on.'

13. Some ships lacked a third of their complement, the *Orient* had just 850 men instead of the 1,130 needed. The *Timoleon* had just 500 instead of 706, and the *Mercure* 600. Decrès noted that the crew of the *Diane* 'consisted of 284 men and that the majority of them have never been to sea before this expedition'. Jean-Pierre Etienne on the *Heureux* had '518 men, half novices, and including 25 men of the 25th Line Infantry'.

14. Had a proper sounding been carried out then Brueys would have seen that he could have brought his line a kilometre closer to the shore. The wide gap between ships and shore proved of enormous significance.

15. Money was very short. General Menou told Napoleon on 16 July that 'I cannot do a thing. I do not have the cash' to buy supplies for the fleet. On 20 July Menou took the drastic step of requisitioning foodstuffs and sending them northwards, the supplies reaching the fleet on 29 July.

'we might too, comrades, be fortunate enough to have the opportunity of distinguishing ourselves at sea through a complete victory over the English!'

Such a trial of strength was not far off. Alexandria was shaken by some broadsides on 31 July, although it turned out to be salutes in honour of the victory over the Mamelukes. Then the following day, the artilleryman Bricard, doing the rounds on the town's battlements whilst the others slept off the effects of the party, caught sight of some strange ships:

> We saw some sails appear on the horizon at one in the afternoon of 1 August. We thought it must be another fleet from Toulon. As they came near we could see they were warships with two decks or frigates, but we could not see whose ships they were as they did not have any flags.

Engineer Thurman must also have been on the walls, for he saw the same ships:

> I was still at Alexandria and attending to my duties beneath the burning sun when, towards noon, we caught sight of a numerous squadron off to the west. We were expecting a second convoy escorted by a Spanish squadron[16] and so we were quite pleased to see them. I dropped my pickaxe and gave my workers some time off whilst I and Vinache climbed the observation tower and stared at the squadron bearing down on us thanks to favourable winds. After satisfying my initial curiosity, I came down for my telescope and saw that everyone was out on the terraces. Our flag was waving from the forts as a sign of encouragement and welcome. I saw how three ships surged ahead and, within range of the batteries, swept past the lighthouse without showing their colours. We could see that there were fifteen ships and that they were heading for Aboukir. Our joy was short-lived for we soon perceived from their shape that they were English.

It was Nelson with thirteen of his seventy-four-gun warships, one fifty-gun ship and a brig, the whole squadron bristling with 1,026 guns. The *Alexander* and *Swiftsure* were the ones sent ahead with an Arab *djerma* (a small boat) evidently acting as their pilot. The midshipman François-Etienne Sanglé-Ferrière watched them sail by before racing off to Aboukir:

> We saw two ships forming the vanguard of a squadron which was soon identified as being Nelson's. These were evidently scouts whilst the rest held back off the coast. It was now that the men required to man

---

16. Antoine Galland, who was working at the printing house in Alexandria, was convinced the strangers had been flying Spanish colours.

the fleet were sent off. I asked that I might be allowed to accompany them ... and it took us two or three hours to hurry over and reach the ships.

Thurman also accompanied this column of sailors returning to the fleet:

Now Dumay had the mobile column drawn up and added to it all the sailors, gunners and marine infantry who were in Alexandria, and there were quite a few of them, and they set off, at a forced march across the desert to Aboukir. It would be the first time I set eyes on this place and under such fateful circumstances. It was around quarter past five in the evening and we were still en route, and surrounded by Arabs, when we heard a tremendous cannonade announcing the start of the battle.

At Aboukir Bay, the lookouts on the *Heureux* had been the first to spot strange sail. Lieutenant Antoine Jequart on the *Guerrier*, one of the poorest ships but unaccountably placed at the head of the French line, and anchored a mile south of Aboukir's little island, also saw Nelson and his band of brothers approach:

At around two the English squadron was sighted by a lookout in the mast and he saw twelve sail bearing down from the west-north-west. They were nine miles off and heading towards us in an easterly direction, meaning towards our anchorage. At three, two more sail which had been detached were also sighted and they rejoined their main body, making fifteen sail in all as there were fourteen warships and a brig. In front of them sailed a *djerma*, a local boat, leading the way.

The French brigs the *Railleur* and the *Alerte* were sent to chase away the *djerma* and Lieutenant Charrier on the *Franklin* marvelled at how 'the brig the *Alerte* sailed within range of the enemy and sought to lure them onto the reefs off the island'. The British would not be distracted, however, and bore down on the French, clearly intending to fight that evening. The French fleet, swallowing its panic, cleared its decks and Brueys issued orders to rig the gallants. A flurry of signals was hauled aloft to urge those sailors on shore to return to their ships, but Lieutenant Frère of the *Guerrier* recalled that 'our boat had been sent ashore that afternoon to get water, the other one was with picking up salted meat from the *Tonnant* and the barge had been sent to Rosetta to source a replacement throat halyard'. This delayed the recall of the crews and, as many were still absent or on the way from Alexandria, Gantheaume remarked that, consequently, 'the frigates and corvettes were ordered to send as many of their men as possible to man the ships of the line'.

That line consisted of a van commanded by Du Chayla on the eighty-gun *Franklin* with six warships and the *Guerrier* at its head, its bow pointing towards the little fort under which the French brigs and bombs cowered. The *Guillaume Tell* and five other ships formed the rear along with the undermanned frigates, whilst the *Orient* sat, glowering, in the centre. On it was Brueys with his captains, the latter having hurried over to the flagship for a council of war during which, it seemed, the admiral changed his mind, suggesting they sally forth against the British, with Decrès even saying he saw the signal 'prepare to sail' go up at a quarter-past three. Brueys, however, soon had second thoughts and at four that afternoon he ordered that, as the officers on the old *Conquérant* recorded, 'the squadron shall fight at anchor and that we should secure ourselves and pass a cable through to the *Spartiate* whilst the *Guerrier* did the same to us'. According to Lieutenant François Talon, Admiral Du Chayla was still being obstinate, urging that the French 'should sail out to encounter the enemy, something which I also saw as advantageous as we could board the enemy, but the commander-in-chief did not agree'.

So the French waited until, at half-past five that afternoon, Nelson's audacious plan was put into effect. Gantheaume watched the Royal Navy ships sweep forward and 'at a quarter to six the battery[17] based on the little island fired some shells which fell into the van of the enemy line'. Then, a few minutes later, it was Brueys' turn to order his line to commence firing.[18] The worn-out *Guerrier* had been amongst the first to open up, followed by the equally infirm *Conquérant*. Then Lieutenant Foutrel of the *Mercure* watched as 'at a quarter past six the van of our fleet was in range of the English as they bore down upon us. The admiral had given the signal to open fire and the action became general, our ships opening fire from the van to the centre. Soon our ships were being attacked from two sides.' Gantheaume confirms the junior officer's observation, noting that 'the attack and the defence was extremely brisk and the whole of our van was attacked on two sides and sometimes raked'.

The British plan had indeed involved their squadron splitting and slipping around the end of the French line. This required some of the British warships to pass between the anchored French and the shore and although the *Culloden*, which made the first attempt, ran aground, others soon succeeded. The captain of the *Goliath* found the water deep enough and the French firing along the shore a mere irritant and, no doubt wondering why the French had not scuttled a few old boats to block his entry, surged into the gap between the enemy and the beach. The French, shackled to each

---

17. The French had only managed to give Captain Blancard and his twenty-five gunners two mortars and four 6-pounders.
18. Poussielgue, based in Rosetta, records that 'at half past five that evening we heard the reports of several guns and this was the start of the action'.

other, were now, as Gantheaume saw, trapped between fire from the left and from the right. The poor *Guerrier* suffered the most, the attack proving 'so violent that in less than an hour all our masts had been cut 10 feet above the deck' according to one officer. Worse was to come when, as Lieutenant Achard noted, 'another enemy ship came between the *Guerrier* and the *Conquérant* firing its port guns into the back of the *Guerrier* and those of its starboard into the *Conquérant*'.

The *Sérieuse* frigate was also caught and sank in the shallows, whilst the rest of the French, anchored and bound to each other, and unable to adjust their position, awaited their turn. Thurman of the engineers, now watching from the shore, saw for himself how they were overwhelmed one by one:

> The English squadron split into two lines and one, despite the accident that had befallen one of theirs, passed the islet and took our line from the south whilst the other faced off to the north. Our ships at the head of our line found themselves caught between two fires whilst our other vessels remained at anchor and unable to assist. The situation was such that the *Orient* at the head of our line seemed to be being attacked by the entire enemy squadron at once.

The fighting was intense, but the French were quickly outgunned. The British pieces were better served, their gunners more disciplined and more numerous, and Captain Le Joille of the *Généreux* also adds that 'our powder was so inferior to that of the English that our shot carried just two-thirds of the distance theirs did, with their shot exceeding ours by a cable-length'. Moreover, British tactics ensured an advantage. They had concentrated on destroying the van whilst the French rear sat in appalled horror, after which the centre became a target, the *Orient* resembling a stag beset by vicious hounds. Riding the back of that stag was Lieutenant Berthelot:

> The *Bellerophon* and the *Majestic* positioned themselves to our starboard, yardarm to yardarm, and maintained a steady fire against us both with their guns and with musketry. They could not match us and the former lost her masts and her gun ports fell silent, forcing her to cut her cables and drift along our line. The latter suffered less but, having lost her captain and most of her crew, she followed in her wake. They were replaced by the *Swiftsure* and the *Alexander*.

The flagship was fighting back. Gantheaume saw how 'the admiral, all the superior officers, the chief commissary and about twenty pilots and masters of transports were on the poop of the ship using their muskets as all the soldiers and sailors had been ordered to go man the guns on the main and lower decks'. Redouté, too, saw how 'the admiral and all the other superior officers were on the poop deck of the *Orient*, firing muskets at the enemy', the French officers conspicuous in full dress uniform. Auguste Lachadenède was on the

Orient and he saw that 'at around seven o'clock the admiral was wounded in the head and the hand. He did not wish to be treated, wiping away the blood running down his face with his handkerchief. Then at half past seven his leg was carried off. We gathered around him and the quartermaster held him and, although his wound seemed fatal, we wished to carry him so he could be tended to. He would not have this and said he wished to die on the deck. He died as calmly as he had fought.'

Still the *Orient* fought back, supported by the *Franklin* and the *Tonnant*. By then the *Conquérant* was on fire and, with its masts down and most of the crew wounded, it capitulated at ten that evening. The *Guerrier* had also lost masts and rigging over her port side, 'obstructing the guns of the second battery'. Ensign Sornin added that for an hour after half-past nine 'the enemy had been calling upon us to surrender but our captain refused to hear them, hoping that whilst we kept these two ships busy our strongest ships in the centre would destroy and sink those enemy ranged against them and so win the battle'. However, it was not to be, and so the *Guerrier*, overwhelmed by Captain Hood's *Zealous*, reluctantly accepted an English officer onboard and yielded.

The *Franklin* was also in a bad way, Lieutenant Talon recalling that 'we had three ships against us and the captain was wounded,[19] Citizen Martinet taking over. The ships before us were no longer firing, we were riddled by shot, had most of our crew wounded and our main and mizzen masts down, but we were tied by a cable to the flagship.' He was anxious because 'grenades and shells lobbed in by the enemy had set fire to the armoury, which was full of cartridges, and the captain's cabin'. The crew managed to put the fire out, but it would not be the same on the *Orient*. Already reeling from the loss of Brueys and the wounding of its commander, Casabianca, the flagship's decks were now burning. Captain Léonce Trullet of the *Timoleon* watched as 'fire took hold of the *Orient* and the flames made terrible progress'. The neighbouring ships began to cut their cables to get away, and not before time. Gantheaume on the flagship observed how

the pumps had been smashed by enemy shot and there were no tubs or buckets to fight the flames. An order was given to cease firing so that all hands could bring water but such was the ardour of the moment that, in the tumult, the main deck gunners continued to fire. Although the officers had called the crew between the decks the flames above had made alarming progress and we had few means in our power to check them. Our main and mizzen masts were down and we saw we could not save the ship. The fire had gained the poop and now the battery on the quarter deck. The captain and second in command had been wounded some time before this.

---

19. The brave Blanquet du Chayla lost his nose in the battle.

He gave the bitter order to scuttle and abandon ship. Lachadenède had already done so, and just as well for the *Orient* then exploded with an enormous bang:

> Motard and I threw ourselves into the sea from the starboard and although I did not know how to swim I managed to find a yardarm and cling to it waiting for the ship to go up. More than 400 of us did the same, clinging to wreckage, but when the ship blew up at 10.15 we were all submerged and only sixty of us resurfaced.

Saint-Hilaire, on dry land, was mesmerised by the disaster:

> It was around nine o'clock when we saw a very bright and very tall flame and three-quarters of an hour later the ship that was on fire blew up. The explosion could be heard 18 miles away and for us it seemed as though an 18-pounder canon had just been fired under our noses. It signalled our defeat for the ship that exploded was the *Orient*.[20]

Antoine Galland in Alexandria could hardly believe what had happened:

> I was at my window which overlooks the harbour and from where I could see the bay of Aboukir. A blast of air hit me full in the chest, such that I thought one of my friends must have hit me by accident. However, they all felt the same blast and the sound of the explosion which followed in its wake soon told us what had caused this. The next day we discovered that it was the flagship the *Orient* that had blown up.

Back in the bay, the loss of the flagship stunned both sides. Captain Trullet saw how 'the *Orient* was blown into the air, and the explosion of this ship was so terrible that it sowed panic amongst the crews'. Some men from Captain Racord's *Peuple Souverain* abandoned their posts and took to the boats but most of the French crews, though shaken, held firm and the action soon recommenced.

Redouté, transfixed by the struggle, watched these final agonies:

> At quarter past ten the ship, still on fire, leapt into the air with a resounding bang which could be heard miles away and which sounded

---

20. Poussielgue, based in Rosetta, records that 'at ten the vessel that was burning blew up and there was a most terrible bang which could be heard as far away as Rosetta. ... This accident was followed by complete darkness and a most profound silence which lasted ten minutes. The time that elapsed between us seeing the explosion and hearing it was two minutes.'

like an earthquake. An ominous silence continued for the next ten minutes but the firing began again and continued without interruption until three in the morning. It finished around five but started again with even more violence.

With their admiral dead and flagship gone, the surviving French captains cut their cables and shifted for themselves. Night added to the confusion, with ships firing on friendly vessels with only the intermittent flashes from muzzles throwing light on the butchery. Daylight enabled Thurman, in the little fort close to the action, to survey the scene:

> Dawn did away with the last of our doubts. It was a spectacle of horror stretched out before our eyes. The sea was covered with debris and with the dead. We could make out our ships, demisted, burnt, sails shredded, surrounded by English ships in a similar condition to ours.

The least badly damaged were stationed in the French rear and, late that morning, two of them, as well as two frigates and a brig under Admiral Villeneuve, took on some sailors from the shore and slipped away 'in the direction of Malta'. Of the rest, the *Heureux* unhappily ran aground, the *Tonnant* eventually surrendered on 3 August, whilst the *Timoleon*, which had also resisted to the last, was scuttled and burnt shortly afterwards by her captain. The infantryman Pierre Louis Cailleux, watching from the shore, was left to survey the sorry scene:

> Of all of our squadron the English took just seven vessels for the others had sunk, burnt or were in no condition to be towed. The English burnt what they could not repair and sent ashore all the sailors and soldiers they had taken prisoner. For several days after the battle the shoreline was littered with bodies and debris from the ships.

Gunner Bricard in Alexandria had initially been told that the English fleet had been destroyed and so 'hopes for peace quickened our heartbeats'. But then the truth emerged and 'this terrible blow shocked everyone. Nobody said a word. The losses were greater than we could ever have imagined.'

The painter Henri-Joseph Redouté was just as devastated by the debacle:

> The consternation on their faces revealed the extent of our disaster. Eleven ships had been lost for France and our best officers killed or wounded. The shoreline of our new colony was now exposed to enemy attack and we were more cut off than ever from our homeland.

The French had lost 1,500 killed and 3,000 wounded. Most of the survivors were traumatised, deafened[21] or demoralised. Of the warships, only two seventy-fours escaped (*Généreux* and the *Guillaume Tell*). Six were taken, two ran aground and were burnt, two were destroyed to prevent them falling into enemy hands, one blew up, and one sank. The frigates the *Justice* and *Diane* also escaped, as did Debout's brig *Railleur* although it was later captured at Rhodes by the Turks and the crew thrown into a prison 'compared to which the prisons of Europe would seem like a palace'. The *Courageuse* was fortunate to have escaped the disaster as it was moored in Alexandria along with the transports.[22] Brueys had been killed, as had Thévenard of the *Aquilon*, and the talented Casabianca had been mortally wounded on the burning deck of the *Orient*. Thousands had fallen into British hands but they were soon sent ashore by a Nelson unwilling to feed them, as Admiral Gantheaume relates:

> Admiral Nelson suggested to me that I should receive the wounded and other prisoners. In concert with General Kléber, the commandant of the town, I agreed to his proposal and 3,100 prisoners, of whom 800 are wounded, have been brought ashore since 6 August.

Those wounded were taken to Alexandria, as Captain Trullet remarked:

> The wounded have gone to Alexandria to be dumped in the warehouses, most not having a bed or receiving any help. Some will recover but most shall perish in misery from neglect. The unhappy navy won't be listened to, their reputation dragged through the mud. They shall be blamed for the disaster of Aboukir whilst, in fact, just one man must bear the responsibility for that catastrophe.[23]

---

21. Antoine Galland noted, 'I heard an account of the battle from a survivor of the horror and he would suffer from deafness and tinnitus for several months afterwards.'
22. Neutral transports were allowed to leave in September but with mixed success. On 8 October thirty-eight came out but twenty-eight were burnt by the British blockading squadron under Hood. Galland noticed that the French transports also tried to slip away: 'Our transports were moored in the old port and a few in the new. They left at regular intervals for Europe but whenever the English seized one they burnt it and sent the ship's complement back telling them to go and die of hunger in Alexandria.'
23. Peyrusse was ashamed that the victors were English: 'By what cruel fate is it that when all peoples have submitted before us only the English continue to resist and even humiliate us?'

Gunner Bricard echoes these sentiments. 'On the morning of 3 August,' he recalls, 'a mass of wounded or sailors saved from the sea poured in bringing the most terrible accounts and everyone agreed that Admiral Brueys was to blame for sending the wrong orders and placing his ships in the wrong position.'

Whoever was at fault, the results were soon clear to all. The expedition had been dealt a fatal blow by Nelson who, although wounded, would enable Britain to form another coalition on the back of his victory. Worst of all for those sent to Egypt, Britain now dominated the sea, stranding the French expeditionary force in Africa. And Africa was covered in French blood, as Henri-Joseph Redouté noted when he crossed the dunes, on 26 August, on his way to Rosetta:

> On that unfortunate beach we saw the scale of the disaster that had befallen our squadron. It was a terrible scene. The shore was covered with wreckage half buried in the sand whilst other wrecks drifted on the water. It looked like a huge shipyard. There were broken masts, a broken longboat, a rudder, oars, cages for poultry, trunks, boxes. And corpses of those who had died in the battle and been washed ashore. These sad remains stretched along the beach for 12 miles. Some of the dead were naked and intact and lay in a peaceful yet horrifying posture. Only the limbs could be seen of some of the others as they were partially covered by sand. Still more had been picked clean by birds of prey and were mere skeletons.[24]

Pausing to reflect on the disaster, he then wheeled south into the deserts and trotted along the banks of the Nile to join an army which, like Robinson Crusoe, was marooned in a strange and hostile land.

---

24. Bricard agreed: 'There was nothing but corpses and wreckage for a distance of 18 miles. One could not go six paces without stepping on a body. This macabre sight filled us with horror.'

5

Masters of Egypt

Word that their fleet had been destroyed inevitably hit the army with a wave of despondency. Gunner Bricard thought their fate was to be 'like Bluebeard's wife, left to dream sad dreams about our families and our situation'. An equally pessimistic Vertray saw dismay take hold:

> Discouragement gripped the soldiers and many of the officers. The hope of ever returning to France had suddenly vanished. The sea belonged to our mortal enemies. Victorious, we nevertheless saw that our victory could not last. Masters of Egypt, we were her prisoners.

Maurice Godet had, for once, good reason to be gloomy. He heard the news on 15 August and confided to his diary that 'this disaster also destroyed our courage and gave rise to sad reflections on our situation. We saw ourselves as prisoners in Egypt until peace could be signed, something which at least seemed likely as we could no longer fight at sea.'[1]

Malus expressed similar feelings in his journal:

> We learned the English had arrived off Aboukir and of the destruction of our fleet. We realised that any communication with Europe would now be impossible. We began to lose hope that we would ever see our homeland again. After spending a few more days at Salheyeh I left for Cairo, tired, sick and depressed.

---

1. The officer of dragoons also saw that sea power was key: 'So here we were more or less abandoned in this distant land as it would be some time before our government would be able to fit-out a fleet strong enough to contest dominance of the Mediterranean with the English.'

Only Napoleon put on a brave face. Still, privately, he was just as anxious. His stepson, Eugene de Beauharnais, confided to his mother Josephine:

> I have never seen my stepfather so sad and so serious. He has just told me that he would rather swap places with your little dog than be in the position he is now.

His position was as pasha and prisoner, the prison encompassing Cairo, Alexandria, the towns along the Nile and a smattering of isolated forts in the Nile delta. Cairo was the capital of France's new African empire, and, despite the disaster at Aboukir and rumours of Ottoman intervention, it remained calm if isolated. To undermine that sense of being cut off, the French established a printing press which began to churn out the *Courrier d'Egypte*,[2] more a bulletin than a newspaper. Still, the botanist Coquebert was an enthusiastic reader as it was 'a newspaper which is badly put together but rather precious because it brings us news, French newspapers are so rare that they are impossible to find'.

Then, in an attempt to recreate Paris in Egypt, Napoleon announced the establishment of his beloved Institute. Monge was delighted, diplomatically telling his wife that 'all we want is our wives and children, then our happiness would be complete'. The scholars, still murmuring after being abandoned in Alexandria, had been drifting south and were overjoyed to be finally granted a place of work. Jollois describes this new institution nestled in a complex of buildings once belonging to Hassan Bey Kachef:

> The commander-in-chief finally turned his attention to the Commission for the Arts and the formation of an institute composed of its members. Some five houses, once belonging to the beys, and each with immense gardens, were given to the commission. One house was specified to be that belonging to the Institute. Monge and Berthollet, regarded as the directors, lodged there. One room was set aside as a meeting room, another as a library and another as a laboratory.[3]

---

2. Marc-Aurel initially printed it, but he did a bad job of it and returned to France. Marcel then took over with the presses brought down from Alexandria. He expanded his workforce to include five Egyptians, one of whom was Yousef Msabky, Egypt's first indigenous printer. It would eventually be edited by Jean-Joseph Fourier, the orphan, former Benedictine novice and zoologist.
3. The new academy was a broad church, and even had an Egyptian, or rather Greek, member in Raphael Antun Zakhur Rahib of Aleppo, a Melchite priest, who acted as interpreter and translator. He came to Paris in September 1803, living at 4, Rue des Enfants Rouges.

The Institute also boasted an auditorium (the old harem), a zoo, a botanical garden, an observatory and a cabinet of antiquities. Something of a university in exile, it was divided into faculties working on scientific questions, or history and economics, and members shared their findings in learned studies and lectures when not out in the sands collecting evidence. The membership was wonderfully productive and it was not long before the auditorium played host to talks on sharia law and Islamic customs. Before long, descriptions of excavating tombs, or drawings of the birds of the delta basin, were being circulated and enthusiastically discussed. Not everyone was excited by this academic activity, however. Bernoyer attended one lecture that winter, and it left him cold:

> On 10 January I attended a lecture at the Institute on the anatomy of the ostrich. It lasted nearly three hours. Our scholars were divided into two to debate all aspects of the ostrich's body, but the argument fixed on whether the ostrich was made to run or to fly. One side defended the thesis that it was for running, the other flying. After three hours of deliberation, each side maintained its own view. The discussion was so silly that it came as a disagreeable surprise. Even a fool could have demonstrated that with such long legs it was made for running, whereas, if it had been intended for flight, then its wings would have been bigger.

We should probably be glad that he missed the lecture on the natural history of the egg. Still, it was not all theory and scholars found themselves given practical challenges such as building gunpowder mills,[4] telegraphs, windmills, hot air balloons and breweries – all the facilities essential to the functioning of a modern state – whilst others assessed the prospects of growing cane to replace the sugar of the West Indies. However, Saint-Hilaire saw that work on assuring a clean source of drink was an early priority:

> The commander-in-chief has nominated the following to direct the institute: citizens Monge, Berthollet, Caffarelli, Andreossi, Desgenettes, Costaz and myself. Everything is organised. The president is Monge, with Fourier as secretary, and we begin at once. Some are working on

---

4. It was Conté who was tasked with launching a balloon. He had brought the Meudon prototype balloon with him but lost most of his equipment when the *Patriote* sank off Alexandria. He worked on a new paper balloon, painted in the French national colours, that was launched on 22 September 1798. Another launch took place on 10 December 1798, this time using a cloth balloon, and then again, more successfully, in January 1799. There were no manned flights, however.

a way of producing beer without hops, others on how to purify the waters of the Nile.

Outside of academia, the military were eagerly awaiting something to drink to. The festivities to mark the rising of the Nile had seen the last of the Champagne consumed, just in time for the teetotal birth of the Prophet. Then, that September, came the birthday of the French republic, always a lively event in the new calendar. When Henri-Joseph Redouté reached the capital, moving into the house of Cassim Bey on Azbakiyya Square, he saw that something grand was being prepared to mark the occasion:

> They had formed a circle of 105 columns and from each of these flew the tricolour. Each of these flags bore the name of a French department and the columns were linked by a double garland representing unity and the nation. One of the entrances to this circle consisted of an arc de triomphe whilst the other was a gate with the Arab inscription 'There is no god but God and Mohammed is his Prophet'. In the centre of the circle was an obelisk covered in red cloth, in imitation of the local granite, 70 feet high. On one side was the inscription The French Republic Year VII and on the other The Expulsion of the Mamelukes Year VI.[5]

On the day itself there was a parade followed by a speech in which Napoleon, for once, misjudged the mood. After telling his men, rather darkly, that 'you will die bravely and your names shall be inscribed on altars such as these or you shall return to your hearths covered in honour and in glory', he seems to have realised his rhetoric was too morbid but made things worse by telling troops nostalgic for their families that '40 million people are thinking of you'. He put an end to the agony with the customary shout of 'Long live the republic' but this time, as Jollois notes, the troops did not repeat the refrain. Luckily, the feasting which followed was more to their liking. Peyrusse marvelled at 'a dinner of 150 places which was sumptuously served' and during which 'the French and Turkish colours were intermingled, the cap of liberty and the crescent, the Rights of Man and the Koran were side by side'.[6]

Bread consumed, then came the circus. It began on the morning of 21 September with a running race, won by François Pathou of the 75th Line, followed by a horse race that afternoon. This had the added frisson of

---

5. General Kléber noted in his diary how 'the soldiers made a hole into it and climbed inside. The found it to be a good place to entertain their Egyptian floozies and it became a den for vice and debauchery.'
6. Bernoyer, a passionate republican, was horrified to see 'the Turkish and French flags intertwined, the bonnet of liberty, the Rights of Man and the Koran treated the same way'.

pitting French horses against their sleek local rivals and the officers, guilty of chauvinism before it had even been invented, were overjoyed to see Simon de Sucy's French horse beat an Arab stallion by ten seconds, having covered 1,350 *toises* in four minutes. A triumphant party of Frenchmen then set off to celebrate by planting a tricolour on one of the pyramids.

As the noisy celebrations died away, new, more sombre, notes began to be heard. Rumours reached Cairo that, over in Constantinople, Sultan Selim, Sovereign of the Sublime House of Osman, Khan of Khans and Commander of the Faithful, had declared Jihad, or Holy War, on the unbelieving French. The Ottoman emperor had indeed done so on 9 September, and his declaration surprised many, not least Talleyrand, then drumming his fat fingers on his desk in Paris, but horrified Napoleon even more. After all, the expedition had been launched on Talleyrand's promise that the Ottomans would remain neutral. Now not only would the French have to deal with the British and the Russians, they would also have to contend with the sultan's armies and, no doubt, with a surge in unrest in a region already prone to religious fervour.

The unrest began soon enough, with a new and rising sense of militancy feeding off the fear and resentment the infidel intruders had generated. Many in Cairo were ready to recall each slight, or an unpaid bill, and pay heed to those who preached extermination of the French and their Coptic, Jewish and Greek collaborators. A new tax levied against the wives of Mamelukes living in property their husbands had abandoned caused much consternation, as did rumours that the French were to force women to appear in public without their veils. That October, the French authorities began to plan for the worst, implementing stricter security measures by closing the seventy-one city gates, patrolling the streets and strengthening their citadels. Even so, when it came, the scale of Cairo's revolt took them by surprise.

There had been some scuffling on Friday 19 October after prayers and, at the El-Azhar mosque, where anti-French rhetoric always went down well, weapons began to be distributed to the congregation and to shadowy groups of young men who had been drifting into the city in recent weeks. Then the signal was given and the standard of revolt was promptly raised on the morning of 21 October.

Redouté saw that the signal was soon followed by violence:

At seven that morning an armed mob composed of people of all kinds began to head to the house of Ibrahim Ehctem Effendi, a man respected on account of his character and morality. The crowd closed the shops down as they swept along. ... They arrived before the house of the Cadi and a deputation of twenty entered his house in order to convey to him the complaints of the people. However, they persuaded him to mount his horse and, escorted by the mob, to make his way to the house of the commander-in-chief. Somebody observed to the Cadi that the crowd was rather too loud and rather too vociferous for the presentation of a simple petition, and he dismounted to return home. The mob, furious, turned on him, beat him to death with stones and sticks and took the opportunity to pillage his house.[7]

Detroye then heard 'the muzzins on the minarets rally the mob' and saw 'Turks armed with clubs and muskets flood into each district. The shops closed and at eight the French were called to arms.' The revolt was becoming general. 'Suddenly,' observed a surprised Malus, 'all the houses were boarded shut, the streets were filled with armed men and any individual who became isolated risked being butchered.' Miot was right to be nervous as he was among the isolated:

> I was trotting back into Cairo on a donkey, its driver holding on to its tail, and no sooner was I in the city than I noticed that it was menacingly silent. The doors were barred and nobody was in the streets. I did not know what to think. I did not dare go deeper into the city, or retrace my steps. I felt it safer to head for the Birket-el-fyl square where the 32nd Line was quartered. I was lucky to arrive and, just as I did so, found General Dupuis, former commander of that regiment, and now promoted to general, coming out of his house preceded by some men carrying sticks and followed by some dragoons. He ordered the infantry to muster and headed off in the direction of the cemetery.

General Bonaparte had been off inspecting the island of Roudah and so it was Dupuis, the city's governor, who bore the brunt of the insurrection and he, as Miot observed, set off to face down the mob. Barthémély of Chios, commanding the capital's Greek police then, rather rashly, fired a blunderbuss into the crowd. This incensed the insurgents and they charged Dupuis, his aide-de-camp Mory, an interpreter named Beaudeuf, and their cavalry escort. Laval reports on the outcome:

> General Dupuis was killed by a lance thrust. The alarm was sounded, everyone rushed to arms and we marched against the mob who had already thrown up some defences around the mosque. Anyone found to be armed was killed or massacred.[8]

---

7. Other accounts say that Sheikh Al-Sara was seized, stoned, dressed in a dead soldier's uniform and sold as a slave for thirteen piastres in the marketplace, a settling of scores for the man's collaboration with the French authorities.
8. The death of Dupuis gave rise in December to rumours in London and Vienna and, briefly, in Paris, that Napoleon had been killed. As Josephine was not being seen in public this was taken as confirmation that she was in mourning.

Napoleon heard the alarm and sent his Guides to support the beleaguered garrison. The Guides pushed through the Old Cairo gate and encountered a scene of desolation. Detroye was at the head of a patrol of eight of them when 'in the Frankish quarter, 200 *toises* from headquarters, we were attacked by 150 rebels and could only escape by cutting through them and blowing out the brains of the one who seemed to me to be their leader'. Most of the mob was away hunting down Christians and Jews and killing any unarmed Frenchmen they encountered, including two unfortunate medical officers emerging from the house of Ibrahim Bey on Birket-el-fyl. The isolated and the sensible locked themselves in and waited for salvation. It did not always arrive in time. Some fourteen civilians and soldiers in General Caffarelli's house were trapped and besieged, as reported by Bernoyer:

> Early on the morning of 22 October a huge number of people assembled in certain quarters of the city and then this mob descended on those places inhabited or frequented by the French. They massacred all those they could lay hands on, even those just suspected of being friendly to us. The first house to be attacked was that of General Caffarelli and it was totally looted.

Saint-Hilaire understood that the besieged officers 'had fired through the windows before being taken by surprise when the mob, which had swarmed over the roof, broke into the house. ... The house was pillaged and the Physics laboratory, which had only arrived the day before, as well as all the instruments of Papa Champi [Champy], my gunpowder, a great number of tools acquired at considerable expense in Paris, fell victim to the rebels.'

Detroye lost 'all my possessions apart from the clothes I stood in' whilst Jollois was devastated to hear how 'most of the scientific instruments and those for astronomy were destroyed along with many tools, two chests of muskets and the property of the general and his staff'. As for the little garrison, the 'officers and scientists had attempted to cut their way through the mob in order to reach the citadel. Eight, including Monsieur Testevuide of the engineers, and Peré the draughtsman, were felled by stones whilst Monsieur Duval and Thévenot, civil engineers, were cut down in the street as they headed for the commander-in-chief's residence.'

The painter Redouté worried that the Institute itself might be next as it was poorly guarded. He watched as

> the members of the commission of Arts and Sciences gathered in the hall of the Institute and there awaited the weapons the commander-in-chief was sending for our defence. We were isolated on the edge of Cairo and therefore we were rather concerned. We spent the day anxiously and it was only at midnight that we received forty large Maltese muskets, one hundred flints and a thousand cartridges from the Gizah arsenal. These guns were too heavy for us to lift and they

were without bayonets. Some fifty grenadiers were sent to protect us but at three in the morning they received orders to head to the Great Mosque. The people of the district gathered and attacked us at around eleven that morning. Based at a nearby mosque they armed themselves with lances and sticks and, uttering horrible shouts, advanced as the muezzins urged them on to exterminate the infidels. The women encouraged their menfolk and brought bricks to serve as missiles against us.

Fortunately, Napoleon was now sending armed detachments into the city to relieve the besieged troops, scholars and religious minorities. He also posted warnings against further unrest, sought out moderate voices to begin negotiations with and then, on 22 October, ordered the guns brought up and the streets swept by cavalry. Still, tragedy struck when, after Napoleon had his aide-de-camp Sulkowski take orders to General Dumas, the young Polish officer was ambushed by the Bab-en-Nassar Gate at the head of fifteen Guides. An officer of dragoons heard how 'the unfortunate S was leading one of our patrols when his horse slipped on the wet ground and rolled on top of the rider. He had no sooner hit the ground than he was cut to pieces and the dragoons could do nothing but seek vengeance for the loss of this noble young man.'

Desvernois, who swore that the locals allowed their dogs to eat the dead Pole, was sent on a similar mission to that of Sulkowski, but enjoyed more success:

Our hussars were resting in our encampment in Boulaq but our repose was disturbed by a sudden onset of savage shouting and threats. It was a riot. In ten minutes the regiment was mounted and ready. They opened the gates and we rode down any of the insurgents who resisted as we made for Cairo. We were soon there and galloped into the square of Azbakiyya where headquarters was located. They sent us to the Djezel Azhar mosque where we cut down a large number of rebels.

Bernoyer, taking up arms, played his part in what was rapidly turning into a massacre of the rebels:

I obtained a sword and a musket, mounted my horse and attached myself to a squadron of dragoons. We rode down deserted streets until we reached the Birket-al-fil square where a large crowd was grappling with the 22nd Light. We brought up two guns and their first discharge angered the Turks whilst the second caused panic as they saw so many of their compatriots fall. The streets were too narrow for them to escape and General Reynier had us charge them, resulting in an awful massacre.

Amidst the bloodshed, General Lannes and a company of grenadiers rescued the stranded scholars in the Institute as General Bon and the 32nd Line turned besiegers into besieged by isolating the remaining pocket of revolt around the Al-Husayn mosque. An officer from the 32nd felt that 'it was now time to be done with the miserable rabble of brigands and assassins, with those fanatics in the mosque who kept on firing and who shot at the emissaries and sheiks Bonaparte sent to negotiate surrender and offer pardon'.

General Bon had been ordered to set fire to the mosque, but the good general hesitated, hoping that the mere sight of his artillery would break rebel resolve. Nevertheless, he was eventually obliged to have Dommartin's four guns fire a whiff of grapeshot, that classic scourge of the mob, and the Al-Husayn mosque capitulated. Still, Bon's men plundered it and the French, unwisely and unnecessarily, defiled it by stabling their horses there. A victorious Napoleon then entered the city, blaming Ibrahim Bey and Mourad Bey of the Mamelukes for having stirred the rebellion and the local sheikhs for having failed to stop it, demanding revenge for the loss of 250 French dead. Poor Sheikh Shams Al-Din Al-Sadat was taken to the citadel and beaten twice a day for not having resisted the revolt and to extract compensation from him, just a part of the 18 million francs the French would fine the city elites. Some heads would roll, too, and the ringleaders 'were led as prisoners to the citadel and the majority were beheaded there during the night'. Detroye heard that at least 300 were bayonetted to death in the citadel, whilst Henri-Joseph Redouté saw how 'as we passed along the street of the Petit-Thouars we saw that two leaders of the revolt were being beheaded by the Turks themselves'. Outwardly forgiving, Napoleon also made sure to seize hostages to ensure future good behaviour, and to order his vizier, good General Berthier, to have those rebels taken with weapons in their hands brought down to the Nile where they would have their throats cut and be dropped into the river.

The French called it peace and François saw how their retribution was extended beyond the deserts to the rest of Egypt:

> The sheikhs of the province of Charkieh came to ask forgiveness from General Reynier, saying that those miserable individuals had only gone to Cairo because Ibrahim Bey had ordered them to do so. Still, the twenty-three villages recognised to have been most active in the revolt were burnt by us and their livestock and grain brought to our camp. All the inhabitants, except for women and children, were put to the sword, some 900 were killed.

Pierre Boyer thought that 'cutting off 100 heads and meting out 500,000 blows with a cane' would bring the region to its senses. The country as a whole was growing used to the sight of punitive expeditions, as French columns would appear whenever food or taxes needed collecting, or chastisement meted out. In the south, Savary and his light infantry would find that they could merely block an irrigation canal to bring a village to its knees and force it to pay up, whilst, further north, the aptly named Adjutant Leturcq was sent to 'this province [Ramanieh] as, whilst the inhabitants are quiet, they are slow to carry out the orders I sent them to supply us with 120 horses. I will find a clever way of obliging them. The village of Damanhour is particularly arrogant and will not obey.' Laporte would have agreed. When Damanhour continued in its disobedience, he was involved in enforcing some respect for French rule:

> The town was told to surrender and to compensate us for the damage that they had caused, however they replied by shooting at us. The entire population had crowded on the poor walls that ringed the place and they had two or three guns. The infantry chased back into the town those of their masses before the walls. Despite raining shot down on us, which was, fortunately, not very accurate, we pushed on with the assault so as not to give them time to recover. However, they promptly made to submit, promising to hand over the troublemakers and a contribution was also paid to us.[9]

Corporal Barallier of the Nautical Legion, just a teenage sailor forced to carry a musket following the loss of Napoleon's fleet, had also been sent into Ramanieh province 'to take part in a mobile column in order to go and force the inhabitants of different villages to hand over contributions'. At Caffra Chabass he recalled how

> our two guns opened a breach and we charged in to this rebel village and nothing was spared. After a quarter of an hour of pillage the drums sounded the retreat, warning the scattered soldiery to assemble. After setting fire to the village, we formed up and left for Galine. The conflagration, which must have been visible across the province, terrorised the people and many came to submit bringing us things to eat, especially dairy products.

A few days later and the village of Galine [Genay] suffered the same fate:

> The retreat again sounded and, once the column had assembled, we saw that there were as many chickens and geese tied to knapsacks as there were soldiers. Such was life and, having set fire to this village we left this blasted place and marched for six miles before halting.

---

9. The French ensured there would be no further obstinacy by taking six elders and four Bedouin women as hostages.

As night fell we camped and the men used their ramrods as spits, cooking the poultry over the flames. It was all so delightful and our conversation consisted of the loud repetition of 'tomorrow at such and such a place, and the day after at the next place, we shall do the same again'. As this racket continued I reflected on my own homeland, and shuddered to think of all the horrors of war.

Bernoyer and a friend thought all this was far removed from the liberation the Egyptians had been promised:

We thought it was a hard thing for republicans to carry out such orders as our ideal is to make people happy and to treat them as brothers. Now we were imitating the example of tyrants, threatening the population with a huge stick. The two of us blamed Bonaparte who could have eased the treatment of these unfortunates and enforced a more humane approach to law.

Napoleon's attention was, however, elsewhere that autumn. After imposing his version of peace, he was thinking of expanding his empire, sending men to the east, to the Red Sea ports, and others southwards down the Nile. The 3,000 troops destined for the deep south were under the command of Desaix, and he was to pursue the fugitive Mamelukes under Mourad Bey and Ibrahim the Small, before turning to the organization of French rule between Cairo and Nubia. Not all his officers were enthusiastic about bearing the imperial burden so far south, and many tendered their resignations in protest. Even so, Desaix's division eventually embarked on barges protected by the gunships the *Hart*, the *Star* and the *Coquette*, everything being so rushed that, according to Godet, 'we had no time to take anything with us'. As they munched on old hardtack seized from Mameluke warehouses, they sailed down into lands unknown to Europeans. Not all of it was unwelcoming. Indeed, Godet noted that they 'passed through several villages where the inhabitants showed a disposition to welcome us, revealing to us several dead Mamelukes they had killed or thrown into the canal'.

After disembarking, and weeks of cat-and-mouse work, the French, hungry and beset by fevers and eye trouble, managed to catch the surviving Mamelukes on 7 October 1798 at Sediman. Belliard, that other laconic diarist, recalled how 'the battle was a stubborn one. Two thousand infantry at the most fought against four charges by eight or ten thousand cavalry. One of the small squares was charged and opened fire at point-blank range. There was no time to reload so they presented bayonets and the Mamelukes threw themselves onto them.'

General Desaix himself adds the detail that the doomed square was that of 'Captain Vallette on the right who told his chasseurs of the 21st Light to open fire at ten paces and fix bayonets. This was done. The enemy was not brought down by this close-range fire and reached the square. They could not break in and covering fire brought them to a standstill. So they threw their carbines, pistols, sabres, daggers and weapons at us. Many of our men fell and they broke in. We had twelve killed and they had just as many whilst we had thirty wounded.'

Despite the Mamelukes then bringing up five guns, and a massacre of the French wounded, the French were eventually victorious and, despite their lack of shoes, set off in pursuit. Belliard saw that the enemy were shedding men, and that 'a deserter, originally from Saxony, came over to us' followed on the next day by 'two Greeks and a Circassian'.[10] Still it took months before Desaix, reinforced by the short-sighted but ruthlessly ambitious General Davout, again caught up with his mobile foe. Desaix, inconspicuous in his simple riding coat, cornered the Mamelukes and 2,000 jihadists from Tunis or Mecca, some of the latter armed with impressive two-handed scimitars, at Samanhout on 22 January. Belliard watched the battle begin from his square on the French left:

The reports we had received were true and, an hour into our march, we came across the enemy vanguard and their main body at Samhoud [*sic*]. The hussars of our vanguard opened the fray and our division advanced. The Mamelukes were reluctant to engage, only making a show of charging at three or four places but our artillery stopping them. So the general ordered the cavalry to attack.

So Jean Rapp with Captain Desvernois led the 7th Hussars forwards and the engineer Jean-François Detroye watched how 'the chasseurs and hussars, to the number of around 100 men, charged forwards in good order and with some courage. The enemy bravely met them and there was a furious fight. We were surrounded and if the dragoons had not been able to reform and open fire then none of us would have been able to survive the Mameluke swords.' The result was another victory of sorts in which Captain Desvernois, a hussar used to scrapes, was wounded eighteen times.

The Mamelukes of the south had been wounded too, and would finally be brought to terms in August 1799 when Colonel Morand captured Mourad's camp, arsenal and slippers. It had been a long campaign and Belliard grumbled throughout whilst Charles Lasalle was much more vocal, lamenting to General Dugua that 'we have never been as unhappy as we are

---

10. The Mamelukes themselves were foreign to Egypt, but their ranks also included European prisoners seized by the Turks. Pierre Boyer put it thus: 'Each Mameluke is purchased from Georgia and the Caucasus, although there are a great number of Germans and Russians amongst them.' Savary says he met a Hungarian taken in the Austrian war against the Turks in 1783. Later, in December 1799, General Dugua was concerned to hear that French soldiers were deserting to the Mamelukes.

in Egypt. We are deprived of everything, exhausted by irritations and the hope that things will improve is also absent. Your Lasalle, dear general, has changed. No more gaiety, that has gone, but serious and depressed, he drags his carcass through the plains and the desert. All is lost, even his eyes are deprived of the joy of tears. What did I do by coming here?'

But, as the depressed officers did their duty, a troop of more enthusiastic auxiliaries was also at work. A party of scholars had been designated to explore the lands and the riches and resources of the south. Villiers du Terrage, armed with just six pencils and food for the journey, 'left Cairo with our party. It consisted of Girard, the chief engineer for roads and bridges; Jollois, Dubois-Aymé and Duchanoy, all engineers; Descotils, Rozière and Dupuy, mining engineers; and Casteix, a sculptor. We formed a sort of commission charged with collecting as much information on the economy, agriculture and arts, as well as on the geography and antiques, of Upper Egypt.'

The young explorer visited the hippodrome of Antinopolis, but was most impressed with the ruins of Denderah where they studied, and set to copying, the zodiac in the temple. Here they stumbled over the body of a strangled traveller, 'an unfortunate man who had died in a strange land, the victim of his zeal for the arts', but ignored this warning sign and pushed on cheerfully to Syout [Assiout]. There, among the orange groves, they met Denon, who had come south to explore, and who quipped that 'I was comfortable in Cairo but I did not leave Paris to be comfortable' before trotting off to hunt hieroglyphs, and to carve his name in the temple. The young scholars set about charting this new and very distant French territory, so distant that the soldiers erected a sign in the camp bearing the legend 'No 1,176,340 Paris Avenue'.

Napoleon was also exploring the frontiers of his sheikhdom. That December detachments had been sent out to Quseer on the Red Sea whilst the rheumatic General Bon went to Suez. There was a fort but the general was obliged to write to Cairo requesting 200 pints of brandy and some cooking pots (as the troops had only brought one with them). Napoleon had galloped out of Cairo on Christmas Eve 1798 to spend time on a pet project of his, a canal running from the Red Sea to the Mediterranean. However, the expedition nearly ended in tragedy, François recounting how the general and General Caffarelli nearly drowned when the tide swept in and the Red Sea refused to part. They soon dried out and work could begin. Martin recorded how 'the commander-in-chief, leaving the caravan to make its way to Adgeroud, rode north to look for the remains of the ancient canal. He found them and followed its course for 15 miles, more or less to the point at which it reached the basin of the Bitter Lake.' Napoleon enjoyed the gallop but soon lost interest in the canal and left Engineer Jacques-Marie Le Père and his brother, along with twelve sappers, some dubious former galley slaves encouraged to act as navvies with an extra ration of biscuit, and forty Maltese soldiers to survey and work on the ancient canal of Ptolemy, the so-called Canal of the Pharaohs, whilst Napoleon and his caravan of staff officers returned to Cairo.[11]

Napoleon's new colony was expanding. He had defeated the Mamelukes and established a colonial administration up and down the Nile. He had sent his scholars and soldiers to explore the outer limits of his empire, and reported glowingly to Paris on how Egypt, straddling Asia, Africa and Europe, would soon be the jewel in the republic's crown. Later, he would retell the history of his expedition as a glorious adventure and his conquest of an exotic land peopled by colourful enemies. But other accounts emerged over time, offering different views of Egypt. Some of the men he had brought with him told other tales. Their experiences of, and their opinions on, the wonders of Egypt, the monotony of the landscape, the endless variety of its peoples, and the purpose and cost of pursuing empire were set down in letters, diaries and memoirs. And whilst there were stories of glory and adventure, and casual nods to the picturesque sentimentality then in vogue in Europe, these writings were more honest than those of their commander-in-chief. They genuinely reflect the experience of these modern intruders into this ancient land, and show what it was like to be part of Napoleon's empire of the sands.

---

11. The surveys of the route of the ancient canal continued into 1800. They were a little rushed and inaccurate and the engineers would claim, bizarrely, that a canal was practicable as the Red Sea was 9.91 metres higher than the Mediterranean.

6

Impressions

Those intruders, products of ten years of revolutionary thinking, had caused disquiet in Europe, reshaping societies and knocking over thrones. Here, in Egypt, where the ordering of society had been established for centuries, their sudden appearance was even more unsettling. Egypt, in return, seemed even more unsettling to them. In such times, and in such circumstances, a clash between the worlds of the occupiers and occupied was inevitable.

Pierre-François Gerbaud was, like every other participant in Napoleon's conquest, new to Egyptian society. He tried to make sense of it, dividing it into types:

> Egypt is inhabited by four kinds of different people. The Turks; the Bedouins, and Bedouin nomads; the Christians (who are Maronites, Greek Catholics and schismatics) and Copts; and the Jews.

The Christians and Egypt's 5,000 Jews were very much second-class citizens, something which seems to have passed over the head of the Neapolitan doctor Antonio Savaresi,[1] who would claim that 'the three principal peoples, namely the Muslims, the Christians and the Jews, are only really distinguished by their difference in religion, otherwise they speak the same language, have the same passions and morality, and the same customs'.

Whatever differences there were between the locals, there was a much starker contrast between the peoples of Egypt and the newcomers. This was partly cultural, of course, but it was also in the nature of the relationship;

---

1. Savaresi had been banished from Naples in 1794 following a police raid in which he was implicated in a plot allegedly organised by republican clubs and secret societies. He took up service as a medical officer in the French Army of Italy.

after all, the former saw their way of life, their family and their property placed at risk by these aggressive intruders, whilst, for all the revolutionary talk, the invaders themselves could not see themselves as equals to the conquered. Still, some, such as Miot, in his fair-minded way, tried not to make too much of these tensions:

> The Muslims see things differently and it would be wrong, for example, to say that their gardens, or their women, are less attractive, because our ideas and way of seeing is so different. Show them our slim beauties with fine legs and elegant clothes, or our most suave Parisian girl, and it may be that they think little of them. For the Egyptians value size and the fatter the woman the more beautiful she is.[2]

Bernoyer would not go so far, even though it was a subject which keenly interested him, but he felt it sufficient to shrug that 'here, custom, manners, clothing, language and religion are so different to those in our country' whilst Saint-Hilaire left it as 'what a people the Egyptians are with their morality and customs so contrary to ours'. Still, such neutral voices died out as an army of liberation transformed into one of occupation. By then most of the French were finding Egypt and the Egyptians entirely alien, and took great pains to show it. Saint-Hilaire, the young scholar, saw that the soldiers took easily to hating Egypt:

> The soldiers yearn for the delights of France. Their hatred for Egypt stems from being denied essentials. They have only water to drink. They cannot be attracted to women who hide themselves in veils.[3]

Monge added some detail, telling his daughter 'the army was against Egypt in the beginning because, one, they had to endure terrible fatigues and privations as they crossed 150 miles of desert; two, because, lacking horses, they were harassed by bands of mounted Arabs who descended suddenly on their camps, or made off with stragglers; three because in this country all

---

2. Dr Frank, an army surgeon, remarked, 'Women here think it a sign of beauty to be plump, or worse. They have a saying here to flatter women with: *beautiful like the moon.*' Galland joked that 'the Turks like a woman with the eyes of a gazelle, a face like the moon and hips like a cushion'.
3. A sentiment confirmed by Bernoyer: 'We had just enough water to sake our thirst and wine was out of the question as it is forbidden by the laws of Mohammed. The more I think about our situation, the more desperate it seems. If we encounter any women or children in the street, they flee as though we were wild beasts.'

the ways of doing things are different to ours; four because as soon as you move from the Nile there is simply no water to be had.'[4]

Perhaps, over time, attitudes might change, or Egypt might be made to conform. After all, France, as the imperial power, had an interest in developing the colony, and the invaders were soon articulating their desire to improve the colonised. The progress of a people was central to the Enlightenment but this noble idea now found itself being applied following a war of conquest. Peyrusse, generally an apostle of liberty, thought it worthwhile, and felt that 'Egypt could be a fantastic colony in fifty years' time' but added, ominously, that first 'the inhabitants have to be civilised, their prejudices squashed and the Arabs broken'.

Monge was also a republican, but he, too, was already thinking like a colonial governor:

It will take some time before there will be any improvements. But, if there is peace, and free trade, and if 20,000 French families come and settle here and involve themselves in trade, industry and so on, then the French will set the tone and both fashion and force will exert influence and the country will be the best, and brightest, and the best-placed, of all our colonies.[5]

Old Captain Moiret echoed the prevailing view, writing that 'we flattered ourselves that we would restore civilisation, so that the sciences and fine arts would reign there, and there would be abundance, fertility and happiness'. Some, however, including General Reynier, went beyond these platitudes and suggested practical ways of restoring Egypt to its former glory:

All the different branches of society in Egypt unite against any form of improvement and only a foreign power has any hope of changing things. The French found themselves in that situation but they were preoccupied with establishing themselves, and waging war, to be able to deal with all the moral obstacles placed in their path. There was the attachment to former customs, pride and superstition, a level of ignorance which

---

4. Laval went as far as to exclaim that 'the French government sent us to this country to be rid of us'. Not all were negative, however. François was actually quite pleased to be there, remarking that 'it was the oddest expedition but I was so pleased for it had long been my ambition to travel in strange lands and here I was in one of the strangest'. Alexandre Ladrix of the hussars thought that 'if it was not for the heat then this expedition would be alright'.

5. An opinion summed up in a letter to his wife: 'When this country has been rebuilt, replanted and run by the French for fifty years then it will be heaven on Earth. The landowners shall winter here to manage their estates and will then spend the spring burning through their income at Paris.'

rejected any new ideas, differences in languages and religion, the morality and social standing of different classes, and so on. The people should be studied carefully, then its prejudices destroyed and law-makers brought forth who will be loved, esteemed and venerated, with this alone giving them the moral authority to establish and consolidate new institutions. This cannot be done at once and will take time.

Lagrange agreed that just such an enlightened government, naturally that of the French republic, would indeed lift the people:

Bonaparte won't be remembered by the monuments he builds in Egypt. There is much to be done for the prosperity and happiness of Egypt. A good government for a people debased and subjugated by despotism, regeneration through good laws, those are the works worthy of our immortal general.

If all this sounds righteous, Hamelin, a merchant who acted as courier, was on hand to reassure us that the French had learned from previous attempts at conversion:

This history of our modern crusade of the French in Egypt will not be like that of the thirteenth century, a story of pious folly. It will be that of a regeneration of a people.

The people in question perhaps had a right to be offended by the imputation they needed to change. Distrust and differences were compounded by an inability to communicate them, and this was often a problem of language. A handful of scholars such as Venture de Paradis and a few Levantine clerics were on hand to assist as interpreters,[6] and Donzelot told Friant that there were 'Italian Catholic priests who could serve you well' even in the distant south. It was also the case that some locals had mastered French or, more commonly, Italian.[7] A few of the invaders tried some Sabir, the pidgin language of Mediterranean merchants, but only a few learned Arabic, Jaubert thinking that the men of Provence made better progress although Coquebert de Montbret, born in Hamburg, proved a capable student:

---

6. Elias Pharaon (1774–1827), from a Syrian or Lebanese family living in Alexandria, was Napoleon's personal interpreter after the death of Venture de Paradis. He later served as a diplomat for the Ionian islands. Jean Baptiste Santi L'Homaca, an interpreter from Salonika, also proved his worth.

7. When the dragoon Augustin Delesalle was captured outside Jaffa, the local tribal leader had someone on hand who spoke Italian. When he was subsequently sent off to Acre, he found the pasha there had an interpreter who could work in French.

I spend much time learning Arabic and I now speak it quite well, such that I can make myself understood. I don't pretend that I can deliver a learned discourse in Arabic, but I can tell a shopkeeper what I want, explain something to a servant, artisan or worker, or find out more about something I am curious about. I can read a little. I think that in another six months I will be quite fluent.

Moiret 'spent a year learning the Arabic they speak here' so he could purchase uniform cloth whilst Bernoyer, more motivated by the desire to chase skirt, managed to sound high-minded when he confessed his wish to be able to communicate:

> The Turks were drinking their coffee on the terrace as was their wont before supper. They were telling stories to each other, something of a tradition. It was a pleasure for me to be among them, not only so I could learn their language but also so I could understand their customs and way of life.

However, most of the French failed to see the need to bother trying. Laval sighed that 'it takes time to learn the Arab language' and he relied on 'a few Jews who spoke Italian and explained things to us and sometimes acted as interpreters'. Alexandre Ladrix was a simple soldier and had no interpreter, so for him the lack of a common language was an obstacle, as he confided in a letter home: 'I shall not attempt to describe the country here, nor the Turks. They speak a language which is unknown to us, and that is quite some barrier between us.' Jollois proved it was a barrier not only to understanding but also trust when he declared that 'the French were almost completely ignorant of the language used in the country and this allowed the population considerable latitude when it came to plotting against us'. Galland saw such frustration boil over, recording that he had 'seen Frenchmen resort to the use of their riding crop or the flats of their swords having failed to make themselves understood with words'.

Henri-Joseph Redouté didn't want to listen because 'when they talk amongst themselves their rasping, guttural voices make them seem ferocious and excitable'.[8] Miot sighed that it probably wasn't worth trying: 'How could there be any understanding amongst people of

---

8. The French were more curious about the unique ululations of Egyptian women, uttered as a mark of honour. Bouchard heard this trilling once as he approached a caravan whilst Major Detroye recalled that 'the inhabitants seem friendly. As we approach the village the men come out to the front of the column to sell water, melons and bread and, once we have marched through, the women express their relief with a kind of bizarre gurgling.'

such different taste and morals and who could only make themselves understood through the use of interpreters?' Joseph Laporte, who had felt at home conquering Italy, also saw language as just part of a much deeper incomprehension:

> The traveller here feels like he has been taken to another world and when he sets foot upon it a mass of impressions bears down on him. A language which sounds barbarous and which has an unsettling effect on the ear, clothes which seem strange and bodies so odd, for instead of our exposed faces and hairy heads one sees with surprise sunburned faces with beards and moustaches beneath shaved heads.

Sometimes, however, both sides overcame the dividing gulf by making an effort and Saint-Hilaire noticed how 'the labourers working for the bey at Nalahio are getting used to our soldiers and they, in turn, are teaching them French of a kind which will make them swear like hussars'.[9]

But, to genuine French dismay, the number of locals wanting to learn French was on a par with the number of French learning Arabic. Indeed, indifference was the standard response to the newcomers. Bernoyer had noted on day one how little attention the Egyptians paid to the new arrivals:

> The beach was covered with caissons, shells and roundshot belonging to our heavy artillery. More than a thousand men were toiling away to move these munitions from ship to shore and from shore to store. Despite this bustle I saw some of the natives come down to the beach, wash face and body, then kneel in the sand and recite prayers, oblivious to what was going on around them.

Sulkowski also remarked that 'as for how we were met, it seemed to be with indifference for they neither feared us nor were curious enough to come out of their habitual apathy in order to study us'. A son of the revolution, and another occupier who liked to blame every woe on despotism, he put this down to the kind of fatalism which stems from being ruled by tyrants. Redouté, on the other hand, felt that the locals were simply prejudiced:

---

9. Arabic was difficult, but Turkish was also problematic. At the end of the campaign, François, who had been in Egypt for a year and a half, found himself fraternising with some Janissaries, and relates that 'the Janissaries were a bit more civilised and they asked us some questions in Turkish but we did not know how to respond, however they were good about it and they showed us respect and expressed their disappointment that they could not understand us either'.

We kept to ourselves as we never managed to socialise with the locals who, despite outwardly showing friendship nurtured, for the most part, feelings of hatred towards us. The people are too prejudiced to be able to change character and they despise everything which is not Muslim and hate everything Christian.

Dubois-Aymé acknowledged some truth in this, but tried to be understanding:

As for the inhabitants of the Delta in particular, they are better than generally supposed. True, they put up a fierce resistance when we first appeared in Egypt, and perhaps more so than other provinces, and assassinated a number of our troops, but we should put ourselves in their place, something one must always remember to do when judging the character of a nation. For had some Muslims landed in one of our more Catholic provinces, and conquered the principal towns, would it be possible that their detachments would be made welcome in the villages and that they would not be attacked if they sought to levy contributions and all that whilst the government, beaten but not destroyed, encouraged the faithful to wage a glorious defence?

Still, for all the seeming intolerance, Jean-Pierre Doguereau found hospitality in some of the distant provinces, something all the more remarkable for the populace having to bear the brunt of the French thirst for resources:

The inhabitants seemed quite attached to us, they showed much friendliness. I often found that, out in the sticks, in those distant villages, I was often most generously welcomed by these unfortunates who had just been pillaged by our soldiers. They often served me dates and coffee.[10]

Such hospitality was welcomed by an army which marched on its stomach and often went without. Bernard MacSheehy, now far from his native Dublin, was soon complaining to a friend that

We are engaged here, my dear Le Maire, in a most fatiguing business. The wars of Europe have nothing in common with this in Egypt. We

---

10. They also refused payment for their hospitality. He adds, perhaps defensively, that 'whenever we pillaged our Turkish servants were always in the lead and stole much more than anyone else, beating anyone who resisted'.

count ourselves the most fortunate beings if we manage to procure some biscuit and water.[11]

For the French, the lack of bread and wine was particularly galling. Corporal Dumas of the dragoons lamented to his mother that 'we are in an extremely hot country where there is no wine and, what is worse, no bread'. Galland was quite put out to find that 'people here drink Nile water, which is fine, but we Frenchmen want to down a few glasses of good Burgundy from time to time'. Alexandre Ladrix was also daydreaming about wine when he told his parents, 'I hope to return and drink a glass of Gisquet wine, although I have forgotten what it tastes like here. In this country wine is 6 francs a bottle and is not good.' Cypriot wine, brought in on Greek ships, could be found and Bernoyer seems to have had a lot of republican fun with it: 'The wine from Cyprus was sweet but went to our heads and engendered in our hearts a keen enthusiasm for Liberty. That noble sentiment inspired each of us to imagine a government designed to make a people happy.'

In the absence of such staples, the French would have to take liberties with the local fare and this came, if it came at all, with its own complications. There were strange things to eat and digest, and even stranger rituals around the eating and digesting. Desvernois was fascinated:

I saw the Mamelukes at leisure on a few occasions and could observe their habits. When they halted for food they would sit on their heels and form two lines opposite each other. They would eat rice mixed with saffron, helping themselves with tortoiseshell spoons and supporting themselves by laying their left arm on the neck of the man next to them. After the rice came the roast chicken or lamb and eggs on a plate and, afterwards, they had fresh dates or oranges. They drank Nile water out of goatskins, or had lemonade or orangeade. They finished with three cups of mocha coffee without sugar.

Eating like this was a challenge for the French, although General Belliard did well enough with the seating, recalling how 'we had supper in the village, all arranged by the Copt, and served on rugs in the Turkish manner.[12] There were three servings of soup, enough to satisfy three or four hundred men, some veal presented in two different ways, and two dishes bearing 500 eggs

---

11. It was just as bad for the horses. Coquebert wrote home about his poor nag's suffering: 'My poor Milord is not so fortunate and I am afraid he will not survive in this country for long. There is neither hay nor oats to be had and horses must be content with beans and a little chopped straw. If he can remember what his life in Turin was like, then he really is to be pitied.'
12. When describing another meal he was more down to earth: 'Bum on the floor, as tradition dictates, and the fork Old Adam made use of.'

each.' However, Saint-Hilaire was perplexed by the lack of furniture, and shocked at having to use his fingers:

> General Menou accepted dinner with a local sheikh. Some fifteen of us accompanied him, escorted by twenty soldiers. We ate on a floor which had been covered with mattresses and rugs[13] and we were served ninety-six dishes as we sat around in a circle. We were treated grandly. The best dishes were the chicken with rice of different kinds. The sheikh had invited us to crouch down and we saw the Turks help themselves to the dishes with their fingers, keeping the liquids on their palms and the solids in their fingers as they took the food to their mouths. We were obliged to do the same as there were no forks or spoons.

Captain Moiret looked more closely and saw that the locals 'always use the right hand for the left is used for washing private places' whilst Detroye looked away as he found 'the way the Egyptians eat disgusting; they do not know about using a fork everyone sticks his fingers into the dish'. Redouté's chief concern was 'the disgusting valets who walked barefoot over the rugs on which the food had been laid out and this, as nobody gave us plates, and nor did we have forks or knives, we had to eat with our fingers'.

Both the French and Egyptians would exchange puzzled looks across the rugs but there were moments of relief, too, as Thurman, attending a banquet with his men, recalled:

> My veterans sat with crossed legs and, having never before participated at such a feast, seemed embarrassed. They were clumsy in so many petty ways but then made a loud faux-pas, one brought about, no doubt by their posture. In revenge the Turks began to belch loudly.

Miot was again ready with a culturally sensitive explanation:

> Our hosts made it clear through considerable expulsions of wind that they had dined well and we rose from the table. Belching is something which we see as a sign of rudeness or bad manners but, with the Turks, it is an indication that they ate well.

---

13. Sergeant Antoine-Mathias Bonnefons noted the lack of any furniture: 'They have little furniture compared to Europeans, the beys and sheikhs having a few bits of marble and cupboards full of Chinese porcelain.' Moiret noted that 'the people do not have wardrobes because they do not have wood and there are no carpenters'. Galland was most surprised by the lack of beds and bedrooms, noting that the locals unrolled a mattress in whichever room suited them.

His hosts had gone to the trouble of finding chairs:

> We were shown into a room where they had set a vast table surrounded
> by chairs.[14] The Turks thought they were paying us a great compliment
> by having arranged everything in the French manner. ... The meal
> began with rice and soup and bottles of Cypriot wine and jugs of
> different sauces were also on the table. Two minutes later the second
> course arrived with plates of beef and stewed poultry. Then came the
> roasts, fish, vegetables, sweets and pastries, all in such quick succession
> that I gave up the idea of counting the different courses. However, I
> do not think I am exaggerating when I say there were nearly twenty.

Such opulence was largely missing away from the grand establishments and
Pierre-Louis Cordier, a mineralogist, was one of the few to record how badly
the poor ate, for 'they count a good meal as being one of a little four-ounce
loaf, an onion and a bit of cheese the size of one's thumb'. Galland agreed,
stating that 'a little bread, dates, rancid cheese, beans, watermelon and a few
roots form the staple diet of the people. I have seen them collect the skin
of watermelons we had thrown out of the window in order to get at the
bits we had missed.' He added that the French ate more in a day than many
Egyptians consume in a year. It is true that some months were better than
others, and Detroye noted that whilst 'they live off watermelons, cucumbers
and other such stuff' most of the year he also added that 'the dates have
arrived. Here in Cairo they eat an amazing number and, along with figs,
grenadines and some sour little lemons are the only fruits here. And bananas
which taste a bit like some of our pear varieties in Europe.'

The Egyptians might have eaten less than the French, but they washed
rather more. The French found bathhouses everywhere and initially assumed
they were the same as Europe's notorious bagnios. They found the reality
rather more mundane. Still, curiosity, rather than hygiene, lead them there.
André Peyrusse enjoyed the experience:

> You do not go into the water but get exposed to steam and then some
> strong Turks come and rub you with flannels so that you are scrubbed
> clean of whatever was on your skin. They say this is the best way to
> deal with skin conditions. ... You feel a bit weak afterwards, but I
> intend to have them quite frequently.

---

14. Bernoyer ridicules his mistress's clumsy attempts with western furniture: 'I saw
she was discomforted by having to sit at the table, for she was unfamiliar with
chairs and first elected to sit on the floor. I lifted her up and had her seated next
to me but she was so uncomfortable that it was funny. She was worried about
falling off, no doubt.'

As did Captain Moiret who, despite being a little nervous when he first donned the towel and red slippers, had a good soak and finished with a foot massage:

> I changed my linen and the boy rubbed the soles of my feet with a pumice stone. He then brought me a pipe and a mocha coffee, which I drank with great pleasure. I gave him a few coins and he went off very happy. I paid the bath owner and went off happy too. After, it seems as though you have just been born and that you are alive for the first time.

However, Miot found it too strange:

> You walk down a corridor which leads to a steam room. The first thing that you notice is the lack of air and it is so bad that I was obliged to stop and sit for a few minutes as I had difficulty breathing. When you have grown accustomed to this you can then proceed and enter a vaulted room where you are soon enveloped by steam. You then go into a second room where it is difficult to see and it is there that the boys begin to clean your body in a way which is so strange for any European. They sit you down on a slab of stone or marble and rub you down with a huge glove to clean your pores. ... Once you have been thoroughly cleaned they take your limbs and, with considerable dexterity, start to manipulate them. They put a knee in your ribs they start to crack the bones around the spine. It does not hurt, but it is quite surprising. They take your head and twist it on its supports, and, finally, place a towel over the face and massage the skin in order to make it elastic and spare you a migraine. You smoke a pipe, drink a coffee and fall asleep.[15]

Detroye was another detractor, remarking that 'there was nothing pleasurable about any of the ceremonies, indeed I would say that I suffered the experience rather than enjoyed it. It cost 30 or 40 sols.' Galland left hurriedly after an attendant 'asked whether he wanted to have some fun' whilst Jean-Pierre Doguereau swore never to go back after being handed someone else's unwashed towel.

Ironically, the soldiers' first impression of Egypt was also one of dirt and squalor. It was not what they had been led to expect. Indeed, Jean Baptiste Lattil communicated a sense of shock when he fulminated against the

---

15. In September 1800 General Menou had to issue an order of the day reminding the soldiers about how to behave in such institutions: 'I have received complaints that some excesses have been committed in the public baths. Some of the men have tried to bring women in with them to bathe with them. In all civilised countries, this is against the law.'

best-known travel writer on Egypt, declaring, 'Savary tricked us when it came to Egypt. It is not the land of plenty he writes of, one does not breathe the scent of rose oil in the morning. This is a land of misery.' Most of those recording this Napoleonic adventure would agree. Antoine-Marie Chamans de Lavalette certainly did, lamenting that 'they would have us believe that all the riches of the east were here for the taking, but all we found was universal misery'. For those who knew of the grandeurs of ancient Egypt the reality of the present condition of the country was painful. Bernoyer had in mind the decline and fall of the pharaohs when he examined the Egypt of 1798. He mused that it was 'odd that the Egyptians of today are born on the same land and in the same climate as their ancestors, although now they struggle to build miserable huts daubed with mud and cow pats'.

Those huts, scattered around the countryside, sheltered Egypt's poor. All agreed that the lot of the peasantry, the *fellahin*, was particularly brutal and miserable. Saint-Hilaire was horrified by the destitution he saw there:

> All in all, the Egyptian peasants are the most wretched individuals, you cannot imagine how miserable. Can you credit that most of the villages consist of mud huts just three feet tall and that the miserable inhabitants of these lairs gain access through a round hole one and a half feet in diameter and which remains open at all times. There is barely enough space for the husband, wife or children to lie down and in order to change position they have to crawl about on their stomachs. An earthen structure for the baking of bread takes up most of the space. There are two stones to grind grain and a pot for coffee, and sometimes a bag for tobacco. That is all the furniture these poor peasants have. They never eat meat but they do drink coffee in the mornings.[16]

Millet agreed, writing that 'they live in horrible huts, built from earth and like a fox's den. You have to bend down in order to go in.' Gratien Le Père was horrified by the homes of some Copts in the north, jotting down that 'I cannot remember encountering a worse smell than that I encountered in these disgusting shacks and where General Menou and myself nearly suffocated as the air there is as impossible to breathe as that in the tomb of the queen in the great pyramid'. Jean-Pierre Doguereau saw that the peasants around Salheyeh were 'very miserable. They are haggard, emaciated, many of them are naked. They live off what the date trees produce ... There are

---

16. Bricard also noted the coffee: 'The peasants live like animals eating herbs, dates, watermelons, a little rice and lots of coffee. Despite this bad diet they are never ill, are robust and live a long time. They are always smoking a pipe. The women are very fertile and some villages consist almost entirely of children who, naked as worms, roll in the sand.'

ten or twenty families in little earth-baked huts, all surrounded by a wall with round towers on each corner, all this forming their village. They all sleep together, man and beast.'

Antoine Galland, passing through another village near Rahmalah, confirmed this, noting:

> It was composed of square or round mud huts, very low, and in which everyone slept together and often with the animals. I saw just two stone buildings. One was a dirty café, the other the house of the governor, a building which would not be fit to serve as a stable in France.

The sight of such evident misery angered Bernoyer, who still thought of himself as a republican:

> You might think that a people living amongst such plenty should be happy. Wrong. Only the rich benefit because they can buy in bulk and save, whilst the poor, whose income is so meagre, are limited to buying the basics. If they are able to economise and buy a shirt or sandals, they consider this the most bountiful good fortune.

There were, of course, some wealthy Egyptians even after the Mameluke caste had been driven from the country. Their houses were marbled examples of refinement, although Sergeant Antoine-Mathias Bonnefons, who on occasion seems to be writing for a disreputable tabloid, was sure that too much ostentation could bring the wrong kind of attention, declaring that 'the government knows how to profit from this wealth, and if you show yourself as being well off you are sure to be crushed by taxes'. The result, he thought, was that the rich confined themselves to distinguishing themselves through their dress. Galland, however, thought the wealthy stood out in different ways:

> The ordinary people, both men and women, have a forthright step and an assured demeanour. The classier women dress well and walk slowly whilst the men of the upper classes have a really confident air but rarely walk. They are all a bit plumper than the poor people, but this is seen as a mark of beauty.

Lacorre thought their behaviour rather high-handed: 'Being rich here means wearing a fine cashmere or muslin turban, having an impressive robe with great sleeves, and having a pack of slaves run ahead of your horse and in your wake.'

Dress was evidently important. 'The costume of the locals,' writes the uncomplicated veteran Pierre Millet, 'is very different to ours but, having examined it closely, I would say it was more majestic. They shave their heads and wear a little red cap, called a *tarbouk* in Arabic, around which they wind a turban some six or seven times. They wear silk or cloth robes and these are very long, stretching down to their ankles. Their legs and sometimes their feet are bare. They have long beards which make the older ones look dignified and respectable.'

Henri-Joseph Redouté had just landed at Alexandria when he gave his account of Egyptian costume:

> The men were half naked and were lazily smoking their pipes, their muscles bronzed by the strong sun. The older ones had a short beard, which made them seem respectable. Heads were shaved and covered by turbans whilst clothes consisted of a blue shirt tied by a belt at the waist.

The French gaze, being the gaze of soldiers, more usually sought out the women of Egypt for examination. Their dress seemed even more exotic, and, as many wore the burqa, they made sure that those glances were quickly rebuffed. This outlandish costume certainly intrigued the French and the *Courrier d'Egypte* obliged with a description:

> The burqa is a piece of white cloth which stretches from below the nose to below the chest, and it hides all the face with the exception of the forehead and eyes. A Muslim woman cannot show her face to anyone except her father, brother or husband.

Revealing the face to the unbelieving Frenchman was, therefore, not going to happen. Lieutenant Laval concentrated on the positive by complimenting Egyptian eyes: 'The Turkish women always wear a veil and before our arrival in Egypt a woman was not allowed to go out without one. They have nice eyelashes and those that do not have them artificially make them black.' Redouté, who, for purely artistic reasons, wanted to see more, had to restrict himself to noticing some colourful refinements:

> As for the ordinary women, for those with means keep their women out of sight, they generally wear a poor-quality blue dress and a borgo, or black veil, which descends to their knees but is designed to cover their entire face apart from the eyes. Their eyelashes and eyebrows are often painted black and their nails are stained bright red. Their legs and feet are bare.

Intriguingly, he also noticed their use of henna, 'a powder made from the dried leaves of henna to stain their fingers and palms orange', as did Bricard who put it simply as 'the poorer ones put marks on their faces, hands and legs and even their stomachs'.

Pierre Louis Cailleux seemed frustrated that 'all the girls and women have their faces hidden by veils which are black or white and which descend to their knees. Only their eyes are visible and they would rather show any other part of their bodies than reveal their faces.' Alexandre Ladrix agreed on this paradox and wrote that 'they wear a long blouse and a veil which covers their faces so that they can be hidden, although you often get to see the rest of their bodies. The rich ones are different. They rarely go out, and when they do they are mounted on donkeys with tall saddles, and with a crowd of servants around them ready to do whatever they want. They wear a huge piece of black taffeta which covers them from head to foot.'

The captivity of Egypt's females, and the fact they could hardly be seen, was frustrating for the invaders, most particularly to André Peyrusse who viewed himself as something of a gift to women everywhere:

> We have been unable to find out if the women here, who have been so much spoken about, are as pretty as our French ones. Those we have seen to date have given us a poor opinion of their grace even though, as a rule, they are mostly kept locked up whilst those who do manage to appear are entirely covered from head to toe in a veil. We just get to see their eyes, which are black.

The idea that the women of Egypt were locked away and slaves to their menfolk was a universal one. Cailleux thought that all 'Turks saw women as creatures sent to earth by Muhammad solely for their men's pleasure'. Bricard complained that 'their women are kept as slaves and they can only look out on the world from behind the shuttered windows' before going on to assert that 'these women do not know how to do anything and never get involved in anything and their only activity is to learn how best to deal with the caprices or fantasies of those who own them'. Grandjean thought it a form of slavery:

> Such is the liberty the Turkish women enjoy, or, to be more direct, such is the perpetual slavery they are condemned to when they are born for, from the age of six, they are shut away with their mothers.

Pierre Millet went as far as to state that wives were purchased on the open market:

> Here women are slaves to their men and they are bought at market as we buy beasts in Europe. The Turks have one real wife and as many concubines as they can feed. They are most unfortunate as they only ever leave home to go to the baths.

Alexandre Ladrix saw when the women encountered any of the French, on their way to the baths for example, they were afraid. 'As for the women,' he lamented, 'despite the fact they wear veils, they always run off when they see us, or, if one of us is passing in the street, they cower by the walls and seem to shake with fear.' The portly antiquarian Denon had the same effect, and he watched as 'the women in their blue tunics, their faces covered by a poor mask of black cloth, their eyelashes and eyebrows coloured with black, their legs and feet bare, their scarlet nails, always run from us as though we were demons or savages'.

The severe shortage of French women, and the anxiety of local ones, resulted in a frustration which expressed itself in diverse ways.[17] Many turned to denigrating what they could not possess, among them Quartermaster François who sneered, 'The Orientals are not so fussy. Here if a woman is white then she is beautiful, if she is fat she is worthy of admiration. They have a saying, which is take a white woman to look at and an Egyptian to enjoy.' Moiret also adds that the Arabs preferred larger women, quoting his Georgian girlfriend as saying that 'the Muslims only love huge slabs of flesh' and that 'her deceased husband would only sleep with her once she put on weight'.

Galland remained loyal to French women, writing that the locals 'have neither the grace nor charm of our French women whose *je ne sais quoi* wins the day'. Joseph-Marie Moiret barely concealed his disappointment, having imagined that every Egyptian 'would have the charms and attractiveness of Cleopatra' but who was now fervently missing the girls 'of the lands by the Po, the Tiber, the Rhine and the Oder'. Jean Baptiste Lattil was also dismissive of Egyptian beauty, claiming that 'the only women I have seen are as dirty as snails and as black as moles. The pretty ones never come out of their dingy houses.' Sergeant Bonnefons sounds as though he had seen some up close, and smirked that 'you are generally astonished when you first get to properly see these women, something difficult to understand if you have not had the chance, for instead of revealing a young, slim thing with a pretty face and petite feet, you actually get to see a hag'. Miot was fairer towards what he viewed as the fair sex, commenting that 'you had to make do with what you could get and some took those women abandoned by the Mamelukes'. Still 'some were pretty and taught us Arabic and learned to pronounce French words. Often not the cleanest expressions.' The predatory Bernoyer confirms in a letter that there were indeed many abandoned women in the capital:

When our generals reached Cairo they requisitioned the women the Mamelukes had abandoned in their harems. They thought they made a bargain there, but when their passions calmed and they studied the objects of their desire, they found they really had got themselves some bankrupt stock. They rid themselves of them and these passed through so many hands that they are now reduced to keeping company with our soldiers.

---

17. Dr Ceresole was worried about the health of the army, implying that the soldiers had once taken other measures, when he noted that 'masturbation, which causes so much damage amongst us, is relatively rare here'.

1. The expeditionary force embarks in May 1798. This scene, set at Toulon, conveys some of the difficulties of loading horses onto ships. The French would take comparatively few horses with them, although they did find room for a grand piano.

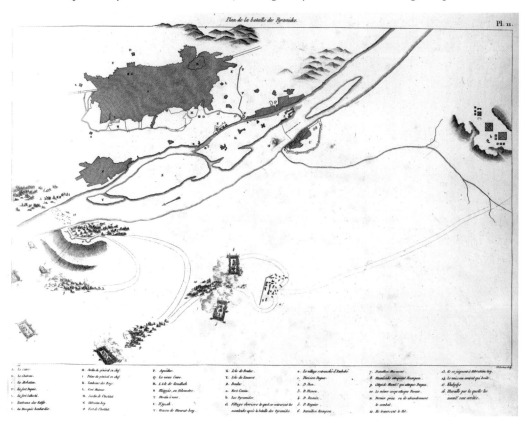

2. Denon's plan of the battle of the pyramids. This shows Cairo on the other side of the river, the principal French squares and, at 12, the flight of the Mamelukes across the Nile.

3. Baron Lejeune's almost panoramic painting of the battle of the pyramids is a glorious depiction of battle, even if a little romanticised when it comes to some of the realities of this first major encounter between the Frenc and the Mameluke warlords of Egypt.

4. Baron Lejeune's painting of the battle of the pyramids shows the French infantry in their blue woollen tunics, bicornes and bearksins, against the Mameluke cavalry armed with scimitars, pistols, lances and the odd blunderbuss.

5. The French infantry storm the village during the closing moments of the battle of the pyramids, triggering a desperate Mameluke attempt to escape across the Nile. Many were drowned, and the French could be seen fishing for corpses for days afterwards, all with the hope of recovering some of the gold and gold coins the Mamelukes carried into battle.

6. This seemingly chaotic, but rather accurate, illustration of a Mameluke charge depicts an episode at the battle of the pyramids. French accounts agree that the Mameluke captains made valiant efforts to urge their men on and against French infantry drawn up in a bewildering formation.

7. Whilst the French were superior in set-piece battles, hand-to-hand combat was a different matter. For this reason, the French tended to shield their cavalry from the Mamelukes as the latter were expert horsemen.

8. Guérin's romanticised depiction of Napoleon pardoning the rebels of Cairo. In fact, Napoleon made sure to apprehend and quietly execute as many rebels as possible whilst shifting the blame for the revolt on to the ruling council composed of locals he himself had selected.

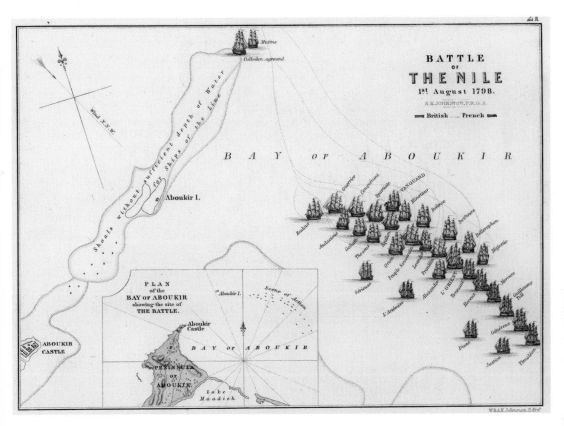

BATTLE
OF
THE NILE
1st August 1798.

A K.JOHNSTON,F.R.G.S.

British ——— French

B A Y   O F   A B O U K I R

Wind N.N.W.

Shoals without sufficient depth of Water for Ships of the Line

Aboukir I.

Mutine

Culloden aground

VANGUARD

Orion

Theseus

Zealous

Audacious

Goliath

Minotaur

Defence

Swiftsure

Bellerophon

Majestic

Orient

People Souverain

Leander

Franklin

Alexander

Tonnant

Heureux

Mercure

Guillaume Tell

L'Artemise

Serieuse

Diane

Généreux

Justice

Timoléon

PLAN
of the
BAY of ABOUKIR
showing the site of
THE BATTLE.

Aboukir I.

Scene of Action

Aboukir
Castle

B A Y   OF   A B O U K I R

ABOUKIR
CASTLE

PENINSULA
OF
ABOUKIR

Lake
Maadieh

W&A.K.Johnston, Edin.

9. Map of the Battle of the Nile.

10. Napoleon's fleet, and his future plans, was destroyed by Nelson in Aboukir bay in August 1799, just a few weeks after the French landing. It not only rendered the return of the army to Europe impossible but also sent a signal to France's rivals that her best army, and best general, would be unavailable for operations on the Continent. Naples, Austria, Russia and the Ottomans soon joined the British in their lonely war against the revolution.

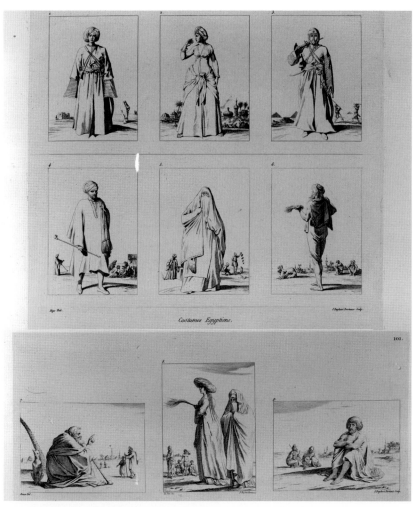

Above: 11. Some illustrations on the costumes of the Egyptians. The man has the obligatory pipe and the woman wears the burkha, a garment which puzzled the Europeans at the time and continues to do so to this day.

Left: 12. Denon's sketch captures what the French imagined Egypt's women to be like, and probably ready and waiting to be liberated from an old man's harem.

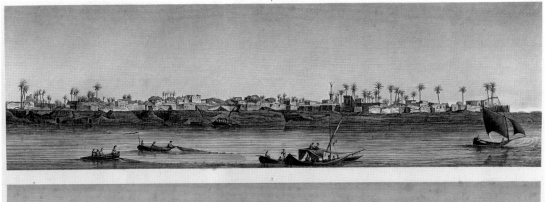

13. Two views of Egyptian villages. The French were unimpressed by the homes of the Egyptians, dismissing them, for the most part, as mud huts worse than French stables.

14. Another Egyptian village, this time sketched by André Dutertre.

15. A British caricature by Gillray has two of the French expedition's scholars ambushed by some Nile crocodiles. The scholar in red drops a volume entitled *The Rights of the Crocodile* and flees, whilst the unfortunate individual in the foreground sees his treatise *On the Education of the Crocodile* scattered into the sands.

16. The scholars accompanying the expedition were housed in a palace in Cairo, quickly turned into the Institute of Egypt, complete with a lecture hall, library, museum and small zoo. Here the members, including engineers, artists, chemists, historians and other useful types, gathered to share their findings or to chat in the shaded gardens.

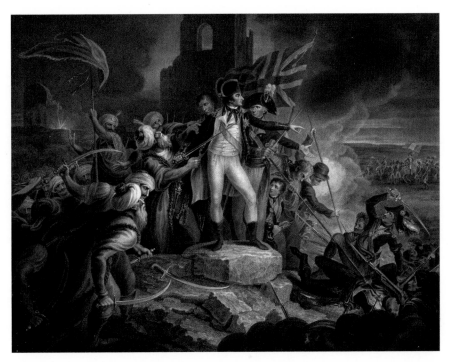

17. Here, at Acre, in the spring of 1799, Sir Sidney Smith and his marines and sailors assist local forces under the Bosnian warlord Djezzar in driving back Napoleon's infantry assaults. In this heroic image Smith directs Ottoman reinforcements against another unsuccessful French attack.

18. Napoleon visiting the plague house at Jaffa. This visit took place with Dr Desgenettes in attendance. Some of these patients were to be abandoned during the French evacuation of Syria, and a few dozen had poison administered to them by the army's chief pharmacist.

19. Some British naval officers visit a Turkish encampment. Britain and the Ottoman empire were in an opportunistic relationship. Both wanted to see the French expelled, and the British appreciated the weight of numbers the Turks could field whilst the Turks needed British expertise in military technology. However, the British were reluctant to see the Turks establish themselves too strongly in what had been a largely autonomous province, whilst the Turks were suspicious of British designs on the region.

20. Baron Lejeune's magnificent painting of the battle of Aboukir when Napoleon, having returned from Syria, surprised and destroyed an Ottoman expeditionary force landing near Alexandria. The fort of Aboukir is in the centre distance and, before it, the little village. To the right of that the Turks are being driven in to the sea by Murat's ferocious assault.

21. The artist's sketch of the same scene, with Napoleon's own Mameluke, Roustam Raza, visible in Napoleon's entourage.

22. General Murat leads a charge into the Ottoman lines during the battle of Aboukir. He was wounded in the mouth but his cavalry broke the Turkish centre, securing a victory for a Napoleon who, returning to France the following month, could again pose as a conquering hero.

23. General Belliard's 21st Light storm the town of Benouth in March 1799. Napoleon had taken most of the French off to Syria, leaving Desaix and Belliard to pacify the endless expanse south of Cairo.

Above left: 24. General Kléber succeeded Napoleon as commander-in-chief of the French troops in Egypt when that general returned to Europe. He proved a popular choice amongst troops who felt abandoned not only by the fugitive Bonaparte but also by the government in distant Paris.

Above right: 25. Jacques de Menou, Baron of Boussay, or Abdullah, the servant of God, Menou, succeeded Kléber when that general was assassinated in Cairo. Isolated and attacked by Anglo-Indian and Turkish forces he was soon besieged in Alexandria and had to surrender Egypt, and the Rosetta Stone, to the British.

26. The battle of Alexandria, or Canope, in March 1801. The British expeditionary force is engaged against Menou's dispirited army, although the French dragoons made a brave show of charging the British lines and breaking into their camp, before being driven off by the 28th and 42nd Foot.

27. General Abercrombie was mortally wounded by a French dragoon at this critical point in the battle.

Above: 28. British and Indian troops in their camp by the Red Sea in mid-1801. This second invading army had been sipped over to drive the French back from the Red Sea and then advance on Cairo. It arrived too late before the capital, however, for the French under Belliard had already surrendered to an Anglo-Ottoman force which had advanced down the Nile.

Left: 29. Some French graffiti, left at the Temple of Philae. The impact of the French was not always as visible as this but it would have a profound effect on Egypt, its government and its peoples.

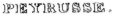

PEYRUSSE.

MADAME VERDIER

Above left: 30. André Dutertre's portrait of André Peyrusse, paymaster and secretary, who left a frank account of his experiences in Egypt.

Above right: 31. Here Dutertre portrays Madame Bianca Verdier, wife to General Verdier and one of the few women to accompany the expedition to Egypt.

DENON.

Murat

Above left: 32. The same artist also drew his fellow artist, Denon, an incorrigible sketcher of everything he encountered and the force behind the seminal description of Egypt.

Above right: 33. General Joachim Murat, France's most flamboyant cavalry general. It took many months before the French cavalry was capable of carrying out a charge against opponents quite superior on horseback.

LASALLE   BELLIARD.   GÉNÉRAL EN CHEF.

Top left: 34. The French horsemen were largely composed of rather lumbering dragoons, a type of cavalry too heavy for the shifting sands of Egypt. Due to a shortage of horses, the dragoons had to do with local mounts but found that their saddles would not fit the smaller, sleeker horses.

Top middle: 35. General Belliard, a diarist with a sharp sense of humour, was Desaix's right-hand man in the south and was the officer who would eventually surrender Cairo to Anglo-Ottoman forces.

Top right: 36. General Bonaparte by André Dutertre. Roustam Raza, a Mameluke apprentice given to Napoleon to serve as a bodyguard, recorded his first sighting of the general in Cairo: 'He was covered in dust and out of breath. he was wearing cavalry boots, white kerseymere breeches and a general's tunic. His skin was dark, he wore his hair long, powdered and tied in a queue. It wasn't a favourable impression.'

37. A full-length portrait by Dutertre, this time of young General Reynier, a military enthusiast for transforming Egypt into a French colony.

Admiral Jean-Baptiste Perrée seems to have been one of those greedy generals. 'I am tolerably well off,' he confided to a friend, 'regarding my table and my other amusements. The beys have left us some pretty Armenian and Georgian girls and we have appropriated them for the profit of the nation.'[18]

Peyrusse had such incidents in mind when he grumbled that 'there are rumours of some gallant adventures and some seraglios liberated and quite a few Frenchmen live with a woman and are working on increasing the population'.

Captain Moiret would be one of these, and would form a relationship with a woman from the Caucasus:

> Whilst I said that Egyptian women are not generally worthy of gracing the court of Amathus, nor capable of winning French hearts, it should not be assumed that all the women in Egypt are unworthy of the attention of foreigners. The beys, their ministers and high-ranking officials brought beautiful women in from Georgia and the Caucasus to serve as wives. These were the equals of the most elegant women of Paris or Lyon.

Bernoyer, too, was also on the lookout for beautiful women, or girls. This libertine, who claims to have even seduced a nun on Malta, apparently had a local procure some so he could select a concubine:

> I told him I liked brunettes as much as blondes, just make sure they are young and pretty. Five or six hours later he came back followed by a dozen women dressed in a long blouse of blue cloth that came down to the knees. ... Suddenly one of them removed her clothes and burst out laughing, as though to mock me for my timidity. Her cheeky look, her ravishing black eyes and her fourteen years captivated me and I proclaimed her my sultana.[19]

---

18. Niello-Sargy gave a similar account, writing that 'the women were frightful although the beys had left behind a few pretty Armenians and Georgians whom the generals seized for, as they put it, the profit of the nation'. Some of these later exchanged hands for money. Miot noted that 'as for whites there was no slave market for them whilst we were there although one could acquire the women abandoned by the Mamelukes for a reasonable price'. Jacques-Marie Le Père apparently bought one of them for 3,600 livres.

19. He thought it harmless fun, adding that the next day 'Lallemant [the servant], under the pretext of wishing me good morning entered my room and asked, rather ironically, whether I had had a good night. I told him it had been wonderful.'

General Desaix proved even more of a libertine than Bernoyer, ranging more widely and also indulging himself in a way which, by modern standards, would repel:

> I loved young Astiza, a sweet Georgian, pretty as Venus, blond and gentle. She was 14, two rose buds. I inherited her as I ruled the province and her husband was dead. I sold her for 6,000 livres. I gave her away, she unsettled me. I received Sarah as a present, a lively Abyssinian aged fifteen who travelled with me. I owned Mara, a native of the Tigris and Fatma, big, beautiful, shapely, unlucky. Imagine that, in the midst of my harem she could witness my pleasures, my ecstasy, my dissolution, she could not join in. For, when she was young her parents had taken a peculiar precaution, sewing up her private parts. That's my harem, and three black women more constitute my household.[20]

He could, of course, have been making it up and Redouté suggested that romantic exploits were largely a figment of the imagination, although much energy had gone into making gallant attempts at trying. 'The local women,' he warned, 'were kept at home but the French tried to court them and, as is our wont, flirt with them, seeming to be ignorant of this important difference between our social graces and theirs.'[21]

Of course, despite the obstacles, there were examples of relationships between French officers and local women or women found in Egypt. Chef de brigade Lambert married a woman called Martha whilst Moiret says he met a Georgian called Zulima, 'the widow of Ali Bey killed at the battle of the pyramids', which, in itself, makes his account hard to believe whilst the claim that they fell for each other over 'lessons in French grammar and maths' makes it impossible. However, General Menou not only had a romantic relationship with but also married the once divorced Setti Zobaidah, even, as per the dictates of sharia law, converting to Islam and becoming Abdullah (the servant of God)[22] Menou.

The happy servant described his new partner thus:

---

20. Sauzet, 'Desaix: le sultan juste', p. 245. This letter was to his mistress, Marguerite Victoire de Tournhem. Bernoyer also found a young girl at the slave market whose private parts had been stitched closed. Dr Louis Frank examined several of the women abandoned by the Mamelukes in Cairo, finding that they had suffered from female genital circumcision.

21. French conduct with local women certainly offended some of the locals. The Christian Niqula al-Turk commented mysteriously on the lack of respect: 'The women went out shamelessly with the French. Cairo became like Paris; there was wine and other alcoholic beverages everywhere and the other things of which our Lord does not approve.'

22. Vertray suggests this name means slave of Allah.

My wife is a good woman, neither ugly nor pretty, large, strong, well-made and with stunning eyes. Her family is an honest one. My marriage was an entirely political one and I don't think everyone will approve.

Peyrusse certainly didn't, sniggering that she was guarded by eunuchs and that anyone catching sight of her would be put to death. Moiret nevertheless saw her and wondered why he had chosen a woman who was 'old, very ugly, without charm', whilst François was, if anything, crueller, writing that 'we heard that the general, aged sixty-two, had fallen in love with the daughter of the owner of the baths at Rosetta and that he had converted to Islam, calling himself Abdullah, to marry her. This conversion made him ridiculous in the eyes of the army for you do not need to change your religion in Turkey to get a woman. You just go down to the market and you can buy one of any colour or age.'

Colonel Marmont went one further, firing an opening salvo of mock alarm, and asking whether Menou would 'follow local custom' and marry more than one woman. Menou shot back that 'the appetite of Turkish women was such that one would satisfies me for now'. And so the joshing continued, with only General Dugua being sympathetic, telling his friend that 'he hoped many bachelors would follow this example, for that is how the conquered grow attached to the conquerors'.

The conquerors were certainly looking for partners. Indeed, the ordinary soldiers had begun their dreaming aboard the transport ships heading to Alexandria. Martin had watched how 'the soldiers put on a play of their own devising and the subject matter was always the same, namely the deliverance of a slave from the harem. She would be rescued from the grasp of an old Turk and would marry the French soldier, her liberator.' When they arrived, the reality was far less romantic. There were instances of the rank and file keeping mistresses and Quartermaster François 'was glad to possess' the fifteen-year-old Anif, another Georgian whom he dubbed a princess and who had been abandoned by her Mameluke owner, and he would have married her had the circumstances been different. But there were also instances of the French violating such norms, and some glaring examples of rape. Of course, the laws of war permitted rape and pillaging whenever a besieged city was stormed, or a village for that matter. In that sense it was common and at Deïr General Murat told Napoleon that he had seen 'a company of grenadiers sling seven of their women over the shoulder and carry them off'. Detroye watched a punitive expedition against the desert Arabs return, noticing 'a few [soldiers] bringing in some extremely ugly women upon whom they had already exercised the rights of conquest'. The bloody siege of Jaffa was worse, and there a local chronicler was moved to write, 'What a terrible moment! They entered the city and killed soldiers and civilians, looted houses, took possession of women, raped girls, and cut the throats of children.'

Bernoyer was in the camp below the walls and watched the women and girls being brought in:

> We saw the soldiers returning to camp loaded with booty of all kinds, but this time, and I had never seen this before, they also brought back some young girls whom they bartered away for other objects. They saw that this quickly became a lucrative trade and brought in more young girls and young women, so much so that the camp became a hotbed of disorder and trouble. They were soon fighting over the most beautiful ones.

Some specific examples of rape occurring outside combat can also be found. Young Eugene de Beauharnais, Napoleon's stepson and aide-de-camp, reports being sent to chase French soldiers 'of different regiments' from a house from which screaming had been heard. Using the flat of his sword he expelled men who, in the quaint language of the time, 'had given way to an excess of brutality that a long period of privation had given rise to and which, whilst not excusable, was at least understandable'. However, Villiers, on patrol near Suez, relates an even more shocking story:

> We came across an Arab family composed of a father, mother and a son aged around twenty. They had a camel. General Boyer had the menfolk brought in for questioning, thinking that they may be spies or informers for the enemy. Whilst he was interrogating them and hitting them with his riding crop, twenty-five of our soldiers subjected the woman to an act of indignity behind the general's back. The father and son were taken as guides but proved of limited use. The son was shot and the father was taken and quietly finished off behind some bushes.

This indifference to human life was witnessed by many, but was routine for most. Coquebert, the botanist, was something of an exception and thoughtfully described one experience:

> I rode through the midst of 3,000 slaughtered Mamelukes, Milord [his horse] trembled beneath me while I fixed my eyes on those poor victims of ambition and vanity and said to myself – we cross the sea, we brave the English fleet, we disembark in a country which had never heard of us, we pillage their villages, ruin their inhabitants and rape their wives; we wantonly run the risk of dying from hunger and thirst and we are, every one of us, on the cusp of being assassinated. And all this for what? Well, we do not really know.

Most of the troops would balk at rape, but many used the prostitutes that were becoming increasingly numerous across Egypt. Gunner Bricard noted that in the capital 'there were prostitutes in this great city. Indeed, a combination of harems having been closed down, and thus many women finding themselves impoverished, and French spending, meant that there were vast numbers of them.' Captain Moiret, who expressed a general prejudice against Egyptian women, thought the prostitutes not worth bothering about:

> As for the joys of gallantry, there was nothing here which compared to Milan, Padua, Livorno, Rome, Verona or Graz, and it was neither possible nor prudent to visit the wives of the rich as they are under lock and key and jealously guarded by tyrants. There were some prostitutes but the courtesans there were so ugly, so dirty, and spoke such gobbledygook, that even the most ardent libertines were put off.

Yet Galland heard how 'a young woman who worked her charms made a lot of money from our Frenchmen, managed later to establish a life for herself in another village where she lived quietly and content'. At Syout, such women would accost passers-by, something which scandalised Dr Vincent Ceresole who thought it flew in the face 'of the admirable laws which govern the reproduction of living beings'. Bonnefons also thought the situation was getting out of hand, and to the detriment of public morals:

> Whilst we were there, the lure of gold led some to prostitute themselves and these told their friends of the freedoms they had among the Europeans and many were tempted to imitate them such that if this general rush to depravity had not been punished, corruption would have been at its height.

Warnings on the decadence and depravity of the east were legion, but the anonymous officer of dragoons sounded even more puritanical when he suggested a solution to preserve the morals, and health, of his charges:

> The cavalry were shut up in Boulaq and many of the soldiers found themselves infected by the prostitutes so that many of them fell sick.[23] Trying to stop them is pointless and to put an end to the matter we should imitate the Turks, namely stuff them [the prostitutes] into sacks and throw them into the Nile.[24]

---

23. This seems to be borne out by official records. General Daure told Damas that in one hospital there were 39 patients suffering from fever, 83 wounded and 176 who had syphilis.
24. François explains that 'the Muslim rule was that when a Muslim woman was found to have co-habited with an infidel she would be taken and placed in a leather bag which would then be tied up and thrown into the Nile'. However, it was a rule adopted by the French. On 23 June 1799 Napoleon instructed Dugua to have drowned any prostitute found working French barracks.

Morals were also at risk from the performing or dancing girls, an exotic temptation. At Metelis, a village famous for its dancers, Redouté accompanied Menou (whilst that general was still a bachelor) to a performance:

At first the sheikhs who owned them showed reluctance to have them perform before us. They probably thought we were unworthy of such a favour and that our profane gaze would sully the reputation of even the most dissolute women. The women also let it be known that they did not wish to appear during the day; however, military authority prevailed, the obstacles were lifted and six rather shy performers came before us. We supposed that a little alcohol would encourage them and offered them brandy and they drank it down in one go as though it were lemonade. It had an immediate effect and they began their chaotic performance. The women were not particularly attractive, not being pretty or graceful. Their bodies seemed to be covered with jewellery and this ridiculous embellishment almost completely masked their bronzed delights which were, in any case, covered in tattoos. The women stay in one place and shake their hips whilst the rest of their body is kept still, they do this rhythmically and are extremely supple, indeed almost indecently so. They hold little cymbals rather like castanets between their thumb and forefinger and accompany their clanging with gestures that are far from graceful.

Horace Say, whilst entranced, found time to take notes:

After performing a song, they present a miniature ballet based around the mysteries of love. Then, when the dancing starts, they drop their veils and the modesty of their sex. A long robe of fine silk flows to their heels. A rich belt is loosely tied around their hips. Long black scented hair in braids falls around their shoulders, and their breasts are barely covered by a transparent blouse, as though the cloth were made from air. When they begin to shake, it is as though the contours of their bodies break free.

Faye also watched carefully, noting that the girls' 'hips and waist are wiggled in a movement in which the bust seems to take no part' whilst Thurman kept his description even shorter, noting only that 'the dancers began their routine and I swear to you it was quite unlike any of the ballets at the opera'. Bernoyer was uncharacteristically prudish after seeing one such dance. 'For us westerners,' he moralised, 'these dances are so vulgar that even the most deprived amongst us could not tolerate them.'

Depravity was all around, however. And it was another institution, that of slavery, that caused the most unease, at least initially. For many of Napoleon's soldiers it would be their first immediate encounter with the antithesis of the liberty they had been fighting for. Yet, as they settled down to life in a society in which slavery had always existed, a certain ambiguity crept into the attitudes of men who had planted a Tree of Liberty in the dry soil of Azbakiyya. Not only was slavery common, but Egypt was a land based on bondage. After all, the Mamelukes themselves were a caste of slaves, and more slaves were continuously being supplied. Pilgrims from Mecca, that 'monstrous army of bigots', according to Bernoyer, brought in hundreds of black Africans each year. However, it was the huge caravans snaking their way up from Darfur which really fed this awful trade. Bonnefons was shocked by the inhumanity:

> Each year a caravan brings 1,000 or 1,200 black slaves from Abyssinia. Humanity revolts when it sees these victims of human ferocity. I shuddered with horror when I saw these poor people, practically naked, shackled to each other and with death written on their faces. They were sold off cheaply as though they were livestock. ... When they see a European approach, they take to beckoning to him and, by casting woeful looks, indicating to him that they earnestly wanted to be freed from the hands of their oppressors. ... The price is 300 or 500 francs in our money.

Louis Frank was also appalled, fuming that the slave drivers 'treated their camels better than their blacks' and that slaves were sold 'as we sell domestic animals in Europe'. He thought 3,000 or 4,000 souls were traded each year at Cairo whilst Laval was vaguer, writing that 'a huge number of blacks are brought to market in Cairo every year and sold to the highest bidder'. But his knowledge of the trade was more intimate as revealed by his subsequent confession that 'I bought myself a female and she cost me 300 livres tournois'.[25] The erstwhile sons of liberty were having their republican morals corrupted. Although slaves had been released from servitude to their Mameluke masters, they instead became the property of the nation. Nor did the French outlaw the slave trade. Indeed, many officers began to make use of it, purchasing servants as soon as Napoleon ended the option of employing soldiers as valets. The buying of individuals became really quite common and, just as Laval had, Malus traded in flesh: 'On 1 December ... I bought Zamour aged around nine from the Darfur caravan which had arrived at Beni-Soues.' François also visited the Cairo

---

25. The livre tournois had been converted into the franc in 1795. Galland says that the price for a woman varied between 200 and 500 francs. Dr Frank was more methodical, noting that 'a boy aged between ten and fourteen costs 50 to 70 piastres of Spain; from fifteen to eighteen years, 70 to 100 piastres. For a girl aged eight to twelve, 35 to 50 piastres; for a girl or woman, from fourteen to twenty, 70 to 90 piastres. A eunuch aged ten to twelve costs from 160 to 200 piastres.'

slave bazaar, and, once, came away with two female slaves one of whom was ostensibly to serve as a maid for his mistress:

> All the soldiers from the generals down to the drummers would go down to the bazaar where the slaves were sold in order to watch what was going on and even to buy one of the wretches. I went a few times and ended up buying two black girls aged fifteen and seventeen. One was for me, the other for my comrades, and they cost me fifty-five and seventy piastres respectively.

Saint-Hilaire the scholar also made a few purchases, but perhaps a tinge of guilt forced him to justify his behaviour:

> For 250 francs I bought a child aged eleven [Tendelti] and I have taught him to take care of my collection and feed the animals. Since then I have also been given an old black woman and she has proved adept at managing my domestic affairs. Slavery here is not quite what it is in the Americas. It is more like adoption. My two slaves refer to me as their father and I am so content with them that I show them the same kindness.

Tendelti was to act as an assistant taxidermist. This was bad enough, but others were used much worse. Galland, who also thought that the treatment of the slaves in Egypt was better than that of slaves in the European colonies,[26] saw them being taken as mistresses:

> An officer took a black to live with him and this was the done thing for most of the French who, for reasons of taste, or for reasons of economy, preferred them to the women of Egypt.[27]

Bernoyer, visiting the market with a companion, badly wanted one like that and it was only reasons of economy, rather than morality, which prevented him:

> On 22 October I met Captain [Joseph Agricol] Lunel from Avignon. He suggested we go down to the bazaar as a caravan had just arrived bringing in a great number of women, mostly blacks. He wanted to buy

---

26. Doguereau had it that 'the black slaves of Egypt live comparatively well' and noted that 'their fate is better than that of the Egyptian poor'.
27. Dr Louis Frank thought that the black women preferred the French to the Mamelukes as the former 'do not treat them as property but admit them to their table and even share their beds with them'.

one. My curiosity got the better of me and I gladly accepted his offer. We went into a vast building built like one of our old monasteries. There in the courtyard we saw around 100 blacks, men and women of all ages crouching on the ground like monkeys. They had a dirty loin cloth by way of clothing and gave off a vile smell. We wanted to know the price of a particular black girl close by and so approached the merchant to ask. Before telling us, he had her uncovered so we could examine her, then he suggested we pay 500 francs. The captain was unimpressed and asked if he had any whites. He replied that there were not many and that they were expensive, having to charge 8,000 francs each if he was not to make a loss. We asked him to show us some, but he refused saying General Bonaparte had forbidden him to sell any before he saw them and that he had first pick.[28]

The bazaar was not the only place slavery was prevalent. Villiers du Terrage saw that some slaves never made it to market, as he makes clear in a deeply troubling statement:

We came across a flock of sheep tended by a nine-year-old girl. We killed the sheep or stole them, carrying off what we could. As for the girl she was loaded onto a camel and taken to Suez where she became the prey of the general's staff. They told me she was later sold on to a merchant from Yanbu.

Some of the female slaves were kept in French households whilst males were treated as servants or, later, as the supply of replacements from France became impossible, found themselves in French uniform. On 22 June 1799 Napoleon had ordered that 200 slaves be purchased, and informed Desaix that he wanted 2,000 or 3,000 more. Gunner Bricard noted that in March 1800 General Belliard's corps included 'a number of black men and women; and most of the drummers and musicians consisted of young blacks who had been bought by the units'.

The anonymous officer of dragoons described this strange form of taking the First Consul's Shilling:

A number of commanders had enrolled Nubian blacks and they did good service. They were tough marchers, very sober and quite bright. They were quite proud to be included in our ranks and citizens Eppler and Lasalle praised them to such an extent that General Kléber

---

28. The merchant then took them to see two black slave girls noted for their beauty. He asked 1,800 francs for them. Haggling proved fruitless, but when the two returned a little later resolved to pay that price they found the two already sold. Bernoyer later found out that Eugene Beauharnais had bought one of them.

encouraged this trend. Anyone who managed to recruit a black capable of bearing arms was to be awarded a bonus of 150 livres.

Slavery divided the French in Egypt. Some, such as Anne-Jean-Marie-René Savary, saw it as acceptable. 'We all thought,' he generalised, 'that it was more philanthropic to permit [the trade] than to ban it, although perhaps it would be better if the government itself took on the responsibility of buying the blacks and transporting them to the tropics, where they would be regulated rather than sold to private buyers.' However, Grandjean and others dissented, thinking it something which corrupted society, making it incapable of asserting itself in its own interest, or working for its own good. He found that, as a consequence, Egypt was corrupt and lazy, and was scathing of Egyptian capacity for improvement, or work:

> The Turks, the most lazy and ignorant of the earth's inhabitants, do not understand the notion of repairing things, all they can do is destroy. Believing in predestination they will not lift a finger to avoid a calamity that could easily have been foreseen.

That the inhabitants were lazy was something Galland the printer also believed, and he railed that 'the Egyptian is careless, and hates anything new, whether it is good or not, and can never drag himself from a state of apathy in order to make use of it'. Vigo-Roussillon agreed, generalising that 'the inhabitants are so negligent that if an animal dies in the street they just leave it there until only the bones remain'. Laziness was a symptom of poor morality for the Europeans of the age of industry. 'It is a shame that so flourishing a country,' pontificated Bricard from Rosetta, 'is inhabited by such lazy people, people who shun work and lack morals.' Gerbaud summed up this litany of complaints when he opined that 'Cairo full of Turks who nonchalantly lounge about smoking their enormous pipes and drinking their little cups of coffee. ... The women bake bread, cook, wash the clothes.' Galland thought the people lazy even when going to the toilet, writing with astonishment that 'when a certain need takes them then they do not make use of a wall or a tree, instead they squat down, as we would for that other function, and do what they need to do right there'.[29] He also thought that the 'Egyptians do not really like to work, and they do what needs doing slowly. When you tell them to try to change their way of doing

---

29. A criticism the chronicler al-Jabarti would have found hypocritical, for he observed that 'whenever a Frenchman has to perform an act of nature he does so wherever he is, even in the view of people, and does what he must, without even washing his parts after defecation. If he is a gentleman, he wipes himself with whatever is to hand, even if it is a paper he is writing on, otherwise he walks off.'

something they reply brusquely that their forefathers did things in such or such a way.'

Talk of those forefathers, however, prompted some to think. For Lacorre the contrast with the glories of ancient Egypt and the Egypt of today was just too much. He lamented that 'they have rendered this place unrecognisable as once it passed into legend as a promised and flourishing land'. Inevitably, the word degeneracy was bandied about. Gérard Lacuée despaired when he looked around:

> Egypt bears not the slightest resemblance to what our writers have said of it. The natives, degraded by slavery, have relapsed into a state of savagery and have retained nothing of their former civilization, save superstition and religious intolerance. I have found that they resemble in every detail the islanders of the South Seas as described by Captain Cook.[30]

Faye thought that the people who had built ancient Egypt 'were a people far superior to ourselves' but Doctor Savaresi opined that whilst the Egyptians might once have sat on the pinnacle of civilisation, they had now fallen very low. He prescribed a dose of European morality and discipline to set things right. Bernoyer was equally disappointed by the apparent contrast between the glories of the old and the apathy of modern Egypt:

> The ancients had built canals and channelled springs to bring drinking water into homes. Nowadays, through carelessness, all has gone to ruin and they have to collect water from three miles away and bring it on the back of a camel. That, my dearest, is the inevitable consequence of a government founded on despotism. The people, accustomed only to obey, never do anything for themselves, worse they allow that which is useful or good go to ruin.

Monge, perhaps reflecting on his own revolutionary past, was quick to blame organised religion, thinking that only once the dead hand of dogma was removed could Egypt flourish:

> The Estates General of Egypt has been convoked to ascertain ways to improve the country. These poor people are good for nothing. They think the Koran contains answers to everything, and cannot be argued with.

---

30. Alexandre Ladrix of the hussars wrote, 'All I can say is that there is nobody among the Egyptians who looks human, and I think their character is reflected in their faces. When I look at them I see savages, but we are not cowards and they do not scare us.'

Many of the French blamed Islam for an unforgivable betrayal of human potential and they, with the possible exception of Napoleon and the definite exception of General Menou, took to loathing the religion, its holy texts, its places of worship, its manifestation in sharia law and the hold it evidently had on the morals and outlook of the population. As men of Reason, they were also disquieted by the strange rituals of daily worship and alarmed at the alien enthusiasms of local celebrations. Villiers du Terrage was one to be so unnerved:

> The people gathered [to celebrate the birthday of Mahomed] at around nine in the evening and began with their singing and strange kind of dancing. They continued with it until they fell exhausted or even dead. Such superstition filled me with pity and doubt.

Lacorre had similar misgivings after watching a family celebrate a circumcision:

> The place was illuminated for eight days, and there was feasting of a most unusual kind. The first was a kind of outlandish buffoonery with the men dressed up in strange costumes or almost naked. Others in white powder and carrying torches shouted and leapt about like monkeys. Some gestured to the women of the chief as they looked down from behind their grills, and these gestures would have shocked the modesty of even the most debased Frenchman. The women replied by singing some rather tuneless song and it was here for the first time that I saw this ignorant and barbarous people laugh whilst we Europeans shrugged our shoulders.

Laval just thought that 'the population are fanatics. The Koran is respected by the Turks much more than the Bible in France.'[31] Gerbaud was more disturbed by the noise from the mosques, complaining that 'the Turks gather in the mosque five times each day and are invited there by the muezzin who, from the top of the minaret, calls them to prayer'. Godet was also out of humour when he was 'woken at an early hour by the noise the Muslims make from their mosques'. Millet was even more forthright in his criticism, lambasting the fact that 'there are 300 temples or mosques dedicated to worshipping Mohammed. Men go up the towers and start shouting at the top of their voices, their warbling bringing people to the temple.'

For those among the French who cared about such things, and there were many, the consequences of this primacy of religion were much more serious. It meant that the people were kept in ignorance, and were prey to

---

31. Reynier commented that 'the religion is not particularly dogmatic, but the fanaticism it inspires is a tool which the priests know how to exploit'.

exploitation and superstition. Chasseur Millet, however, thought that it was centuries of subjugation, rather than religion as such, which had taken its toll:

> The people are not like the ancient Egyptians so celebrated for their literature and their wisdom and about whose achievements so many volumes have been written. No, they have only kept the name and lost the ways, Egypt having been prey to so many wars and subjugated by so many different people, such that fires and terrible massacres have destroyed their spirit.

Bernoyer the tailor, after having embroidered on his hope that Reason might save Egypt's virtue, blamed tyranny but also ignorance for this state of affairs. 'It is certain,' he declared, 'that an educated and enlightened people would not be able to tolerate the kind of tyranny they have here and that they would rise up against their oppressors rather than suffer under such a yoke. However, these people are so ignorant they do not think about it and so tolerate it all with patience.'

This made the Egyptians seemed fatalistic, and Antoine Galland thought that this trait killed any sense of natural curiosity. For example, on 14 July, he saw how

> on the anniversary of Rivoli they launched another balloon but it was scarcely more successful than the first attempt. It is impossible to imagine the complete indifference of these people when they saw this aircraft. As it passed over the square they hardly lifted their eyes whilst the French stared upwards.

This seemed to confirm Dolomieu's view that 'the people have neither curiosity nor the desire to emulate. They have an absolute indifference to everything which is new.'

Attitudes such as these caused despair in the likes of General Reynier, a believer in the power of education, and he complained that 'one never sees a man who has improved himself through the arts or the study of science'. Perhaps he had in mind Sheikh Al-Mahdi who, upon visiting the Institute, surprised his hosts schooled in the art of Linnaean taxonomy by dismissing their curiosity in the natural world with the curt declaration that 'the Prophet had declared there are 30,000 kinds of animals, 10,000 on land and in the air, 20,000 in the sea'. Berthollet noted another such example, this time when sheikh El-Bekri, visiting the Institute, watched as Berthollet demonstrated electricity, and then afterwards earnestly told him, 'That's all very well but can he make me be here and in Morocco at the same time?'

Bricard, who was self-taught, and therefore more scathing, thought the problem deep rooted, complaining that 'the majority live in unparalleled ignorance, and do not even know how old they are or how it is they are alive, and whilst a few of the richer ones have some education, the people here are like wild beasts'. In December 1798 Napoleon himself chided Al-Sadat that 'the Arabs had cultivated the arts and the sciences in the time of the Caliphs but now ignorance dominates and they know nothing of the wisdom of the ancients'. Others averred that the pyramids could not have been built by the Egyptians of today given their ignorance of mathematics. Thurman, for whom that science was central to existence, was stupefied to see that, after teaching an astonished Egyptian how to multiply 250 by 30, the man then chanted sacred texts under his breath as though he had just witnessed some devilish magic. Redouté was also horrified by the tendency to confuse science with magic:

> Menou had a knife with him which had a magnetic blade and he showed them how it could attract fragments of iron from the sand. They were astonished and thought it was some kind of magic.

Laporte also saw how French technology and progress was quickly branded the stuff of evil spirits:

> They sent up a superb balloon which flew above the city for two hours. The Turks thought it was witchcraft and we had to take a great deal of trouble to persuade them that it was the effect of hot air which did this.

Galland would generalise that there is 'no need to add that the Arabs are ignorant, credulous and superstitious, something they share with all Orientals', but he was particularly dismayed to see that 'they treat the sick by placing on the patient's head a piece of paper, on which some mystic's words of the writings of a dervish are written'. He was more amused when, having killed a weasel in his bedroom, the servants 'said that his ghost would haunt me for four years'.

Superstition and credulity were bad enough, but the French went further and saw in such ideas the enemy of dignity and the root causes of much of the debasement they felt they were encountering. Godet, who had risked his life for liberty and equality, and had a sense that fraternity could be useful, was shocked by the degree to which the people were inclined to prostrate themselves before their old masters and their new:

> Out of gratitude one of the villagers kissed my hand and then immediately kissed me on the feet. He did this so quickly that I, taken by surprise, could not stop him. That a man can be reduced to this degree of abjection and baseness!

Bricard thought this was all pure hypocrisy, and was convinced that the Egyptians were really glowering behind his back whilst they rushed to kiss his hand:

Those that live in the cities are a little politer but he is more than likely to deceive you. He will do nothing unless you show a coin and he is inclined to be arrogant, cowardly, nasty and duplicitous. He is devoted only to his pipe.

Redouté went even further in his condemnation:

They are nothing but fanatics, hypocrites and traitors and at the least opportunity they turn haughty and insolent. As we pass through the streets we are obliged to tolerate the insults they utter and they curse us in their own tongue whilst throwing hostile glances in our direction. The greatest danger was of being stabbed, for they carry blades under their garments.[32]

There were other dangers, too. Millet, who was also inclined to think there was little to admire, thought the populace vicious. He went as far as to state that 'the Turks are coarse and viler than animals, and with less shame. Most of them are sodomites and there are as many public houses containing young men in this city [Cairo] as women, and they carry out all kinds of perversions there.' Jaubert, too, heard stories about men being raped when taken prisoner, writing that 'the Arabs and the Mamelukes have treated some of our prisoners as Socrates is said to have treated Alcibiades [i.e. sodomy]'. Moiret told an anecdote about one such atrocity:

A French officer was seized by the Arabs and subjected to that most cruel act of indignity one can inflict on a man. His wife had been taken too and the tears and wailing of this unfortunate woman did not curb the lust of these wretches. The French recaptured the officer and his distraught wife, who recounted this atrocity in the most singular manner. 'Those wretches, those villains! I offered myself to them but they preferred to go back to buggering a poor man aged fifty.'[33]

---

32. Although one local, a certain Al-Jabarti, wrote, 'The French soldiers stroll through the capital without carrying weapons and without harassing anyone. They jest with the people and are willing to pay a high price for their needs. This encourages the people to forge relations with them.'

33. Dr Savaresi was of the opinion that Egypt's women were to blame for the prevalence of this vice. He had it that their genitals were too wide, diminishing the pleasure and leading to an increase in this 'infamous and detestable vice which has deep roots amongst Orientals'.

Quartermaster François describes another incident in this earlier series of the disasters of war:

> Some civilians, sappers, bakers and engineer officers were seized by the Arabs and raped and then they had their noses, ears, arms, legs, privates, etc, cut off. Those who were spared were thrust into the ovens by these cannibals. When we arrived we saw these miserable victims had been roasted in the oven. We took revenge by burning the hamlets where these eighty men had been killed.

Bricard saw more examples of cruelty, recalling an incident in which 'the Bedouins ambushed some men coming out of the town [Alexandria] and they seized two. They had the ferocity to kill one of them, an officer of light infantry, by burning him alive.'[34] Bernoyer came across yet another case, one which sealed his opinion of the local population for the rest of the campaign:

> A commissary officer was sent into a village to procure corn. He and his servant were seized by the Arabs, tied to a tree and burnt. We saw their corpses, they were still giving off smoke. In the face of such barbarity Bonaparte grew angry and ordered that the village be burnt and for the inhabitants to be shot or run through. Such an example did not mean that such atrocities ended, at every step we came across other victims who had been tortured to death in different ways by this ferocious people. I saw one scalped, others with their faces skinned or with the soles of their feet burnt. I won't say more.

Such atrocities, and accusations of other crimes, prompted men like Bricard to see enemies everywhere, and to distrust the population as a whole:

---

34. This brutality sowed fear in the French, and indeed Maltese, ranks. Thurman recalls how his escort of Maltese troops was thrown into disorder by some Arab horsemen: 'My Maltese imbeciles, little accustomed to such a menace, took fright and began by throwing away their canteens in order to lighten their load. They quickened their pace and the column fell into disorder. ... The officers and I grabbed their muskets and along with the six grenadiers, fired back. The men were running now and so we, seeing the enemy attacking us from behind, formed a rear-guard. We walked amongst haversacks, hats and tunics, thrown down by our rabble in order to get away.' Major Vincent at Suez was also sure that 'the Maltese can't live peaceably in the land of the Turk, for, at the sight of a turban, they are seized by complete panic'.

These savage brutes filled us with horror. Their barbaric costumes and faces, along with the crimes they committed every day, repelled nature itself. Their black, rugged faces made them look like monsters and despite their attempt to seem friendly they did not win our trust.[35]

The war made the population seem cruel. But it was the war itself that was crueller. Few prisoners were taken by either side, and the laws of war were frequently reduced to those of survival. The French were horrified by the Ottoman habit of decapitating the wounded and dead to present heads for monetary reward. Augustin Delesalle, captured in March 1799, recalled,

> I was struck in the side once more and this blow unseated me and I fell to the ground where I was at the mercy of the Arabs. They threw themselves on me like famished vultures and stripped me down to my underclothes and shirt. One of them, hoping to get my ear-rings, made as if to cut off my ears but instead they struck me with a lance, even though I was naked and covered in blood. I parried the blow with my arm, but the lance went through it. Meanwhile, I watched as fourteen of my companions, including Terrand, were hacked to pieces and they brought over, and made me kiss, their bloodied heads.

Lieutenant Pierre François Xavier Bouchard, who, in happier times, discovered the Rosetta Stone, recalled an incident at El-Arich when a detachment was ambushed and 'they decapitated the three soldiers who had fired and tied the others to their horses' tails and dragged them to Karroub. ... They were then taken to Jaffa to be presented to the Grand Vizier. They had to carry the heads of their comrades as they were marched in triumph around the city and camp.'

In the face of such atrocities, the French were inclined to take an eye for an eye. Łazowski felt that 'any politeness or compassion is taken by them to be a mark of fear or weakness. I am not convinced that we should behave as the Turks do, but I think that in this place a rigorous severity is as necessary as justice.' Peyrusse was more concise but just as brutal when he wrote, 'We have to murder in order to avoid being murdered.'

The ferocity escalated and sometimes took strange forms. Detroye was in Cairo on 23 January 1799 when he saw 'four Arab heads were carried through the streets and brought before the windows of the

---

35. Distrust was mutual. A local scholar, Niqula al-Turk, thought the French 'sociable, incredibly tolerant and superior in their behaviour to all the other nations. They pardoned their enemies easily and showed themselves patient and indulgent, observant of justice and dedicated to making sure that good order and worthy laws are enacted. And yet, despite all their efforts, they could not win the confidence of the people.'

commander-in-chief before being placed on the gates of Fort Sulkowski to deter others. This sight, which would have horrified Paris, made little impression here in Cairo. Indeed, the Turks barely looked at them.'

Executions were sometimes extrajudicial. François-Etienne Sanglé-Ferrière provides an instance of everyday barbarity, of casual killing by soldiers who saw an enemy in everyone:

> Whenever we saw a group of *fellahs* or Bedouins assembled on the banks of the river we would fire a few artillery rounds at them in conformity with our orders. However, I have to say that we paid too much attention to our sailors who said that any such assembly was a threat, and thus permitted themselves some target practice. I am sure I can blame myself for the deaths of some poor peasants.[36]

Denon, too, felt the triumph of harshness, confessing that 'we, who boast that we are more just than the Mamelukes, commit wrongs almost daily, the difficulty in identifying our enemies ... leads us to massacring innocent peasants'.

Despite such general hostility, the French did indeed manage to find and cultivate some loyal collaborators even amongst a hostile population. There were some rare examples of locals genuinely won over by the French, including the Syrian scribe Mikhail Ibrahim Sabbagh, but, more commonly, it was the temptation of a salary which decided the matter. The occupiers found that paying some of the defeated Mamelukes proved effective when it came to controlling the cities, those islands of order in a sea of disobedience. Most such auxiliaries were rebranded Janissaries after the Ottoman empire's elite warriors, and were offered 8 médins a day and their daily bread. Gerbaud saw a similar company raised by the local Divan at Damietta. They were, in one sense at least, shock troops:

> Formed and reviewed a company of Janissaries, all inhabitants of the town. Nothing more ridiculous for a European than the sight of this company of old men armed with whatever can be found, all without uniforms and all useless.

Choosing allies and collaborators was apparently a difficult process, but there were some notable individuals who ended up serving the French. Urban elites who wished to retain their status complied, and even Mourad Bey eventually preferred collusion to life as a fugitive. But there was also a host of forgotten collaborators such as the individual Thurman encountered:

---

36. Another officer commented, 'The soldiers thought that any Arab dressed in a long coat was a Bedouin and so mistreated them and so rendered them hostile to us when otherwise they would not have been.'

The sheikh of Bourges, Ismael Ben-Aven, an intelligent man who spoke Italian, had served as a pilot during several naval campaigns and had been held prisoner at Malta, proved to be of great use as we laid the foundations of the fort as he knew all about the local tides.

In June 1799 Murat also made use of the Henady tribe to wage war on some traditional rivals who had molested French convoys. He thought them 'great rascals'. More reliable were those on the fringes of Egyptian society, who could act as intermediaries between the ruler and the ruled. The Greeks, 'no strangers to the sentiments of liberty', crewed the French Nile flotilla but they also contributed to the police with 100 men at Cairo under the infamous Barthélémy of Chios, 100 at Damietta and 100 at Rosetta. Eventually a legion of 1,500 men, serving under Hadji Nicolas Papazoglou the T'chesmeli, and Nicolas Kiriako, served in French uniform. Redouté once watched these green-coated troops march past: 'They were led by the Greek Legion and this auxiliary unit carried a tricolour flag on which featured an inscription in Greek and Arabic.'[37] General Dugua singled them out for praise, telling General Damas that 'those we recruit here are, apart from a few of the Greeks, never going to make soldiers who can be relied upon'.[38]

The Christians of Egypt, too, were seen as outsiders, and they were often hated for having served as stewards for the governing classes, and as tax collectors for what had passed as a government. The French made use of these willing auxiliaries, keeping many as agents and administrators but also raising a 900-strong Coptic legion under Gabriel Sidarious and Jacob Youhana or Mo'allem Yacoub. Black slaves were also enlisted and Vigo-Roussillon saw how the French ranks were filling up with foreigners:

> We had lost so many excellent soldiers in all the revolts, in the street fighting and in battle that it was impossible to replace them with men of the same calibre. To boost our numbers, General Kléber introduced Syrians, Copts and even negroes into our ranks. All the drummers of the 32nd Line were of that latter race. They were dressed in black with silver ornamentation.

As well as finding allies among the Christian peoples of Syria, and the black slaves of Darfur, the French also courted the Jewish merchants. This was easy for, as Reynier noted, 'there is prejudice against them, as in all other

---

37. The French infantry carried flags bearing the phrase 'discipline and submission to military discipline' rather than that more famous motto of the revolution, Liberty, Equality and Fraternity.
38. Some 340 of the Greek soldiers would leave with the French when they eventually evacuated Egypt.

countries'. Indeed, Bernoyer thought that 'Jews and Christians are regarded by the Turks as being inferior. They treat them like domestic animals, things which are for carrying heavy loads and to receive, without complaint, the most infamous treatment.'[39]

These were classes of men who were already alienated, making their switch of allegiance more understandable. Still, in general, the French were unimpressed with all those who chose to side with them. Menou, for one, thought that the Jews in particular 'corrupted and vile, of no use and the greatest robbers the human race has ever produced'. Niello-Sargy went further, thinking all those who offered their services suspicious:

> We found a gang of intriguers, Jews, Copts, Greeks and Europeans, at Cairo as they had come here to practise the art of pillaging and exploiting people and they now became our agents, rendering us hated for depredations real or imagined.

With few local allies, and with the bulk of the population remaining indifferent or hostile, the occupation of Egypt was destined to falter. An occupying army, badly prepared and badly advised, and floundering in the complexities of an alien land, was never the best institution to build trust. Still, with a return to Europe impossible, the occupation was forced to continue and so the soldiers, and the population, would have to adapt to these strange new conditions. For the Egyptians this meant waiting and seeing. For the French it meant not only coming to terms with the peoples of Egypt but also reconciling themselves to Egypt itself. This was a land which constantly reminded them how precarious and hard life was, but also, of course, how grand and glorious it had once been.

---

39. François Leclerc D'Ostein thought that 'for the Turks, a dog and a Christian are the same thing, with this difference. When it comes to dogs, they tolerate them but they kill Christians as easily as you'd kill a hen.'

7

Reactions

If the peoples of Egypt were strange to French eyes, so too was the landscape. Egypt, with its deserts, harsh climate, suspicious creatures and unnerving ailments, was a hard land to trust. Some would never manage but a few tried, including some soldiers who attempted to adapt to local ways. Peyrusse was only half joking when he wrote,

> The way things are here has little in common with our ways of doing things, but we have to get used to them. We have to learn how to smoke, sit on our heels and grow a moustache if we want to be taken seriously by the Turks.

Any concessions to local custom were partly about compromise with the conditions but also about making the alien French presence less menacing. Napoleon himself set an early example, letting it be known he was toying with conversion, even hoping to be called Ali Bonaparte in a bid to replace the Ottoman viceroy and legitimise his rule over Egypt. He would also flatter the inhabitants through his choice of clothes, and Horace Say saw him wear 'oriental costume' on the Prophet's birthday. Detroye also saw 'the commander-in-chief put on Turkish costume today and they say he did so to persuade the Divan that if he could wear their foreign dress then they could wear the colours [a tricolour sash] of our nation. His aide-de-camp, Eugene Beauharnais, son of Citizenness Bonaparte, often wore Turkish clothes with a French [tricolour] turban.' Moiret, who had trained as a priest before joining the army, cast a suspicious eye on the rumour that 'the French sultan would soon be circumcised, that he would wear a turban and by following Mohammed's teachings convert the rest of the army through his experience. ... Most of our soldiers would have been happy to enter the paradise of the Prophet so long as there was Burgundy and Champagne there, and that they would be spared the ceremony of initiation.'

Thurman was probably one of those who preferred not to give up wine, and his foreskin, but his appearance, like Eugene's, was going distinctly native:

> I have a long beard and moustache and am dressed in a torn shirt tucked into some wide but faded blue trousers and with a handkerchief acting as a kind of turban covering my long hair. I have no undies, and wear yellow shoes. I have a curved sword, a big pipe and a Bedouin tent.

Hervé Charles Antoine Faye described his own costume as 'a choirboy's cassock, with a turban, a beard and long whiskers, baggy trousers and huge yellow boots'. Beards and hair offered some protection from the sun, but also from local contempt. Saint-Hilaire saw that facial hair was an important attribute:

> We are following Turkish customs and all have moustaches for the bare chin is a mark of the slave. Even though we are the masters, the power of prejudice is such that the Turks believe that a Frenchman without a moustache belongs to another Frenchman.[1]

Whilst for Miot smoking also seemed like a habit worth adopting:

> We quickly began to borrow some of their customs. We began to smoke pipes, and soon found how beneficial this was. In hot countries the pipe serves to keep the mouth moist and one is less prone to feeling thirsty. Soon you could recognise the true smoker amongst us as those who, like the Turks, did not spit. We carried pipes everywhere and drank coffee with all our meals.[2]

Many of the soldiers posted outside the towns soon lived a life that was part French and part Egyptian. Marc-Antoine Geoffroy of the engineers, sent to fortify Salahie, took up residence in an Egyptian camp where European habits were kept under the bed:

---

1. Perhaps the style of the local barbers put the French off having a shave. Pierre-Amédée Jaubert saw that at Alexandria 'the barbers in the bazaar place the heads of their customers between their knees and seem more inclined at first to break their necks than shave them'.
2. Pipes were better than the alternatives. Pierre-Amédée Jaubert noted that 'in order to keep our mouths moist we kept a bit of lead shot in them and then kept silent, convinced, along with the Turks, that the action of talking made one more thirsty'.

I live in a dwelling constructed from the branches of palm trees. It has four rooms. One for me, one for my brother, that of Bouilly, who is in charge of the fort, and a fourth for guests and where my servant now sleeps. There is a constant breeze as there is a corridor down which the north wind blows. I have a bed, some benches, a table and stools. At the door and windows I have curtains made of muslin so the air can circulate. No sunshine gets into any of the rooms. Under the beds we have casks in which Bouilly is fermenting a good wine made from dates and fresh water.[3]

Such a dual existence was inevitable, but it did not mean that the French had given up on France. Most still yearned for a comfortable place in which they could imbibe their favourite liqueurs,[4] gossip and watch the world go by. After all, what good was life to a Frenchman deprived of a café or restaurant? The local establishments were quite unsuitable according to Antoine Galland:

I went to one of their cafes. The best one was a kind of shack or barracks without any furniture other than some big rugs on which you sit cross-legged. They only had some cafetieres, some dirty little cups which are smaller than the ones we use, and a few pipes for smoking. The Egyptians do not put sugar in their coffee, they had to go off and look for some for the French. I asked for a spoon with which to stir my coffee and the waiter picked up a twig from the ground and handed it over to me. As there was nothing else, I was obliged to make use of it after wiping it on my handkerchief.[5]

Pelleport was just as dismissive, writing that 'there were canteens for the soldiers but some went to refresh themselves in the Turkish cafes. These were often in dingy dives where a few dirty rugs were scattered on the floor

---

3. The French doctors thought the date brandy pernicious and a drink which gave rise to fevers. Then there was order of the day for 9 October 1800 which reads like the sermon it was meant to be: 'The use of a liquor which some Muslims make from hashish, as well as the smoking of its resin, is illegal in Egypt. Those who make a habit of drinking this liquor or smoking this resin lose their minds and become violently delirious to the extent that they then go on to commit all kinds of excesses.'

4. The French were still managing to obtain strong drink. In October 1800 Desgenettes had to warn the troops off drinking too much 'to the cost of their liberty, their life or, perhaps worse, their honour'.

5. He noted that whereas 'they pay a parat when they leave for each cup they drank whilst we were in the habit of always paying a bit more, and usually paid two or three per cup'.

for you to sit on. Those Turks and Arabs who frequented such places often spent much of the day there smoking and listening attentively to a man who, for a cup of coffee or pipe of tobacco, would recount verses from the Koran or epic tales. Our soldiers preferred to watch the jugglers and belly dancers.'

Following similar disappointments, efforts were soon afoot to create France in little corners of Egypt. Moiret noted that, in order to meet demand, 'a few Frenchmen opened inns or cafes here but they were expensive and the wine there was no bargain at 10 francs a bottle, and, in any case, it was watered down or of bad quality'.[6] Perhaps this fostered the demand for beer which resulted in Africa's first brewery, a Cairo establishment run by Royer and charging 9 médins a pint. The capital also had at least 'two Turkish gardens transformed into ones in the French style' and there was also the aptly named Café of the Victorious Army, in the house of Ibrahim Bey in Azbakiyya Square. Pelleport also notes that 'an emigrant opened a Tivoli garden but only those wearing a lot of lace and the top brass went there'. This Tivoli was also in requisitioned Mameluke property, namely the house of Eyoub Bey, and it boasted a library and a little theatre as well as its restaurant. Villiers du Terrage enjoyed his visits:

A certain Dargenel [or Dargevel], a former guardsman, established a Tivoli garden, a residence and garden where one can meet and where orange and citrus trees make the place agreeable. One can play cards, listen to music, refresh oneself and chat.

Peyrusse, still chasing skirt, recalled that there were even some dances held there:

A select group did get together and did what they could to make life bearable by bringing together those few French women who had come with the army and, once a week, organising a dance.

Detroye also noticed that 'what really drew in the crowds was the presence of the fifteen or twenty well-turned-out women who met there' and, indeed,

---

6. Gunner Bricard also lamented that 'there were a number of French men who had opened businesses and so there were cafes, restaurants, billiard halls. In such establishments one was served as one would be in Europe, but unfortunately at four times the price.' One such establishment was Guichard's wine shop selling 'all kinds of liquors, syrups, brandies, wines, sugar, coffee and perfume'.

Napoleon famously met his mistress there.[7] This did not stop Galland from being ungallant about these particular females:

> There were around 300 [French women] for 40,000 men and, with just a few exceptions, they were all plain. A few Frenchmen married local women or lived with them and went along with the local practice of not showing them in public. That which scandalised the Egyptians was to see our women[8] walking in the streets with their faces uncovered and accompanied by men. They told us that had this happened in the time before our arrival, then the woman would have been stoned.[9]

Tivoli was entertaining enough, but it would not last long, some officers accusing the manager of greed and rudeness, others resenting the monthly subscription of 30 livres. Meanwhile, the French also tried to recreate the cultural life they had left behind and opened a theatre in December 1799. Villoteau was to direct it, whilst young Fauvy of the engineers was tasked to build the stage machinery. It opened ominously with *The Death of Caesar* by Voltaire followed by Moliere's lighter work *The Affected Young Ladies*, although the Anglophobic farce *The Frenchman in London* was its true runaway success. Of course, Bernoyer found time to go and to complain about the dearth of pretty actresses:

> They have just completed a play house. There are plenty in the French army who can act, but finding French women for even the smallest of

---

7. Marguerite Pauline Bellile, quickly dubbed Cleopatra (her ugly griffon dog was given the nickname Caesarion), met Napoleon on 30 November. Detroye heard that 'scandalous rumours say that the young and pretty wife of a Chasseur officer has caught the general's eye and that the husband has been got rid of by being sent on a mission to France'. Napoleon had indeed sent Fourès of the 22nd Chasseurs back to France with despatches on 18 December. He was captured by HMS *Lion* ten days later and the British sent the crew to Rhodes but gallantly returned the husband to Alexandria.
8. Not just French women. A local chronicler was mortified to see 'Cairo become like Paris, the women coming out immodestly with the French, intoxicating wine and liquor being sold and such goings-on as would certainly offend the Lord of the Heavens'.
9. Some local women attended these dances. At the ball organised by General Songis des Courbons and Jean Constantin Protain in September 1799 at the commander-in-chief's residence, some local women danced whilst others watched from behind a screened balcony.

female roles is impossible. We are having to make use of delicate young men to play them.[10]

He should have gone to see the performance of *The Deaf* in which three French women volunteered to perform and were enthusiastically applauded for doing so. More often there were women in the audience. 'A few important Turks,' noted Galland as he scoured the stalls, 'many eastern Christians, very few of their women, some blacks and black women, and the pretty Georgians and Circassians of our generals, were in a box opposite and then there were some French women, most of whom were not quite so pretty but were gentler and more charming.'

Beyond Cairo and Alexandria, the French found some of their remoter garrisons deadly dull and an entertainment desert. Jean-Pierre Doguereau at Belbeis saw the French attempt to lighten the evenings with gaming, drinking and womanising:

> The commissary, a friend of my friend, had us for dinner and received us rather well. The dinner party was attended by quite a few officers and civilian employees. We played cards,[11] and drank some punch. A black woman and a washerwoman were the objects of the attention and gallantry of our chivalrous knights. Even when there were balls at Cairo, with staff officers in attendance, the army's washerwomen were present. After all, you need women if you are to dance.[12]

Bonnefons, deprived of even these diversions, came to resent the lack of basic facilities, such as inns, cafes or shops, in any of the villages, sighing that 'the smallest hamlet in Europe boasts of more resources for the weary traveller'. Still, shelter could make all the difference between life and death for that traveller. Villiers deemed himself lucky when he encountered a very simple refuge:

---

10. Napoleon had in fact requested Mahérault in Paris to organise a troupe of actresses and ballerinas for Egypt, but it took so long to screen candidates that Napoleon was back in Paris by the time these crucial reinforcements were ready. A troupe of twenty-six actors was despatched on the *Prudent* but this prize cargo was captured off Alexandria in June 1801.

11. He and his friends spent their time mostly playing bouillotte or brelan. Cards could be the downfall of honest men; two officers of the 25th Line were cashiered in January 1799 for playing cards with some grenadiers of the 32nd who were supposed to be on sentry duty.

12. He notes, later, that they could not hunt, for hunting was forbidden. A billiards table at the Salheyeh fort was a godsend.

There are many caravanserais in the plains of Thebes and these are of enormous value. It was the noble sentiment of disinterested hospitality which has led to them being established in a thousand places across Egypt. There is one such establishment on the left bank of the river, surrounded by palm trees. In order to appreciate their worth, one has to have been out in the heat and here, in Upper Egypt, the temperatures can climb to 54 degrees at noon. It is foolish to touch a rock that has been in the sun.

Sunstroke was just another enemy in a treacherous landscape. Villiers and friends discovered what effect the heat could have, and he recalled that 'Kom Ombo was the one place in Egypt where the heat was impossible to bear. The sand was so hot that one could not stand in the same spot for more than a minute without the risk of burning the soles of one's feet.'

These high temperatures were a challenge for the temperate French. François-Michel de Rozière, an engineer attached to the expedition, saw them reach '15 degrees at night and 27 or 28 by day, but on the 5th it was 34 degrees at three in the afternoon. We don't suffer so much for we sweat. The thermometer reached 46 degrees in the full sun. The sun burns one's feet even when wearing shoes.' The doctors worried that the 2nd Light, which had been based in Flanders, was suffering more from the contrast than the more acclimatised Army of Italy. Even so, everyone found it hard going. Joseph Laporte had spent five years in camps and roughing it outdoors but he too found the fierce sun and hot sand an ordeal:

The heat was bearable before eight or nine o'clock but there was an arid wind which was horrible as it picked up the sand we had to march over and swirled it around us. ... The sand was so fine that it always managed to get into even the best-fitting shoe and this was such an inconvenience that some chose to go barefoot, although the sun then heated the sand to such an extent that it was impossible to walk.

And much harder to survive. Doguereau recounts a brutal example of how heat could kill:

We rode past a soldier whose camel had died and he followed us, even though we were moving fast. When he reached the point of exhaustion and he saw that he was going to be abandoned, he called out, begging us to wait for him. The general who, like us, had too much to carry already, did not wish to stop. The soldier fell behind. Two gunners remained with him a little while longer.

Laugier also marked the lethality of this arid land:

We entered the desert a few miles from Alexandria and by ten that morning the heat was so intense and the thirst so overpowering in the midst of the sands that the men, deprived of water, began to collapse. Some recovered and rejoined later but they told us three had died.

The desert had fatal qualities, but its sheer relentlessness was also dispiriting. 'When a European, accustomed to a diversity of views and to an ever-changing sky, sets foot in Egypt and crosses the delta,' opined François-Michel de Rozière, 'then he is faced by a landscape which comes as a surprise not only on account of its novelty but because it is so sad and depressing. There are no hills, no valleys and the monotony of the terrain renders it less than charming. The soul is left a little emptier by this lack of variety whilst the eye, at first engaged, soon grows indifferent to these endless plains which stretch off as far as it can see.'

The desert could also play tricks on those eyes. Pierre de Pelleport describes one of these unexpected torments:

The heat was excessive, especially when the wind blew in from the desert. We had to breathe that intense air and deal with clouds of dust that was so fine it penetrated everywhere and particularly affected the eyes. In addition to these tortures was added that of the mirage, an optical phenomenon prevalent in the plains when the ground is excessively hot. It was a true punishment of Tantalus. Monge explained the phenomenon but it was only really understood by the learned, and there were few of those amongst our ranks, so the idea persisted that there was water ahead.

Godet gives further details:

As we marched along we often saw vast masses of water, like lakes or marshes, amongst which were scattered villages as though they were islands and all of which seemed to be barring our route. The distance of these visions from us depended on the heat. In normal temperatures our visibility was four or five miles, a distance entirely covered by water, water which, to our astonishment retreated as we advanced and which appeared behind us as we moved forwards. We were played for fools by this as we knew there was no water around us and we realised we were experiencing the effects of a mirage which is something sometimes experienced at sea but which, for us, was hitherto unknown.

Eyes were tricked, but also put at risk by the intense glare, and the scorching sand and dust. Bricard was soon observing that 'a third of the army was attacked by eye complaints and many lost their sight. It was a universal affliction.' Many had conjunctivitis, or trachoma, and ophthalmia (granular conjunctivitis) was the most serious kind. Godet noted in his journal that 'ophthalmia had shown itself in the last few days and was making inroads.

Everyone feared for the health of their eyes when they saw their comrades in danger of losing their sight.' On 26 August he was anxiously writing that 'I awoke to find that my left eye was in a bad way'. His subsequent diary entries chart his decline:

1 September: eye complaints are so common here that barely anyone is free from blindness, or blindness in one eye, largely on account of the immense amounts of dust ... I awoke to find both my eyes in a bad way. ... 3 September I awoke to find both my eyes glued shut. I went to General Desaix and he kindly insisted that I go to Cairo to have my eyes seen to.

Godet, ever curious about the world around him, however dim a view he took of it, was looking for an explanation for his condition:

Could it stem from the incredible heat, the great wind, the effect of the dust or the reflection of the sunlight on the sands, or a combination of all of those? Some had their eyes glued shut for ten or fifteen days. The locals use cumin mixed with egg white to soothe them.

Godet would be lucky. 'I saw Doctor Larrey,' he noted on 18 September, 'and he advised me to leave for Europe if I did not wish to lose my left eye first, followed by my right one. He told me that a membrane between my left eye and my nose had split and that the fistula could not be operated on.'[13]
Many of the French doctors were more at a loss than the local healers and most victims were subjected to the time-honoured remedies of bleeding, leeches, purgations or, if lucky, the application of verdigris, vitriol or zinc sulphate, which was sometimes dissolved in rose water. Such treatment did little to stem what was soon a crisis. Savary, with Desaix in the south, witnessed some horrendous scenes:

We were more like a hospital than troops on the march, for there were more blind men than men in good health. Every soldier who was able to see, or who had the use of one eye, guided along several of his blind comrades as they carried their arms and equipment.

Further north, Vaxelaire also recorded how eye disease blighted the army:

---

13. The most senior doctor of the expedition, Desgenettes, was convinced that the contrast between hot days and cold nights was behind the complaint. He recommended covering the eyes at night. His remedies were still better than Dr Bruant's remedy of 'a few laxative tisanes, for example those made from tamarins or similar'.

We camped in the plains of Mansourah where some of the army of Saint Louis, king of France, died of plague and other diseases. There they gave us tents, a pound of tobacco for a month and some coffee, although that did not last a month. That was in August and many were suffering from eye trouble, indeed three-quarters of our officers and men were hit by this condition. Sometimes, of a hundred men, only three were capable of preparing the soup.[14]

Soon, convoys of the blind were being sent off to Alexandria and from there some took ship for Europe. One transport, the *Liberté*, unfortunately ran aground on Sicily where seventy-eight blind soldiers, along with a young midshipman who had lost both legs at Aboukir, and Napoleon's friend, Sucy, were massacred by enraged locals. In March 1799 Captain Gaudfernau's flotilla transporting 212 invalids made it to Toulon, but they were hardly welcome there, either. Talleyrand, in an early instance of bad news management, sought to have them hidden away:

The government thinks that should these men be allowed into the interior of France then there is a concern that they will create the wrong impression and cause needless worry regarding the situation of our army in Egypt. It therefore intends that these men are kept at Toulon. In no way should they be allowed near Paris where their malady and exaggerated rumours will have a very bad effect.

Those left in Egypt did what they could to prevent themselves from becoming myopic outcasts. Young Jollois was at Rosetta where he was 'busy today [24 July 1798] designing glasses which I wanted to use to protect my eyes from the glare of the sun. The number of cases of eye problems amongst the soldiers led me to take measures to do what I could to preserve the health of these precious organs.' Desvernois found such sunglasses less effective than he had hoped, confessing that 'I had some blue-tinted glasses but I could still barely see, still I refused to go to the hospital at Alexandria despite the insistence of my comrades and the colonel.'

Just as well, for the hospitals were often dirty ('the hospital ward is full of vast numbers of chickens and pigeons', ran one report) or overcrowded. Still, the harsh climate, strange food and universal ignorance of elementary hygiene meant there was a steady stream of patients. Some were suffering from scurvy, some were plagued by parasitic worms or leeches, whilst others were brought low by local, and mostly unnamed, fevers. Saint-Hilaire was preoccupied with eye problems, but also suffered from the bloody flux, or

---

14. Alexandre Ladrix was one of the fortunate ones, as he admitted to his parents: 'The local diseases have left me alone. I have not been seriously ill and have not had any eye trouble, although few of my comrades can say the same.'

dysentery. Auguste Colbert, later a cavalry general, was struck down by just such an epidemic at Damietta:

> At first I thought it was the plague, but instead it was something which knocked me out for a month. I thought myself better then, but convalescence here often lasts longer than the malady itself. Mine was cruel indeed and my poor stomach could not accept any food and my nerves were such that I was a wreck.

Peyrusse was also affected, twice, by this debilitating ailment:

> At my age, and if one has enjoyed a robust health, you tend to believe that whenever you are exposed to a new climate then you pay a price once, and just once, for that. Having suffered so much from one bout of dysentery I therefore believed myself acclimatised. But how wrong I was as this horrible period in my life has shown, again reduced to lying on my sick bed for the last two months.

Bernoyer also suffered from the intestinal scourge:

> The pain I felt in my guts and throughout my body was such that it felt like nature was fighting its last battle against death. It was a curious thing that the day I felt myself closest to the tomb was also the day I started to feel better.

The scale of the problem, as well as the complaint's underlying causes, again puzzled the French doctors. In response, they counselled against moving too quickly from the hot to the cold, and urged that feet should be covered at night. For those already suffering, the Neapolitan doctor Antonio Savaresi suggested wine to settle stomachs, and a puree of lentils with lemon juice to build up strength (but also effective against intestinal worms). Others recommended a dose of ipecacuanha or rhubarb, whilst crueller colleagues advised emetics and purgatives. Instead of the soldiers' choice of pick-me-up, lemonade, these unfeeling men of medicine also insisted they drink oxycrat, a mixture of water, vinegar and sugar.

Those who survived the disease and the treatment emerged considerably weaker. The officer of dragoons was able to note that 'many of our officers had been so weakened by the climate and by such tribulations during this campaign that they were reduced to shadows of their former selves'. Peyrusse could only agree:

> There is a kind of affliction, a dysentery or diarrhoea which, in just a few days, renders you unbelievably thin and wan, as I can confirm myself. My illness lasted thirty-five days and I am no longer recognisable.

This ailment was bad enough, but Egypt was prey to an even more sinister disease, and one which had long tormented European imaginations: bubonic plague. In September 1798 General Vial, the rapacious governor at Damietta, saw how 'a warehouse guard was seized by a high fever and was taken to a military hospital. He was delirious, his eyes inflamed, his muscles weak and he had a bubo on his right groin. He was pale, his testicles were swollen and his eyes were set in a rigid stare. He weakened and on the morning of the third day, died.' Thurman was in Alexandria when he saw similar symptoms appear and he guessed the cause:

> The plague is here. The detachment composed of the Maltese and the men of the Legion Nautique arrived and were placed in garrison. The next day one fell sick, then another and now they drop like flies. Out of twelve men on sentry duty each day four or five collapse.

Captain Malus caught it and confirmed that it struck quickly:

> I started to feel sick on my eleventh day at Jaffa. I had a high fever and violent headaches, such that I was obliged to stay in and rest. I had continual dysentery and, one by one, the symptoms of plague began to manifest themselves. Around then Adjutant Grezieux died and most of the garrison fell ill. Some thirty soldiers a day were dying. It was then that a bubo appeared on my right groin. Until that point I had hoped that my illness was not the same as the wider epidemic. The fact that I had survived so many days since the initial attack made this a possibility, but only until the bubo appeared. I could no longer deceive myself. My turn had come. I therefore sent to Franceschi, who was with the wounded General Damas, all those objects which I wanted passed on after my death.[15]

François-Etienne Sanglé-Ferrière's friend, Dubuisson, fell ill with the plague in Alexandria, the episode revealing how plague patients were often shunned, even by the doctors:

> I told my men not to follow me and entered the little room we shared. What a sight met my eyes. My friend was stretched out on his back and barely conscious. I turned in order to go and fetch help but as I did so he called out asking for water. I went for it and returned and as I brought it to his mouth all he could do was utter the words 'I am burning up'. He drank and fell back. I went to fetch a doctor but they refused to attend him. Only by insisting could I get Doctor Dubois to follow me. Dubuisson

---

15. Malus survived and was shipped back to Damietta and from thence to the hospital at Lesbeh.

was barely alive. The doctor approached the bed and lifted the sheet with his cane. When he saw the buboes he sprang back, exclaiming 'we are done for, it is the plague'.

Bricard gives another example of a terrified doctor, this one too cowardly to treat plague victims:

A man called Boyer, a naval medical officer, refused to treat patients who had the plague so he was condemned and stripped of his post and then carried through the streets of Alexandria dressed as a woman and riding a donkey. He bore a sign which bore the words 'he is unworthy of being a Frenchman for he is afraid of death'.[16]

Perhaps such poor material did not matter, for all the doctors seemed to have a poor understanding of what they were up against.[17] Desgenettes was brave enough to try to find out:

To calm imaginations, and the fear prevalent in the army, I pushed a lancet into the pus forming in one of the buboes which had formed on a patient and then introduced the pus into an incision I made into my own groin and armpit. I then washed the wound with soap and water.

He survived, to the surprise and relief of the army.

Even without any medical qualifications, Gerbaud thought he knew that the disease was of two types – airborne and direct contact – and remarked that 'when the plague is in the air it is difficult to keep free of it but when it is of the kind passed on by contact, then it is easy to control it. The remedies are more numerous than effective and one of the chief ones is to blister the skin.' Apparently keen on lists, Gerbaud jotted down the kinds of symptoms one should expect:

According to what the chief medical officer says, there are three versions of this disease. The first consists of a strong fever and delirium, then buboes and various red marks, followed by an intense headache. Nobody recovers from this one.

---

16. Gerbaud cites the same version but it was all a misunderstanding, apparently. Boyer had worked his shift and then, as new cases arrived, he was told the army surgeons would deal with them and so returned to his quarters. Marmont then accidently reported him as negligent.
17. A post-mortem of Grenadier Roubion of the 32nd Line was of little scientific help as the doctors found out little more than that his stomach was full of green onions.

Its reputation was so terrifying that young Pierre-Amédée Jaubert, who had lent his shoulder to what he thought was a wounded soldier at Jaffa only then to find that the man had been sick with the plague, noted that 'for the next few weeks, whenever I had a headache or was indisposed, I was immediately sure it was the plague'. In truth, the French were still unsure precisely what disease this was or what caused it. Saint-Hilaire, who, as a naturalist, should have known better, thought that 'the plague has been much less deadly this year [1800]. The French have barely taken any precautions against it. It has just struck down those who drink too much brandy and who have an excessive number of women.'

The doctors were on firmer ground when it came to limiting its spread. Desgenettes insisted that the belongings of plague victims be burnt rather than washed and reused, and some effective attempts were made at quarantine. Vigo-Roussillon found this out the hard way:

> Arriving at Damietta on 14 November a few of our men fell ill with the plague and a few died, including a fourier [clerk] from my company with whom I had shared a blanket. As soon as he fell ill I was put into quarantine on the other bank of the Nile. I was kept in a chapel and isolated. They brought food to me each day but as it was forbidden to communicate with me, they left it on the river bank.

More systematic measures were imposed when the disease threatened key urban areas. The French established a lazaretto at Boulaq for Cairo, and the official response at Alexandria was outlined by Gunner Bricard:

> No soldier could enter the city unless absolutely necessary. In each office documents were picked up with tweezers, sprayed with perfume and washed in vinegar before being passed to you. A lazaretto was established for everyone who fell ill or who left hospital. There were barriers set up everywhere in order to prevent communication but the saddest thing was to see how the sick were so poorly treated. ... The locals were unaffected by this disease and they said that it was not the plague but some French epidemic.

Thurman saw how some officers also made novel attempts to disinfect their men:

> The drums summoned the men and they were not forewarned as to what was to happen. Everyone arrived with arms and baggage and the last of the sick had been sent off to Alexandria the day before. Drums beating, we went down towards the coast and onto the beach where we formed a single line. Then, after the soldiers had been ordered to imitate us, the commander and myself went into the sea fully dressed and we waded out so that the water was up to our chests. The soldiers followed with all their equipment, without exception, i.e.

with muskets, pouches and knapsacks. The artillery went in with guns, limbers, ropes, etc. Washing commenced and continued for the next two hours. Everything was washed, soaked and dried, even documents. As this continued some workers went through the barracks removing sheets, straw etc, and burning it all.[18]

Others heard that fumigating a room with smoke from burned sugar helped drive the disease away, or that, as the oily lamplighters of Cairo never fell ill, the vigorous rubbing of the body with olive oil could serve as a preventive treatment. Galland added garlic to his oil as an extra precaution. Still, quarantine proved a more effective measure than this waste of a good salad dressing, and it seems to have helped stifle a repeat outbreak in 1800.

These, then, were some of the challenges of life in Egypt, a land full of manmade or natural danger, with risk lurking around every corner and beneath every rock. And it was not just the population, the climate and disease which troubled the French and their imagination, for so too did the local wildlife. The danger posed by plagues of flies, biting insects, and all reptiles or arachnids, kept the expeditionary force's medical officers on edge. An early order of the day was even dedicated to scorpions:

Being stung by a scorpion is a common occurrence in this country. Consequently, the troops should be informed that the sting of a scorpion in this part of the world is not dangerous. There has never been a case of anyone in Lower Egypt dying from one, despite the many exaggerations you will hear. The sting only causes a painful sensation, some swelling and a light fever which soon passes. The sting can be washed with warm water or, for a more efficient and stronger remedy, by water in which iron has been boiled.

The advice was intended to stave off the sort of rumours Laugier was hearing:

A number of soldiers were stung by scorpions and word went around that you could die from it, although I am sure this is just not true.

Laval agreed that the risks were exaggerated:

Many of our men were stung by scorpions which are very common in Egypt and even more so in the ruins of ancient Alexandria where we were camped. They are less venomous than those in Europe and all you

---

18. Richardot, bizarrely, thought that the heat suppressed the spread of the disease, writing, 'The pestilential miasma must have dissipated, destroyed by the 40 degrees of heat in the desert.'

need to do is crush the insect as it makes the wound and then you will be fine and avoid feeling any pain. An oil was available to treat its sting and it proved an excellent remedy.

Miot had first-hand experience of being stung, and the healing oil:

We halted at the foot of a hill by the gorge which leads from Nazareth to Saffet. At the crest of the hill we had a redoubt built out of rocks and we were to camp within it. Every time the dragoons picked up a stone in order to carry it off they discovered a host of scurrying insects and scorpions under it and we were all stung. We were so used to being stung that we thought little of it. And the oil we used to tend the bite dealt with any inflammation in a couple of hours.

Godet, however, had been terrified by the sight of scorpions as big as crayfish. He had also been unsettled in Alexandria when 'returning to the regiment by walking along the inside of the wall, I saw this was covered with all kinds of enormous lizards and other reptiles and insects, the appearance of which was rather troubling to a European'. His nerves had not improved by the time he reached the Nile, for there he was startled to see a huge crocodile dead in a ditch. Belliard saw a live one '15 to 18 feet long and I fired at it twice with my musket and so it disappeared into the Nile'. François Vigo-Roussillon was also concerned when he heard that 'although the waters of the Nile were delicious, a number of men were savaged or carried off by crocodiles'.

The dragoon Merme and his men not only had to risk fetching water from rivers and canals, but also had to water their horses at them. They found that there be dragons there:

We learnt that it was dangerous to send soldiers down to the river for water at night for the Nile is full of crocodiles and these amphibians will ambush and seize a man, swallowing him down as we would swallow a date. From that point on it was forbidden to go to the Nile at night time.

Vigo-Roussillon, however, felt that his soldiers were still not taking these monsters seriously enough:

In amongst the sugar cane I saw a crocodile which was 25 feet long.[19] It had been captured and was kept in a ditch with its head secured. Its

---

19. Denon confirms the dimensions: 'We saw some crocodiles as we approached Esneh. There were three of them and one, much bigger than the other two, was at least 25 feet long.' However, General Kléber ridiculed a certain tendency to over-report the size of unusual beasts: 'Laroze saw an eagle and assured me that it had a span of 200 feet. These are not French feet, nor German feet, but feet of pure exaggeration.'

eyes were closed and it had not eaten for a week so everyone thought it was dead. One of us decided to ride it and climbed on its back. It made a sudden, violent twist and knocked down the insolent jockey but also a mound of sugar and the worker guarding it.

Strangely enough, few snakes seem to have been encountered, and those that were mostly belonged to snake charmers. Godet cites an example of one such performer, and his unexpected reception:

The peasant tapped the snake on the head with a stick and its head turned into the shape of an arrow; in order to have it return to its more slender shape, as before, a second tap was needed. The man then put it back in his sack. When he showed it to General Belliard, the general killed it.

Sergeant François shared the general's passion for killing and, for want of more mundane prey, he and his men took to tracking down Egypt's biggest birds:

We went hunting gazelle and ostriches. We killed a few but found hunting ostriches was great fun. Bringing one down always amused us. They are very tall, do not fly much but run very fast, throwing up stones behind them. Most are black or grey and we used their feathers as plumes.

The scholars were more humane, and were fascinated by this ungainly bird. Villiers du Terrage was tasked with collecting some for the Institute's little zoo at Cairo:

There are some ostriches in some of the principal houses and they were brought to the garden of the Institute. I went to fetch one from the Aga of the Janissaries [Hassan Aga Muharrem, police commander]. I then had to go and fetch another from the pasha at the citadel but his people had cooked it when their master left with the Mamelukes.[20]

Alexandre Lacorre was impressed by those he saw:

I went to see some of the various animals of the country at Mourad Bey's. That which made most of an impression on me was the ostrich.

---

20. Saint Hilaire seems to have been given the same task: 'I am being kept busy as I have taken it upon myself to collect all the exotic animals which, I have been told, are still in the former residencies of the Mamelukes.'

This extraordinary bird has something in common with a camel, well it does have the same neck and legs.

The swathes of bugs, mosquitoes and biting flies which seem to have plagued our diarists and letter writers also made an impression – followed by red soreness and swelling. The engineer Jacques Marie Le Père encountered these minute enemies:

We are all in good health and if we were not deprived of sleep by innumerable species of insects which consume us alive, we should find ourselves tolerably happy amidst all the embarrassments and privations to which we are constantly exposed.

Another irritation was Egypt's population of stray dogs. Antoine Galland observed that 'these dogs are all of the same breed and they are usually brown and look like, and are as big as, a wolf'. Godet observed that these worryingly large beasts 'covered in wounds and seemingly belonging to no one, lived off waste and spent the night barking to such an extent that it was impossible to sleep'. At Damanhour Belliard found that 'the streets were as dirty as Alexandria's, and twisting, narrow and full of dogs which prevent us from walking about by day and sleeping at night'. Gerbaud agreed and thought them a real nuisance, complaining that 'they say that their religion prevents them from killing them. The dogs spend the whole night barking.' He further added that 'the streets are filled with curs who won't get out of the way, even if a horse is bearing down on them'. Joseph Laporte saw that, indeed, the locals did look after the strays, but he, too, was less than sympathetic:

One of the more unpleasant sights in the streets of Cairo is the enormous number of stray dogs. They do not have owners but the Turks look after them by putting out little stoneware bowls with water and putting out any leftovers from their food at the corner of the street.[21]

The French seemed to have tried poisoning the dogs, but Bernoyer saw that a more extreme measure was resolved on to deal with these disturbers of the peace:

---

21. Pierre Louis Cailleux saw that a different kind of animal was being kept captive: 'There are a lot of monkeys kept as pets and they make them dance in the streets and in the squares. Some were as large as the dogs we keep to guard our courtyard.'

Every evening, at around nine, the barking of the street dogs would begin as they gathered in the main square to give their discordant concert. Here they are at liberty to do so, they belong to nobody but the doors are left open for them and they are welcomed in. I think the Turks would prefer to kick a Jew or a Christian than a dog. Bonaparte grew tired of this nocturnal barking and ordered the 22nd Light to destroy these dogs. The 22nd marched into the square, blocking the exits, and went at the dogs with their sabres. In order to kill them all they returned the second evening.

These dogs, and the herds of donkeys deployed in place of taxi cabs,[22] were a memorable feature of Cairo. Donkeys also doubled up as beasts of burden, as the local horses were unaccustomed to being harnessed to wagons, carts or artillery limbers. Richardot saw that some effort was made to train the horses but that an altogether different animal stepped in to provide horsepower:

The local horses were trained to pull wagons and experiments were made with young camels pulling the artillery limbers as the Arab horses resented the harnessing needed to pull the guns. The camels seemed docile enough.

Bernoyer was most taken by the camel, marvelling that 'it seemed as though nature had placed them in these inhospitable regions for the service of mankind, something they do very well. Sands are their element. Camels in the desert are like fish in water.'

The French were so impressed that they also experimented with using camels as suitable mounts for a kind of dragoon. In January 1799 a dromedary regiment was established having taken ten volunteers, all veterans aged twenty-four or older, from each infantry regiment, including the Maltese and, bizarrely, the Nautical Legion. An impressed but anonymous officer in the 32nd Line recorded that 'Bonaparte had formed a new kind of regiment, that of the dromedaries. Two men could sit back to back and thanks to the grace and strength of these animals, travel for 75 or 80 miles without halting.' François claims he was one of the first volunteers to join this dromedary corps and got to grips with his new mount:

In this unit each of the soldiers was mounted on a camel. These animals are good-tempered and we used a saddle across its back which

---

22. Antoine Galland noted that the 'price of a donkey ride is not fixed but depends on how far you wish to travel or how long you are mounted for. Before we came, you could go from one end of Cairo to the other for 3 or 4 sous. Now it is double that. They are well cared for; their mane is shaped and sometimes dyed red. The rich ride mules … the horse is usually just for soldiers.'

was strapped beneath its stomach and around its sides. ... For the bad-tempered ones there was a kind of bit in the nostril.

These local ships of the desert also had another advantage, and not a small one either considering the general dearth of food: they could become a source of nourishment. Antoine Galland drank their milk: 'I bought a glass of milk to sake my thirst and even though it was camel milk, and therefore naturally unpleasant, I found it delicious.' As for the meat, those who tasted it preferred it to that of the horse.

Camels would brand themselves on the European imagination, and represent Egypt and her deserts in the same way that the pyramids would represent Egypt's ancient glories. And despite the obstacles, barriers, risks and dangers posed by man and nature, there was much to see when it came to ancient glory, and in the French ranks there were many who took a professional or amateur interest in searching it out. Of course, there were others who would spend their time in Africa not impressed by anything, even imperial grandeur. Girard of the engineers 'only wanted to see the pyramids and then leave Egypt', but then he was a man who 'spent four hours at Denderah but slept for three of them'. Galland, who had perhaps seen a hundred things although a thousand others had escaped him, was also rather dismissive of the pyramids and sphynx, thinking them worth less 'than the movement of a watch, and of less use than the water pump of Marly'. Jean Marie Merme, not exactly an ignoramus, was also unimpressed:

> Our column passed Thebes, an old town which was in ruins. As it was only of interest to the scholars attached to the army we did not pay it very much attention.

Perhaps he would have agreed with General Lagrange, who was putting duty before curiosity:

> You might find it surprising that in the three or four months that I have been in Egypt I have said nothing about the beautiful ruins scattered across this country, a source of great interest for the curious. You would be right to reproach me if it were not for the fact that I am a soldier and service and duty have not allowed me time to reflect on these remains which poke out of the ground here and there and reveal that, here and there, once great cities existed.

Jean-Pierre Doguereau on the staff might have been more curious had it not been so dangerous to be so:

> This life here was dull even though we were a group of young men. It contrasted with the life we had led in Europe and was extremely difficult to adapt to. The heat was bad enough, one could barely go out.

In any case, where could we go to? Into the sands, among the ruins? Even that needed an escort. If you left town you were attacked by the Arabs. We had few books and we ardently desired to return to France.

Sulkowski was frustrated that local hostility was repressing any sense of adventure:

Egypt is the one country in Africa which has captivated the literary world. A mass of travellers has set out to track down the remains of its ancient splendour, whilst an ignorant and barbarous people have done everything in their power to stop them.

Belliard had hoped to spend the night in the temple of Apollo at Hermonthis [Armant] but 'the locals had used it as a stable for their goats and the stink was so repulsive it made it uninhabitable. I spent the night in the open cursing these barbarians who spoil everything.' They certainly spoiled one of Jollois' expeditions, and he records an incident in which 'the inhabitants of the island of Philae were just as suspicious of us as the rest of the Egyptians. They did not want us visiting their island because they thought we had come to seek out treasure. As we visited three times they grew extremely concerned and told us they would destroy their monuments so that we would no longer trouble them.'

Given the risks, and the natural hazards, Egypt's past glories could seem inaccessible to any but the most determined. Miot thought it worth the trouble:

An ignoramus pushes on past without regret, whereas an educated man will pause and reflect at each moment. There is a stone, there a monument which will call to mind a battle which decided the fate of an empire or the destiny of a hero. A knoll will go unnoticed by one but for the other will call to mind a great event of history or the siege of a great city which time has erased. Thus the ignorant stagnate whilst the wise man sees into the past, the present and perhaps even the future.

Miot was not alone, for there were many who valued the opportunities to discover a half-sunk or shattered visage in the lone and level sands. Bernoyer, always inclined to the picturesque, marvelled at the ruins he encountered and appreciated their significance:

I spent some time thinking on those ancient times. I could not understand what error, or what culpable negligence, had allowed man to just let these vast and useful works fall into ruin. Nowadays we are inclined to say that the sciences and art have reached their apogee amongst us in Europe. But the things I come across here every day show that we still have much to learn.

He reflected on the experience:

> Thinking about those monuments, it seems as though time had left to those generations to come some clues as to what glory the talent of man can aspire to. I surveyed the vast ruins. They gave an idea as to what once stood here. I was transported by my enthusiasm and rendered homage to the glory of past centuries in which so many men, motivated by the love of their land, created so much extraordinary beauty.

Denon was another in awe, this time at Tentyris:

> I cannot express my feelings as I stood below the gates of Tentyris. I felt I stood in the sanctuary of art and science. The sight of that monument conjured up such visions for my imagination. How many centuries had it taken to enable a nation to produce such perfection, such sublimity, in the arts? In the ruins of Tentyris the Egyptians seemed like giants to me.

He added that he worried that 'my paltry sketches would not capture such sublime objects'. Villiers, who reached Thebes to sketch its ruins with Jollois, was also struck to the core, but found time to consider the impact their discoveries might have on culture and those back home:

> We took such delight in thinking that we would take back to our country examples of the industry and culture of the ancient Egyptians and that this in itself would be a great victory for the arts. How many times did we endure long and difficult expeditions solely to gaze upon a new monument or examine some ruins. How many times had we traipsed across the plains of Thebes, running the risk of being butchered by the Arabs.

Costaz agreed about Thebes:

> With the help of a few feeble candles we passed through vast and sombre rooms in which it was impossible to avoid a feeling of almost religious ecstasy. One is struck by the vast number of sculptures and paintings one is surrounded by. Everything is decorated, the walls, the ceilings, the pillars, everything. Each step reveals something extraordinary, enigmatic or downright bizarre. One can only marvel at the age of these remains for they have survived for thousands of years.

Even General Desaix, in amongst his dry reports on troop movements and demands for cartridges and musket flints, found time to tell Bonaparte that 'Thebes really exceeds its reputation; nothing compares to its scale and the wealth of the visible ruins. There are two obelisks here of such size and workmanship that Rome has not the like; taken to Paris they would be quite something.' The anonymous officer of the 32nd Line also shows how everyone, not just the classically trained gentlemen officers, joined in marvelling at these ancient structures:

> As the army marched back along the Nile it passed through some magnificent ruins. At Denderah, the ancient Tentyris, all were overcome with respect and admiration when they saw the majestic temple built of enormous stones. Scholars, officers and soldiers were all struck dumb by the awesome grandeur and simplicity of this monument.

He was also impressed by 'Thebes where some of the rooms were so vast that they could easily accommodate the biggest of our churches, indeed Notre Dame would have been swallowed whole'.

Jollois, too, was sometimes impressed by the sheer scale of the stones, in this case the colossi of Memnon:

> On seeing the colossal statues on the two sides of the river one cannot be affected by admiration. If just one such monument were created in our times it would be enough to immortalise the rule in which this feat were performed. Their mechanical knowledge must have been incredible and it is difficult to see how we, with what we know of the subject, could complete such a task.

The scholars would agree that such ruins would come as a surprise to a Europe only familiar with Greek or Roman remains. Jollois noted this culture shock when he encountered 'the temple of Denderah ... one of the finest Egypt has. It will astonish anyone who has only seen Greek architecture. The edifice makes such an impression on account of its size and the precious ornaments with which it is decorated.'

Villiers du Terrage nearly killed himself with exhaustion when he fell in love with the vast ruins of ancient Tanis:

> There were quantities of blocks covered on all sides by hieroglyphs. There were also avenues of columns and obelisks, although almost all of them had been knocked over. I only had a few hours in which to explore these curious antiquities and could not make a thorough study. However, I saw as much as I could and on the way back was so exhausted and seized by the desire to sleep that I could not even mount my horse and fell down. I would surely have died in the desert had not a soldier from the escort woken me and helped me along.

But it was the pyramids that excited near universal acclaim, curiosity and interest; after all, these martial visitors had come with the expectation of seeing those famous landmarks. Denon saw them early on, telling Menou that 'so far I have only been able to see the general, the festival and the pyramids which, as a certain scholar known to both of us judiciously remarked, are in the shape of a pyramid'. Alexandre Lacorre was a little more serious in his appraisal:

> We went to see the pyramids. There are three, with two large ones and one small one. There are some smaller ones but they are in ruins. We were astonished by the amount of work needed and it must have been long and difficult, for each slab is enormous.

Bernoyer could not hide his astonishment:

> We stood in ecstasy before these enormous masses of huge stones, piled up on top of each other without cement. Throughout the time they have stood there they have elicited surprise and admiration.

But he, republican as he was, could not hide his puzzlement that 'the vain glory of absolute monarchs had forced ignorant slaves to build something as strange as they were useless'. General Lagrange was also a pragmatist, and laconically remarked that 'there was no practical reason for them to be built [pyramids] and they are just there to reflect the glory and magnificence of their maker'.

The pyramids and their maker were of considerable interest to the scholars, who made several attempts to survey and measure them. Jacotin studied the pyramid of Cheops in December 1799, and assessed it as being 137.531 metres high. Jean Claude Vaxelaire also tried his hand:

> As we marched along we passed close by the pyramids of Egypt which were once counted as one of the Seven Wonders of the World. They are very ancient, the most ancient that time has spared, although nobody knows when they were built.[23] There are three main ones and they are 400 paces from each other and the biggest is 500 paces high and each face 680 paces wide. ... A few paces from this pyramid there is an enormous sphynx made from stone.

Millet was also inclined to attempt some measurements:

> I was a chasseur in the 2nd Light and we were sent to camp by the pyramids, spending two weeks camped there. We spent the time

---

23. Joseph Laporte hazarded a guess that they were 'founded 850 years before the birth of Christ'. Galland was more vague, content to offer that 'some say they were built before the flood'.

exploring the ruins of Memphis, once the best town in Egypt and the tombs of their kings, now a ruin. There are four pyramids and the biggest is 500 feet high.

Indeed, this mania for measurement seems to have infected many of the French soldiers as much as it did those on the Grand Tour in Europe. Captain Moiret reckoned the great pyramid was 313,590 cubic *toises* in volume whilst the curious Joseph Laporte of the 69th Line went further, calculating that 'a pyramid is 1,128,000 cubic *toises* and the stones could build a wall which was four *toises* high and 563 leagues long'.

Lieutenant Laval joined in:

Six miles to the west of Cairo lie the pyramids, masses of stone which are one of the seven wonders of the world. They are built with huge blocks which have been carefully arranged. I measured one of the biggest and found it was 100 *toises* squared ... you can go into the pyramid through a rather dismal entrance clogged up by sand which has blown in there.

The brave Laporte passed through this forbidding passageway:

There is an entry which is quite a little below the surface and when you go through the tunnel under this enormous monument then you come to a dark chamber where the tombs are. You need a torch and white spirits to keep off the cold and the bad air. The room is decorated with hieroglyphs of various kinds. There are no more mummies for they have been carried off.

Galland, fainting in the infected air, found the walls of the king's tomb to be so black from the smoke of torches that he could not even carve his name. Pierre-Louis Cordier, a mineralogist, took a professional interest in the interior and participated in what seems to have been a common experiment:

After striking the sarcophagus and making it ring we then did what all visitors do and fired a pistol. The effect was like that of a cannon going off for the explosion echoes off distant walls and gets repeated a thousand times.

However, he was just as keen to reach the top of the monument, something which he reckoned could be done, 'if you hurry, in twenty minutes'. Denon, a little less sprightly now he was in his fifties, took thirty-five minutes. Still, this race to the top became one of the de rigueur escapades for the invading hordes and Galland even says that some tried to force their horses up the lower slopes, although the sensible creatures refused. Jollois did not give in so easily and reached the top:

> After examining these enormous stone structures as a whole my first instinct was to climb to the top. It was incredibly difficult to get even half way for the blocks are so worn and covered with debris from those further up that it is almost impossible to be sure footed, indeed it happened more than once that the stones themselves would crumble under one's feet. That, combined with the stones that those above me had dislodged, and which came down with such force that they could knock someone out, convinced me to turn back and try a different route.

Saint-Hilaire describes setting off with Napoleon and his staff to see the pyramids in September 1798. They cruised down the Nile but 'once we left the barges we climbed a steep and sandy embankment in order to walk for fifteen minutes beneath the scorching sun and on the burning sand. Then we were there, before the pyramids, the goal of our expedition!'

As they drew closer, Napoleon, competitive regardless of context, encouraged the obligatory race by shouting, 'Who will reach the top first?' Saint-Hilaire met the chief of staff, General Alexandre Berthier, halfway up and the general stopped him to 'complain and ask whether it is really necessary that one goes right to the top. I am exhausted! When we return to Paris and say we have been to the top, who can contradict us?'

Berthier gave up and climbed down to where Napoleon was waiting for him, teasing him with a 'back so soon?' All this despite Napoleon himself not even attempting the climb. Niello-Sargy heard a rumour 'that he [Bonaparte] did not want to go up the pyramid as he had torn his nankeen breeches'.

Villiers took part in this excursion, and confirms that Napoleon remained on the ground:

> Dubois-Aymé and I learnt that there was to be an excursion to the pyramids. This was kept secret so as to keep the curious to a minimum. However, it was too good an opportunity, and another like it might not come soon for one had to be escorted there. We did not tell our colleagues about it but that night crossed the Nile to Gizah where the select few had gathered in order to leave at dawn. We climbed into the barge which had been selected for the trip and were comfortable when the heads of the commission arrived after having dined, slept and breakfasted rather well. ... Our barges took us to the end of the canal and from there we walked to the pyramids. Our enthusiasm meant that climbing to the top was our first priority. Bonaparte encouraged us from the ground. We were most surprised to find that the pyramid was topped by a plateau some 30 metres square because, from afar, it looks like it ends in a point.

Indeed, Napoleon does not seem to have enjoyed himself that much. Villiers closed his account with the statement that 'on the way down I had enough time to go inside the pyramid. Bonaparte refused because it would have entailed him crawling under the entrance stone on his stomach.'

François Vigo-Roussillon was on duty during the Bastille Day jaunt, serving as part of the escort. But he, too, could not resist climbing to the top:

> On 14 July 1799 the division's grenadiers quit Cairo on the pretext of escorting the commander-in-chief on a tour to the pyramids. We slept at Boulaq and reached the pyramids early the following morning. I climbed the highest one and we lunched at the summit. Before descending I carved my name into the rock with my bayonet. I was a sergeant of grenadiers in the 1st Battalion of the 32nd Line.

That November, after a bracing breakfast, François also set out to pay tribute to this wonder of the world, and carved his name on it:

> At six in the morning four of my friends from the 18th Line, having obtained permission from their commander, Monsieur Froment, came with me to see our pharmacist and we found him with a saddled and harnessed donkey all ready for the off. After knocking back five or six cups of coffee with brandy we headed for the Azbakiyya square where the scholars had assembled along with some artists and soldiers, for a trip to the pyramids. I carved my name, my place of birth, my rank in the 9th Line, and the date, 4 November, in the king's chamber, to the right of the sarcophagus, in the second pyramid. I also wrote my name, rank, etc, on the middle of a rock on the outside, at the end of the fifth row of stones which were six, seven or eight feet high and where people climbed up.

Desvernois, the hussar, saw that the carving of one's name was common, a little stab at eternity scrawled across these seemingly eternal remains:

> After resting for half an hour, during which we had a snack and a glass of Roussillon wine, we approached the south-face of the pyramid, the only one which seemed to permit an ascent. So everyone, generals, officers and three charming ladies, set off at once, hurrying to begin the climb. It was really quite difficult as the blocks were 28 or 30 inches tall. However, as I was young and fit, I outstripped the others climbing this face and arrived at the same time as generals Reynier, Belliard and Lagrange, and Mesdames Verdier and Sauvage, who had come up the north face. We exchanged compliments. Soon there were thirty-nine of us including five young and pretty women. I admired the view from the top for some two hours before I noticed that everyone else, with the exception of three of my comrades, had

left. Some had engraved their names with the blade of some scissors or a dagger.

Coming down, Desvernois had dinner beneath the sphynx where the colonel gallantly toasted 'the French women in Egypt, particularly those who had climbed the pyramid with us today'. Then, he adds, 'five days later I returned to the pyramids and climbed up with two of my comrades and the brave Louis Pisler, adjutant of the 7th Hussars and a man from my region of France. Each of us carved our names, Christian names, place of birth, rank, the number of our regiment, our branch of service and the date onto the rock.'

François-Michel Lucet saw some of these carvings when he explored the pyramids:

Took leave. I visited the pyramids and the ruins of Memphis. I measured the tallest pyramid and each face of it is 300 paces. A number of Europeans have engraved their names on the enormously sized stones at the entrance to the chambers, tombs or staircases and the stairs are quite regular.[24]

The pyramids were fascinating, and received most attention, but so too was the nearby sphynx. Malus, a gentleman with a keen sense of historical appreciation for this ancient site, visited the monolith with General Kléber on 27 December 1798. He provides us with some more measurements: 'We also saw the sphynx and we managed to enter the head, gaining access through a hole that had been bored in the neck. The head is 26 paces from the chin to the top.' Jollois also went to see the sphynx, and seems to have preferred it to the pyramids: 'I did not go inside the pyramid, instead I went to see the sphynx. It is a figure cut out of rock and which seems to me to be 20 or 25 feet high. The nose has been mutilated but the profile most closely resembles that of a negro.'

---

24. The French would continue the tradition across Egypt. Costaz and Antoine François Ernest Coquebert de Montbret engraved their names on the eastern wall of the temple at Philae. At Abu, or Elephantine Island, Castex carved an inscription on the entrance to the temple which commemorated 'beating the Mamelukes at the Pyramids, with them being pursued by Desaix commanding the 1st Division beyond the cataracts'. He then added the names 'Davout, Friant, Belliard, Donzelot (chief of staff), La Tourmenie (commanding the artillery) and Eppler (commander of the 21st Light)'. The inscription '1800, 3rd Dragoons' can still be seen at the Beni Hassan tombs at Al-Minya. A more vulgar example of graffiti was found in Alexandria where an anonymous soldier had scrawled 'Bonaparte Trash' with charcoal on a barrack wall.

He also spent some time exploring the immediate area and found much of interest, but also much that was falling prey to a local form of iconoclasm:

> We saw that in one of the caves cut into the rocks close by [the pyramids] the walls were covered in hieroglyphs and saw the remains of a row of twelve Egyptian statues which had been destroyed, only the leg below the knees of one remained and served as a support for a lamp. Parts of three or four other statues were scattered about. A Frenchman who had been here seven or eight years ago said they had been intact then. The religion of the Turks forbids them from having statues and so they destroy those they find in ancient monuments.

The French contributed to the destruction, for their historical appreciation included making off with a great deal. So much did they take that Villiers, when describing Philae, mentions that 'the locals thought the temples must contain great treasure and that the Europeans were just coming to seize it'. The locals were more willing to help when Savary and Denon were exploring the south. Denon recalled that 'the populace, seeing us examine monuments they largely ignored, came to show us some so-called medals that those working in the fields had dug up, or when they were building their houses amidst the ruins. When they saw that we were treating them as valuable objects they brought many more. They were Roman coins.'

There were riches to be had. Dr Antonio Savaresi observed that 'if the Europeans undertake some excavations around Alexandria, I am sure they will find some interesting remains. This is because every time the French dig some earthworks they throw up all kinds of gold or silver medallions or statues or other things in marble.' Lieutenant Bouchard of the engineers would have agreed for when he was supervising the digging trenches around Rosetta shortly after Bastille Day, the pickaxe of one of his men hit a large, and very hard, slab of dark rock which lay concealed amongst the sand-coloured stone. Bouchard halted the work and had his men extract this curious block of black granodiorite, and, on 19 July 1799, informed his superiors that he had unearthed what would soon be called the Rosetta Stone.[25] Bricard, also working on digging ditches, had a similar but less celebrated experience, noting that 'every day our digging brought up all sorts of ancient curiosities: coins, vases, stones with writing on them'. Villiers in the Valley of the Kings managed to pocket some of these keepsakes: 'I collected three idols made from red granite and around a foot

---

25. Bouchard's find was, and still is, famous, as it helped unlock the mysteries of hieroglyphs. However, in addition to the Rosetta Stone, the French also unearthed a demotic and Greek inscription at Menouf in September 1799, and Caristie found a stone at Nasrieh, Cairo, in 1800 with hieroglyphs, demotic and Greek inscriptions.

long, plus another one in black about half a foot longer and another, much smaller, which looks like it can be polished.'

Idols, coins and tablets were all sought-after trophies and souvenirs. However, it was Egypt's famous mummies that these avid collectors really wanted to acquire. Saint-Hilaire was seemingly obsessed by these ancient artefacts and recalled his first encounter with them:

We went into the underground cavern of the birds where, for the first time, I saw mummies still in place. These caverns lead to enormous underground caves which lead to other caves from which there is no issue. These caves are quite deep and are filled with pots containing Ibis laid out rather carelessly as they are just set to lie down like bottles of wine in a French wine cellar.

He acquired three complete mummies encased in sycamore coffins as trophies. François-Michel de Rozière was equally enchanted by his first encounter with a human mummy:

We found a complete mummy swathed in white cloth with irregular patterns in blue, red, yellow and black. There was no flesh left but the cloth was thick. The arms were folded over the chest and the head still had hair and a beard, both cut quite short.

Villiers was also on the hunt for these mysterious and exotic remains, and had to enlist the early equivalent of a tour guide to help him as he searched through some caves near Sydout:

To the left of the mountain there were ten Egyptian statues, perhaps caryatids. No doubt their heads had been struck off by the Turks whose religion forbids them from representing faces. We made a thorough search of the catacombs for preserved mummies but then turned to one of the men who make a living out of scouring the catacombs for amulets and then selling them on at a high price. He seemed to know the place but put on mysterious airs. He told us that two or three years ago they had found the bodies of dogs wrapped in linen. He said they had been buried with great care because the people that existed then thought of them as gods. It seemed as though he knew something of the history of his land but I cannot think it was handed down through tradition. More likely, he was told such stuff by European travellers. He went off and two days later brought us to the base of the hill and to a point where he had made a hole through the wall. We could see a large number of mummified animals, many of them in bad condition, separated by rugs. We brought out a few birds of prey, cats and what seemed to be monkeys. Most seemed to have been jackals or wolves.

Eventually they found what they were looking for:

> We found a human mummy amongst these remains and it was quite well preserved. Its hair was quite straight and we took some of it away with us. It had not been terribly well embalmed and the bandages had not been arranged particularly well, even so we had seen worse examples in the catacombs of Thebes.

They then continued further on, and their guide, apparently thinking they were interested in any kind of corpses, took them to an ancient ruin which turned out to be an abandoned monastery. There he showed them a 'white man whose muscles, skin, teeth, nails and beard seemed to be perfectly conserved'. However, the thought of disinterring a Christian body filled the Frenchmen with horror.

The search for mummies of the right denomination continued. Laval was one of the few to wonder about the reasoning behind this Egyptian ritual:

> Three miles from the town there are catacombs cut into the rock as well as a few burial chambers. They say that in those times they believed in reincarnation and put their dead in these underground rooms. I went in and looked at seven chambers using a torch. There were a few bones there, both human and animal.

In many Egyptian cities and villages, the ancient monuments were experiencing a kind of reincarnation too. Many slabs and columns found themselves incorporated into more modern constructions. Denon saw that in Alexandria 'columns of granite scattered around, littering the streets, squares or shoreline, where many had been gathered up. Egyptian monuments, covered in hieroglyphs, serve as lintels or benches to rest on.'

Redouté was there too and saw a few examples by the port:

> As one walks about one notices that stones from ancient times have been incorporated with barbaric ignorance into more modern buildings, for example the capital of columns serving as a base and bases serving as capitals. Columns in mosques and private houses have the same origin and blocks of granite covered with hieroglyphs serve as doorsteps or foundations.

Elsewhere, Fourier saw how 'the peasants now live inside the former palaces of the kings of Egypt'. Scenes like this made Alexandre Lacorre, like Shelley, reflect on the fleeting nature of fame, even of emperors and cities:

> We went to visit the site where Heliopolis, that famous and wealthy city of King Nectenabo, once stood. Is this what remains of that superb city, I asked myself. What became of its industrious inhabitants? Where

are its magnificent palaces? What became of its economy? What destroyed the city and its population? Ignorance and ambition, replied a voice from deep within me.

Even so perhaps the glories of today were even more fleeting than those of ancient times. Villiers certainly saw that ancient glory could still impress when he and hundreds of tramping French troops marched past Denderah:

> The temple excited the admiration of the army that had conquered Sa'id and it was a remarkable thing to watch as each soldier spontaneously turned to gaze upon Tentyris and its magnificent buildings. These brave men will enthuse about this moment for a long time and wherever fortune takes them they shall not forget Denderah for it shall be impressed upon their very souls.

Those brave men were indeed enthused by such sights. As for fortune, it had not finished with them yet. Having brought them to Egypt, it would also propel them on to Syria and the Holy Land.

8

Syria

Egypt was Napoleon's. But even after the revolt of Cairo had been suppressed, the Red Sea littoral explored and the Nile delta pacified, he could not rest. An occupation never can and, besides, there were forces gathering which heralded more war. The French knew that the Ottomans were intent on restoring their grip on the Levant by driving out the French. The Sublime Porte now had powerful allies in the British and Russians, and ambitious ones among the elites of the Middle East, particularly those of Palestine and Syria. These local warlords eyed the infidel newcomers warily and their suspicions of Constantinople waned in proportion to the rise of French influence. These pashas and beys also sensed the material advantages of an alliance with the great powers, and the reputational benefits of waging jihad. So, soon after the French first appeared, the provincial warlords had welcomed fugitive Mamelukes, watched which way the wind was blowing and then mobilised their feudal armies and mercenaries. And soon enough, once they determined on war with France, the Turks began to lavish men, money and supplies on these belligerent leaders.

By the time 1798 closed, Napoleon was faced with the real danger of a hostile invasion through the isthmus separating Asia and Africa. Around then he had, it seems, briefly contemplated a return to France, but, with the oceans out of bounds, he turned instead to the security of his colony. He began by garrisoning a wooden fort at Qatiyah, improvising a *cordon sanitaire* along the frontier and sending spies into Palestine. He reasoned that, should the British and Turks strike from Rhodes whilst the warlords of Syria struck from the east, then he would be lost. So he first began a diplomatic offensive, signalling to Djezzar 'the Butcher' Pasha, the *capo dei capi* of those chieftains, that he hoped to agree an *entente cordiale*. However, when Napoleon sent his envoy, the ironically named Calmet Beauvoisins, to ascertain his neighbour's intentions, Djezzar had him mishandled at Jaffa before sending him back to Bonaparte as the bearer of bad news.[1] Djezzar, having been awarded by Constantinople the title of governor general of Syria and Egypt, would fight the French in the coming war of power and belief.

Napoleon therefore took the very Napoleonic resolution of launching an offensive before his foes could do the same, perhaps also hoping that success might trigger a wider revolt of Arabs against Turks across the Levant. An expeditionary force was therefore readied that January and 14,000 men, and 500 camels, prepared to march off to the promised land. Joseph Laporte, the curious young infantryman, was overjoyed to be on the move again:

> The 69th, in which I served, was to be included and I was again delighted as I loved distant travels and that part of the world would give me something to talk about one day should I make it back.

Miot was also keen, claiming that 'we were about to enter a land in which the French name had been immortalised during the crusades'. Perhaps this historical allusion was not the most auspicious, but at least it sounded heroic and leant a sense of purpose to a mission that was all too vague. Lacorre at least knew they would be marching into Syria, perhaps to ensure supplies or to seek allies amongst the region's Christian minorities, but the kind of rumours that surrounded any large military undertaking were already circulating, and he felt the need to challenge them with facts:

> Some thought we were marching on Constantinople whilst others said we were to aid Passan-Oglu [in Albania], although those with any sense or judgement refrained from making such conjectures. In any case it was not difficult to discern what we were about: we were advancing against Djezzar, the Pasha of Acre. Most of the army thought we would then move against Damascus.[2]

Desvernois, who lacked for neither sense nor judgement, got carried away by barrack-room chatter and soon convinced himself that they were

---

1. Poor Beauvoisins was chastised for his lack of success by being sent to garrison the backwater of Belbeis. When, after a bad case of eye disease, he dared appear in Cairo, Napoleon had him stripped of his rank and arrested.
2. Kléber informed Napoleon on 8 February that 'it will be hard to detach the men from the idea that we are not returning to Europe via the Dardanelles'. In Paris, military planners had actually worked on a scheme to send the army up to Constantinople where it would be joined by another French army coming over from Brindisi. They concluded it was too impractical. Another plan, by General Belair, suggested the French should capture Aleppo and force the Ottomans to surrender by strangling their trade.

destined for India. He dreamt how 'we would arrive at Bengal and raise the standard of revolt in Ceylon and Orissa whose populations would see us as their liberators'.

Bernoyer also thought this highly likely, having long suspected his commander of Alexandrian hubris. He warmed to the theme in a letter addressed to his long-suffering wife:

> They had it that his intense ambition to rule like a king nurtured in him the idea of leading his army as far as the kingdom of Persia once he had taken Acre and there proclaiming himself king. This scheme suited him well enough on account of his pride. However, it did not suit everyone, especially those who yearned for their homeland or those who, like me, had left a loving wife behind and would not swap her for all the kingdoms in the world.

General Lagrange also knew his superior would sell them all for glory, but he had those soldierly qualities of duty and loyalty that Bernoyer so evidently lacked:

> I know little of where we are going, besides everything is being kept secret. Bonaparte is just as difficult to read in Africa as he was in Europe. However, if forced to speculate, then I would say that the huge amount of supplies we are stockpiling here suggests that we shall be carrying our flag to the one quarter of the world which has not yet seen it. I sleep in Africa and spend the evening strolling around the edges of Asia, and so I think the desert which separates us from Syria won't be able to stop us. I have to say that I am not enamoured by the idea of making new conquests, although I like the idea of visiting new lands and seeing new peoples a little more. Still, under our valiant general, I would go to the ends of the earth.

First stop towards the ends of the earth would be Djezzar's castles of El-Arich, Jaffa and Acre. He could draw upon his own warlike followers and 20,000 North African mercenaries to resist, as well as some embittered and exiled Mamelukes, but the resources of Damascus and Constantinople were also behind him. Napoleon, always one to make a virtue out of risk, therefore pinned all of his hopes on a quick and decisive victory.

Things were therefore done in a rush. Gerbaud, arriving in Cairo on 20 January, saw 'huge activity for an expedition to Syria. Strict orders go out to collect canteens, bowls, wineskins, etc.' Lessons had evidently been learned from the horrendous desert crossings of last summer. Still, Pelleport felt that these preparations were inadequate, observing that when 'the three battalions of the 18th, then present in Cairo, were ordered to prepare to march ... the officers, recalling the tribulations of Alexandria and Ramanieh, sought to lay their hands on all kinds of material which would be essential whilst crossing a desert. The administration, careless and often cruel as it was in the best of times, did nothing for the soldiers but only looked after its own whims.'

Peyrusse, reaching Salheyeh, having marched past seven or eight dead grenadiers from Lannes' division, was also angered by the waste of life brought on by official negligence:

Had there been a good administration then we might have avoided all these problems, but when the expedition was planned, the most essential part of it was neglected: there was no food for no measures had been taken to have it transported forwards to various magazines.[3]

Instead, Laporte reports that 'each Frenchman taking part in the expedition was ordered to obtain a canteen to carry water as well as supplies of biscuits and rice to last several days'.[4] All this meant that the infantry would be weighed down like beasts of burden.[5] The officer of dragoons, on the other hand, was weighed down by worry for his horses. 'So, we are finally off on campaign,' he remarked. 'I have never seen horses carrying such a heavy burden moving off at speed. As well as a rider and his weapons each horse carries four days' rations, 20 litres of water and camping equipment too.'

The army moved off in early February and it would eventually consist of divisions under Reynier, Kléber, Lannes and Bon, supported by Murat's 800 cavalry and eighty-eight men of the new Dromedary Regiment under the arch-disciplinarian, and Calvinist, Major Jacques Cavalier of the 12th Light. A portable printing press and Napoleon's coach, containing three curious scholars, brought up the rear. 'Those quitting Cairo,' averred Lacorre, 'marched out in the greatest possible order and with the bands playing at their head.' The general himself delayed his departure until the 11th in order

---

3. Durand saw some humane reactions from among those responsible: 'The generals, commanders and officers had horses and, in a gesture of generosity, that was much needed, gave their horses to those unfortunate soldiers who had collapsed from exhaustion. General Lagrange was the first to do so.'

4. For example the 75th Line was to be issued with 1,000 canteens, but funds were so short that the money to manufacture them was drawn from the regiment's pay.

5. They were also to carry pikes. Charles Richardot of the artillery writes that 'tests were carried out to see if short pikes 4.5 feet (1.5 metres) long, chained together and fixed into the ground, and thus forming a kind of palisade, could be positioned in front of our squares. These were actually carried into Syria.' Bricard confirms this bizarre order: 'All the infantry were issued with 5-foot pikes to form a barrier to keep the enemy cavalry off. The infantry was trained in their use.'

to meet with the merchant Hamelin, then digesting his news from Europe and taking part in the celebrations marking the start of Ramadan.

The soldiers soon had to fast, too. Many of the heavier foodstuffs were dumped by the troops whilst whatever water they had been able to carry was consumed before the real desert even began. Laval's men had been issued a bottle each, which was scarcely sufficient for a day in the dust and sand, and Niello-Sargy, watching from the comfort of headquarters, soon saw 'our soldiers straggling through the sand only to find some brackish water, which a horse would refuse to drink, with which to quench their thirst. They were bitter on account of such want and they soon turned to pillaging and insubordination. It proved hard to keep them off headquarters' baggage.' Vertray was already enduring 'a battle of the will against exhaustion and suffering' before he had gone very far, and was soon complaining:

> During my entire military career, I have not seen an army as exhausted as this one. Discipline had broken down and only the rearguard, composed of officers and non-commissioned officers, maintained order. We could not see four paces in front of ourselves, and we sank up to our knees into the moving sands. Our artillery found it impossible and ground to a halt and we were obliged to stop and push the gun wheels to get them forward.

Pierre Louis Cailleux was also finding conditions difficult:

> I can assure you that I have never suffered like I suffered in that desert, overcome by hunger, thirst, the heat and having to march through the shifting sands.

Even François, with the better-supplied vanguard, notes that shortages were plaguing the army before it had left Egypt. 'We reached Qatiyah,' he lamented, 'dying from exhaustion but even more from thirst. No sooner had we arrived than we ran for the village wells. Some were dry but one, which was behind a wall, had water in abundance and we could make our soup.'

Durand, a musician in the 75th, records the almost general sense of desperation as the French neared the Promised Land:

> We were on the way to El-Arich which is in the desert and is three fatal days from Qatiyah. It is impossible to describe the suffering we endured in that arid and burning land and every face bore an expression of consternation. Our canteens were empty and it did not look like we would be able to fill them. Whenever we found a spring we would drink but the brackish water would not even quench our thirst. Despite our misfortune, we could not help but laugh when we saw the soldiers run off clutching their breeches after drinking that

water. No purgative medicine could empty the stomach more quickly than that stuff. We slept at this pharmacy.

François saw what happened to those who could not get fresh water:

A number of soldiers blew their brains out. This plain is so arid and is scourged by hot winds which suffocate even the most robust. On 8 February, having left at two in the morning, and after several hours of marching, we saw the sea. The soldiers, tortured by thirst, threw themselves into the waves. Some died and others, having drunk quantities of salt water, blew their own brains out because their bodies were on fire from the salt.

He even saw General Reynier urge his soldiers to dig in the sand, thereby obtaining a little something to drink, but when the march recommenced 'more than 100 men of all ranks were left behind, dead'. Lacorre also saw that 'many of the soldiers died from exhaustion and want of water, others would happily give a Louis for a bottle of it' whilst Richardot was just as affected by the impact on the unfortunate horses and beasts of burden:

The wells we came across had been destroyed during the retreat of Ibrahim Bey's Mamelukes and the muddy water they contained was barely sufficient for one company. ... But the horses, the camels, the dromedaries? We had nothing to give them. The young horses especially simply collapsed and died.

Gerbaud saw that the dead animals were put to some use by the starving soldiers. Supply depots had not been established, and food was now as rare as water, so he watched as 'the men cut up the camels that had died in the fighting and ate them. The soldiers ate dogs, camels and horses. Only four ounces of biscuit per man.'[6] Lieutenant Laval ate a dog and a mule whilst Joseph Laporte noted that 'many soldiers died as did some camels from fatigue and no sooner had they expired than the men fell on them and cut them up ... other animals, such as horses and mules, were stolen from their owners and also killed and chopped up. Everything you could lay hands on was fair game, even dogs and rats.' The young soldier also found and cooked more exotic fare, recording that 'we found some dock leaves and

---

6. Malus confirms this with his observation that 'there was a great famine in our camp and we were eating camels, horses and donkeys. We were reduced to the last extremity.' General Reynier cites an anecdote in which, after Major Pépin's horse goes missing, he chides the soldiers only to be told 'we promise to defend you from those buggers who had wanted to eat you instead'.

a few tortoises and these came as a great relief to us. The following day, after resting for eight hours, we set off at dawn, keeping an eye open for more tortoises and dock leaves. Order had broken down and there was no discipline now, the soldiers were exhausted and worn out by the excessive heat and the sandy ravines.'

Discipline was indeed something of a mirage, and an atmosphere of recrimination and blame had also taken hold among the officers. Vigo-Roussillon faulted Napoleon directly, complaining that 'the commander-in-chief had managed things so badly that not only had he only issued us with ten days' rations for a march which could have lasted a month, but that he had also neglected to order convoys prepared to resupply us'.[7]

Bernoyer must have been listening in:

I heard my first criticism of Bonaparte here. They said he had been careless for not having established a single magazine for food or munitions to supply those troops who formed the expedition. They also said that however confident a general is, and however brave his troops, he should always take precautions in case he meets with a setback.

Pelleport saw how the complaints were carried right to Bonaparte's tent:

The soldiers were complaining and so Bonaparte issued a proclamation in which he spoke of Philistines and Crusaders. To those soldiers who had approached his tent to complain in person he told them that they would never equal the Romans who, in such circumstances, would have rather eaten their knapsacks. 'General,' one bold soldier replied, 'your Romans did not carry knapsacks.'

As in July 1798, the prospect of battle saved the army. Through the dust kicked up by feet and hooves emerged the fort of El-Arich, defended by Ahmed the Great, Ibrahim the Abyssinian, Hadji-Kadir, 500 Albanians and 600 North Africans and Mamelukes.

As soon as François arrived he saw a stone village under the ramparts and that 'the walls were covered in Syrian [*sic*] troops and a large number

---

7. Miot was one of the administrators tasked with providing food so his point of view was rather different, and rather defensive: 'The civil employees avoided getting too near the columns throughout this difficult march as they were on horseback and inevitably ran afoul of the caustic mood of the soldiers who complained when they saw someone better off than themselves. Their suffering exacerbated more than is usual two traits which are inevitable in any army, insubordination and selfishness. Our men, worn down by fatigue and deprivation, no longer respected anyone.'

of flags and we could see that there were lots of them and that they would resist'. The French resolved to clear the village first and so 'Adjutant Devaux led us, the 9th Line, in an assault with fixed bayonets. The Syrian soldiers would rather be stuck with bayonets than surrender. We stormed into the village but were soon forced to stop because the streets were narrow and because they were shooting at us from the houses and throwing stones and burning material down onto us. However, our courage was such that we pushed on, kicked the doors in and bayoneted the Syrians. You cannot imagine the carnage we wreaked.'

Resistance was desperate because, as François added, 'the governor of the fort had barred the gates and so the unfortunate soldiers fought on grimly through despair. Some North Africans held out in a well until some of the 3rd Battalion of the 9th Line threatened to have them burnt alive or massacred. They then surrendered and we took them to the field hospital in the gully.'

The French had suffered from the impetuous nature of their initial attack, Laporte reflecting that 'the excessive ardour of our troops cost the lives of a good number of them as they did not realise the fort was so well defended and so approached without taking precautions'. But Vertray, arriving later, saw that they had exacted more than enough revenge, counting sixteen bodies bayoneted to death in just one house. Bernoyer casually blamed this murder on the enemy's ignorance of the civilised norms of warfare:

> They preferred to have themselves killed rather than surrender, as, not knowing the laws of war as established in civilised countries, they did not expect quarter. So they defended themselves desperately.

The French settled down amongst the corpses. Fortunately, one of Reynier's detachments encountered a convoy under Kassim the Muscovite and, despite the barking of a stray dog, seized it and 'a mass of supplies'.[8] This meant that by the time Napoleon marched in on 17 February, siege works could begin on full stomachs. A mine under the walls had been tried and failed, so batteries were completed by 20 February and, from then on, the 8-pounders began to pummel the 30-foot battlements. Some shots fell short, and there were instances of death and maiming by friendly fire, but this bombardment also provoked a violent response from the fort. Such pugnacity impressed Gerbaud:

> They kept up a steady fire against our gunners, troops and staff officers who had positioned themselves on some heights just within range. The besieged were quick to repair a demolished tower using wooden

---

8. And money. François made 1,200 francs largely because he spared the life of a Mameluke called Ali who presented him with 700 francs out of gratitude.

beams and they bravely fired back despite the effects of our batteries. 300 dead or wounded on our side.

But they could not resist for long and, at five in the evening of Friday 21 February, the governor requested surrender. François was there as the gates opened:

> Their envoy had a white handkerchief on a stick and he was talking all the time. I did not understand a word he said but his gestures made it clear the fort wished to give up.

This led to an armistice and, the next day, to a capitulation that spared the garrison on condition they would not serve Djezzar. The fort's governor swore on Abraham, the Prophet and the Koran that this would be so,[9] and Malus then saw the enemy file out:

> The enemy garrison issued out at four in the afternoon and passed before us bearing their weapons and bringing with them a certain number of horses and mules loaded with baggage. When they had gathered in the plain they were surrounded by General Bon's division and divided up amongst the divisions of the army, the idea being that they would serve with us. However, they all soon deserted.

Gerbaud provides further details:

> Some 200 took up service with us and kept their weapons whilst the rest, some 500, were kept in the El-Arich fort for three days without being issued any bread. Reduced to eating grass. A further thirty then took service with us whilst the rest, Turks, Arnauts,[10] North Africans, were disarmed and taken 3 miles into the desert with a little ration of bread.[11]

Jean-Pierre Doguereau tallies the French trophies as '300 horses, a lot of biscuit and rice, 500 Albanians, 500 North Africans and 200 from Anatolia

---

9. The French had said that the garrison would conserve its weapons, but, following the surrender, did not abide by these terms. Some of the garrison then made their way to Jaffa saying that they too would not abide by the terms of surrender.
10. Arnauts were Albanian or northern Greek infantry in Ottoman service.
11. Richardot says there were '300 Albanians and North Africans who were to be sent to Baghdad but asked to go to Egypt to serve the French, although the Albanians refused'. However, three companies of North Africans and one of Albanians were actually formed.

and Carmania'. Alexandre Lacorre was glad of the horses but also frowned at 'the dead bodies of Turks seen everywhere, at the foot of the towers, in the fort itself and in the village. It was clear that the enemy had lost at least as many men as we had.'[12]

With these supplies, and this key to Palestine in his hands, Napoleon pushed on to Refah and crossed the threshold into Asia. François-Michel Lucet records that 'we left El-Arich, marching through the desert. Camped in Asia at the point where that part of the world meets Africa. There are two granite columns there ten feet apart.'

First impressions of Asia were marred by thirst and Laporte observed how the men were 'issued with two ounces of rice and, after some difficulties, enough water to cook it in (we had to dangle twenty canteens on the end of ropes, musket straps and handkerchiefs to get at it in the well)'. It was no improvement on Egypt, and, as befitting men entering the Holy Land, the troops resorted to telling scriptural jokes about how even Jesus had only spent forty days and forty nights in the wilderness. Still, Detroye was lucky enough to catch a partridge whilst each division at Colionnes had to sacrifice six camels so the men could have meat.

The situation was dire, but then came a surprise. François was there to record it:

> At two that afternoon something extraordinary happened. There was rain which added to its own charms by also cooling the air. We stripped off to greet it and purify ourselves in this heaven-sent shower.

Miot was delighted:

> It was a charming day for me. The sky was cloudy and the heat not too excessive, and I even felt a few drops of rain. The sight of some olive trees made me feel like I was in Europe.

Laval even saw some grass and, in a tasteful homage to unexpected greenery, 'ate it to quench my thirst'. Temperate weather meant other much-needed improvements. Vigo-Roussillon saw that as they approached Gaza 'the land was cultivated and shade provided by fruit trees blossoming in the beautiful spring and, the day after we arrived in this promised land, it rained for the

---

12. Dr Larrey, touring the fort, noted, 'I found fifteen [Turks] in the cellar lying in the airless dark on horrible matts and covered with vermin. These unfortunate wounded had not received any medical attention. Their wounds were not dressed and they all their wounds were gangrenous and were full of worms.' Larrey treated the prisoners, cleared the fort of bodies and lit little fires to purify the air.

first time in a year and continued to do so for a second, third and even fourth day, recalling to mind our wet, cold and humid Europe'.

The infantryman Millet was also reminded of home and described how 'all around Gaza, for some six miles, the land is covered with gardens in which all kinds of fruit grow. This place is like Provence, with its large number of olive trees.'[13]

Gaza even had shops. Sergeant Antoine-Mathias Bonnefons watched as 'every bakery was besieged by a mass of soldiers hoping to buy some bread. However hard they worked they could not satisfy everyone.' In this land of milk and honey, some inevitably overdid it. Laporte observed that 'there was brandy made from dates, not much wine, but poultry, eggs, beef, mutton and goats and our exhausted bodies could not stomach such fare and we had to be careful and that those who did so were glad of it as all the others were afflicted by dysentery'. The drinking and rights that came with conquest quickly led to pillaging and Gaza was soon a scene of devastation. The officers were disappointed that the evils of famine were so quickly followed by those of violence, but Detroye at least took consolation that 'the soldiers were again singing around their campfires'.

The rain soon put an end to that, too. Doguereau and his fellow officers had pitched their tent in a gulley by the gates of Gaza but they found that the downpour transformed the ground 'into a marsh; I don't think I have ever spent a worse night in my life. I was literally lying down in water, something which I felt all the more for having spent six months in the parched lands of Egypt.'[14]

Miot was also nearly drowned, 'spending a peaceful night on a mattress in the tent of the Commissary General Daure and our sleep was so deep that we did not hear the storm. However, there was a flood and this soon came and swept away our tent.'

He spared a thought for the ordinary soldiers:

The soldiers, dressed in blue cloth, were initially grateful for the rain but they were soon soaked through. In Egypt marching by day was hard but the soldiers could sleep under the starry sky at night. In Syria the soldiers would be covered in mud and could not change

---

13. The engineer Jacotin thought 'the olive trees bigger than those around Aix-en-Provence'. A homesick Vertray also made the comparison to France: 'At least here we would wage war without the risk of dying from thirst, hunger or sunstroke. I returned to camp satisfied with what I had seen for the land looked like Provence.'

14. The situation worsened when his horses escaped and he spent two hours running through the bog trying to catch them. 'I have never sworn so much in my life' was his final comment on the episode.

their clothes, so they set fire to olive trees in an attempt to dry themselves out.

Laporte adds that they were 'up to our knees in mud' and Doguereau, riding ahead, 'came across a division in which the troops were cursing and in foul humour; the men had been marching through a bog and in the constant rain since leaving Gaza'. However bad it was for the soldiers, it was worse for the camels, as Richardot observed after four days of constant rain:

> The camels were in a pitiful state, they could barely walk or remain standing as their round feet were designed for sand and so they died, even the best and strongest amongst them. Their loss did not go to waste for the army lacked meat and camel flesh is pretty tasty.

Leaving a small garrison in the fort, the damp and increasingly shoeless French then marched to Ramallah '9 miles from Jaffa, a beautiful village, lots of Christians'. It had an Armenian monastery, and the local women, who went unveiled, seemed delighted to see the invaders, but Élie Krettly of the Guides was more pleased to find 'a jar of Cyprus wine and some flat bread, which looked like the pancakes we eat at carnival, and which, for famished men such as ourselves, was quite a stroke of luck'. Jean-Pierre Doguereau was just as pleased when General Junot shared with him a pâté and a bottle of Bordeaux, delicacies 'we had not tasted in a long time'. Laporte was also lucky, finding '20,000 quintals of biscuit, less good, it must be said, than our own, but when you are hungry everything is good. Unfortunately, much went to waste as the soldiers had pillaged on the night of our arrival and even the monastery and its monks in the village were not spared.'

Nor were the cave dwellers in the cliffs 4 miles from Jaffa, for the hussars came and took their grain before riding over the undulating land towards that fort. Jaffa itself was the next objective and its bastion, high on a broad plateau, was defended by a formidable body of opponents, as an officer of the 32nd Line observed:

> This town was protected by high walls, garnished with a good number of guns and garrisoned by a force drawn from all races: North Africans, Albanians, Egyptians, Anatolians, Arnauts, all full of bravery and bold.

François adds that 'the enemy were North Africans, Albanians, Kurds, people from Aleppo and Damascus, Anatolians and Negroes, all motivated by religious fanaticism'. Malus saw that, whatever their religious feelings, they boasted some fine artillery:

> The enemy wished to demonstrate the strength of his artillery and so fired off several salvoes aimed at those divisions taking up positions around the place. They fired some shells despite the long range. We

did not dig trenches, instead sheltering ourselves in the gardens which surround the town.[15]

Bonaparte was on the receiving end of this enemy broadside, the artilleryman Doguereau watching as the general 'was covered in earth' when a roundshot landed close by. The French then countered by establishing their own batteries, despite a lack of wood, tools and heavy-calibre guns. Then, just as the French were ready, the enemy launched a surprise sortie. Malus, along with nearly everyone else, was caught off guard:

> The enemy managed to reach our batteries without being spotted, killing our sentries and a few workers. I was asleep and woke up in the chaos. Those guarding the position had fled shouting 'to arms' whilst dropping their own. We only managed to rally some way beyond the battery, all the time being exposed to the artillery fire. The Turks carried back to the town the heads of those Frenchmen they had killed as the governor had offered a generous reward.

Gerbaud watched amazed as a 'North African boldly cut off the head of a sergeant of the 32nd Line he had killed despite coming under fire from ten volunteers who were at short range. After removing the head, he showed it in triumph before running back through a storm of bullets without being hit.'

Still, despite such bravura performances, the sortie was beaten back and, soon after, Laporte was relieved to see how the French guns 'brought down one of the towers on the ramparts, opening a slight breach in the walls as it came down at three in the afternoon'. With a breach effected, the French, in conformity with military custom in Europe, sent forward an envoy on 7 March offering terms to the garrison. The envoy's fate was a gruesome one and Élie Krettly watched as 'the enemy put on a horrible show for the French army, raising aloft the bloodied head of the French envoy on the end of a pike'.[16]

Bernoyer confirms this, and the fury it inspired in the ranks:

---

15. The garrison included some French-trained gunners from Constantinople serving the guns, twenty of which were of French calibre manufactured in Austria.

16. François Vigo-Roussillon, of the 32nd Line, saw how 'a breach was opened which was deemed sufficient. The governor was then summoned but his response was to cut the head off our envoy.' Richardot adds that 'the head was thrown into our trenches, the body into the sea'. Monge comments that 'the general summoned the garrison twice but they made no reply other than to cut off the heads of the unfortunate Syrians who had carried the messages'.

A few moments later and they displayed the head of the officer who had taken in the summons on the town's ramparts. Seeing this atrocity, our soldiers did not wait for the order to attack.

That afternoon, General Lannes had the 22nd Light and 69th Line formed into columns to the sound of some martial airs from their regimental bands. Joseph Felix Łazowski then led the men through the smoke with his detachment of engineers:

No sooner had I received the order to lead the grenadiers to storm the breach, and establish themselves beyond it, than I set off at the run with twenty sappers carrying three ladders and tools, some pioneers and six miners. I left some of the sappers with Lieutenant Vernois so that he could widen the breach and, with the rest of the sappers, miners and pioneers, occupied the right and left of the breach in order to secure communications and defensive positions for our troops.

Six companies of grenadiers were close behind and Vaxelaire watched as the French, under a young Swede called Netherwood, 'swarmed up the walls like ants out of the ground'. Major Jean-François Detroye of the engineers was also on hand to watch them climb up to the breach:

The attack on Jaffa was my first experience of a siege. And if something helps me to forget the horror of such a sight, then it was the sheer courage of the troops involved. ... You would not believe their bravery. As soon as the commander-in-chief gave the signal they quietly ran across the 200 paces between the trenches and the breach. They climbed the slope under heavy fire and in a flash had cleared the houses around it. After that, however, they showed that they much preferred chasing loot to attacking their enemies.

The French had overrun the place by five o'clock, and the night and the following day were dedicated to sacking the place. Jean-Gabriel de Niello-Sargy watched as this hunt for plunder was combined with a desire for revenge:

The entire army, mad with a fury it is impossible to describe, charged into the town. Rape, murder, destruction filled the town with blood and mourning as all inhabitants, regardless of age or sex, were put to the sword.

André Peyrusse also saw that no quarter was given:

Men, women, children and the elderly were mercilessly massacred and no sanctuary was spared. The women were raped and then stabbed to death and thrown out of the windows. I saw a pretty woman who had been stabbed five or six times with a bayonet dying amongst a group of four mutilated children.

Malus was horrified by the violence:

The carnage was deafening, doors were kicked in, houses went up in flames, women screamed, fathers and children were cut down together, girls were raped on the corpses of their mothers, bodies smoked under charred clothing, there was a smell of blood whilst the wounded cried and the victors argued over what booty could be extracted from their dying prey.

Lacorre saw that the 'soldiers, drunk on rage and victory, could not distinguish Christians from Muslims and North Africans' and Laporte adds that the 'massacre did not spare 200 or 300 Greeks and Christians of different sects who were dressed like Turks but who could not make themselves understood and so were killed'.

The sack of Jaffa was an extended killing spree and Chasseur Millet surveyed the result:

We reached Jaffa just as the soldiers were returning to the camp from the city which they had just taken by storm. They were loaded with loot. There had been a terrible massacre, men, women, children, all had been killed with bayonets. The massacre was only halted when the drums sounded the call to arms. It was a hideous sight to see so many innocent victims breathing their last in the streets and houses. The French, with death in their eyes, killed everyone they found, not sparing age or sex, and even the suckling babies were not spared.[17]

There was more murder in the coming days. Bernoyer heard that most of the garrison had initially sought sanctuary from the infuriated French:

Some 1,500 of them held out in a mosque. Bonaparte offered them terms, and they accepted having been told that they would be conveyed to the Syrian frontier. They therefore came out trusting in the word of Bonaparte.

---

17. The pillaging lasted four days according to François, who was not there. Word was brought to his men by a detachment who subsequently showed symptoms of the plague and who were quarantined 400 paces from the camp and shot at if they tried to come any closer.

A large contingent had only surrendered on the promise of safe-conduct from Napoleon's aides, the young Eugene de Beauharnais and his colleague Captain François Croisier. The following day Malus noted that 'some 4,000 Turkish soldiers who had escaped the carnage had been collected. They had laid down their weapons on the promise of being spared and they were kept by the camp and only lightly guarded. They remained there for three days during which time they received the same rations as our soldiers and were offered service in our ranks. Many did so.'

Peyrusse also saw the '3,000 men who had laid down their arms were brought into the camp on the orders of the commander-in-chief. The Egyptians, North Africans and Turks were separated and the North Africans were then taken down to the beach the following day.' Doguereau thought that 1,200 Egyptians, and those from Aleppo, were to be spared whilst the rest were to be dealt with infamously, for that trek to the shoreline about a league towards Gaza would be their last. Miot describes this march of death:

On the afternoon of 10 March [the prisoners] were set in motion and brought into the middle of a huge square formed by Bon's division. Rumours of their fate persuaded me and a number of others to follow this silent column of victims in order to see if there was any truth in it. The Turks marched along in groups and seemed to suspect their fate. They did not cry, they remained silent, they were resigned. A few of the wounded who could not follow were finished off with the bayonet. A few others went from group to group and seemed to be warning them of imminent danger. Some of the braver ones perhaps thought they might slip past the battalion which guarded them and into the fields but measures had been taken and there was no attempt to escape.

He continues as they reached the fateful beach:

They eventually came to the sand dunes to the south-west of Jaffa and they were brought close to the yellowish sea. The officer in charge of the troops had them broken up into small groups and taken to different points in order to be shot. This horrible execution required a great deal of time despite the number of soldiers involved. These showed themselves to be utterly repelled by their abominable task.

The massacre continued for some time. 'Our soldiers eventually ran out of bullets,' confessed Miot, 'and had to resort to the bayonet or swords. I could no longer stand such a horrible sight and I turned away pale and barely able to stand.' Peyrusse was sure that there were actually two massacres, first of the garrison's infantry and then of the artillery:

All they could do was to attempt to swim away and many did not hesitate and threw themselves into the water. These were then picked off at leisure and the sea was soon tinged red and covered in bodies. A few managed to reach some rocks but soldiers were sent out in boats to finish them off. The following day some 1,200 Turkish gunners, who had been kept without food by the commander's tent, were led off for execution. This time we were to spare our powder and the unfortunates were bayoneted.

Detroye, who had an eye for detail, noted that 'they shot 1,041 Turks from the garrison including the gunners from Constantinople who had been trained by the French. The execution was a terrible sight. The men had been kept by headquarters for the last three days. Then four battalions surrounded them and led them to their deaths.'

Later Cadet de Gassicourt would write that Adjutant Leturcq refused to take part in the massacre, and young Eugene de Beauharnais claimed that Pierre Boyer likewise refused. Laporte, also an eyewitness, agrees there was much reluctance to kill in cold blood:

The prisoners were shot the following afternoon, despite the fact that they had been promised mercy. The army grumbled as they knew how to fight an enemy which was resisting but took against the idea of butchering unarmed prisoners who had been granted quarter. Even though the Turks did not take prisoners, our men would have preferred to let them go rather than to allow such an act of barbarity which stained the laurels they were accustomed to wear. ... Of the generals, some were of the opinion that the guarantee should be respected, and that, as they had been granted their lives during the fighting, then there was all the more reason to observe that promise now, otherwise we would be in breach of the usages of war and we would cover ourselves with shame.[18]

Élie Krettly went as far to suggest that 'no one, or nearly no one, felt able to strike so they were herded towards the sea and they threw themselves in hoping to make it to some rocks half a mile or a mile out and whilst this meant that our soldiers were spared the ordeal of killing them'. However, he nevertheless felt compelled to justify the killing on the grounds that there was no spare food for the prisoners:

18. Richardot, who would see the remains of the prisoners on the beach on 25 May, admits there was reluctance, noting that 'the unfortunates had been shot, the officers in charge reluctantly carrying out their orders'.

It was impossible for us to save the prisoners as we did not have food enough for ourselves and sending them back to their army was impractical. I remind everyone of the morality of the men we were fighting against. So, a court martial was convened and it was determined that the enemy would be put to the sword.

Vigo-Roussillon added his own reasons to defend the indefensible:

The garrison of Jaffa when combined with that of El-Arish numbered some 6,000 men and the French army was too weak to guard such a large number. Nor could they be exchanged for the Turks gave no quarter and therefore had no French prisoners. They could not be sent back to Egypt as that would weaken the expeditionary force by a third ... Nor could they be fed for there was insufficient food even for us. The commander-in-chief, determined to pursue the enemy northwards, found himself in an impossible position regarding these prisoners. He took an awful resolution – one which his enemies would rebuke him for – but which could be explained by the reasons just given. The order was given to finish these prisoners off with the bayonet in order to preserve cartridges. The prisoners were divided up between our units, squares were formed around them and then they were attacked with the bayonet. All were killed. The army obeyed, but not without disgust and horror.

Millet, however, even went as far as to state that the enemy deserved their fate:

The general had the 700 or 800 soldiers bound two by two and they were taken down to the sea where they were shot without exception of age or rank. These barbarians merited such a fate for their barbarity had cost the lives of the population of the city and those from round about who had fled to Jaffa and been forced to defend it.

The reasons put forward were questionable, but there was also little agreement on the numbers killed. Gerbaud thought that 'nearly all the Turks were killed by four battalions and they say 2,400 were shot, either Turks or North Africans'. Laval gave a figure of 1,100, with the Egyptians being spared, whilst Lacorre says the dead 'numbered about 1,500 although, as they were executed on the beach, a few managed to escape by swimming'. Vertray, who was exploring the ruined churches of Ramallah when the massacre took place, thought that 'the majority of the 2,000 killed were bayoneted'. François claimed 3,563 as an overly precise death toll but Detroye, attached to headquarters and an enemy of hyperbole, listed 800 shot on the first day, 600 on the second and 1,041 on the third.

This was the butcher's bill of the murder at Jaffa, but, however unsettled or disgusted the French were, they soon had something else to worry about. The plague had arrived. Doguereau thought that 'the soldiers caught it from germs in the clothes of the Turks'[19] whilst Detroye watched its horrible effects:

> There has been an outbreak of disease these last few days. It has affected the army, particularly Bon's division. It is a violent fever accompanied by red swellings and you die quite quickly. A number of soldiers have died, many of them suddenly. They say it is the plague. ... The chief medical officer denies it. The commander-in-chief therefore went to the hospital, touched some of the patients and helped lift up a soldier who was dying from the buboes. This gesture has had the best effect.

On 11 March, in a scene subsequently recreated in a heroic painting by Gros, Napoleon had indeed spent an hour and a half among plague patients in a Greek monastery. His tunic had been smeared with pus, something too gross for Baron Gros, but the general's laying on of hands had reassured many and Bernoyer saw the army visibly relax, a process which reanimated his 'admiration for the French character. A little time spent in enjoyment allows him to forget all the woes, all the dangers, he has been through, as well as those to come.'

Unfortunately, death came in many guises that spring and there was more danger around the corner. As the French quit Jaffa, a detachment of twenty-five dragoons was ambushed in the groves by Arab horsemen. The following day, Detroye saw 'them ride up carrying on the point of their lances the heads of the unfortunate dragoons killed the day before'.[20] It was an ominous prelude to the next murderous episode, the siege of Acre.

The army was initially optimistic, Bernoyer jotting down that 'our soldiers thought that it would be as easy to take as Jaffa'. However, Miot was abruptly brought to his senses when Djezzar's capital revealed some of its capabilities:

---

19. An early example of the idea that disease could be transmitted by *germs* rather than the air. His memoirs were written in 1803 or 1804, when such an idea was gaining ground.

20. Their commander, Lieutenant Augustin Delesalle, survived the massacre. His account records how he was 'stripped to my shirt, and driven 12 miles through the mountains that evening and, after inflicting a thousand abuses on me, they came and showed me the heads of eight or ten of my poor dragoons'. He was later taken to Acre and, after Sir Sidney Smith's intervention, handed over to the British.

On 18 March I climbed a wall and some earthworks the enemy had erected and then abandoned for the safety of the city as we advanced. The commander-in-chief came up and inspected the city walls with his telescope. After having studied them for some time he issued his orders to push the enemy back from the gardens surrounding the city. I remained on the heights, gazing down at the sea, something which had always given me pleasure, and at Acre itself, with its walls and minarets and, to my right, the peaks of Mount Lebanon. I allowed myself to be carried away by thoughts of my homeland. Then suddenly a shell landed in the midst of Bon's division at the foot of the earthworks, killing an officer and two NCOs and tearing me from my reverie.

Napoleon, too, was nearly hit when a shell buried itself in the sand just three paces away from where he and his aides-de-camp, Merlin and Eugene de Beauharnais, were standing. Djezzar's 250 guns were evidently effective, and Acre, locked on a spit of land by impressive ramparts, was energetically defended by the pasha's clan and fierce mercenaries. The sea not only provided protection, it also brought help as Djezzar received support from a British flotilla under Sir Sidney Smith. Despite Nelson's reservations about Smith, thinking him an upstart and too soft on the French, or 'modern Goths' as Horatio dubbed them, this gallant commodore had been given an independent command to harry the French across the Levant. He had quickly recognised the strategic implications of Napoleon's siege of Acre, and the consequences of its fall, and so, after begging Constantinople to send even more help, he set about landing marines and guns to bolster the besieged. He also sent ashore his secret weapon, codename Perrin. This was the talented engineer Louis Edmond Le Picard de Phelippeaux, a former classmate of Napoleon who had fled the revolution and now fought for the royalist cause. His skill in managing the port's defences, combined with the garrison's energy, meant Acre would be no easy victory.

It was soon apparent to the French that there would no alternative to the hard toil of siege work, with Lieutenant Cailleux, who arrived on 21 March, recalling that 'we encamped and began digging trenches and establishing batteries right away'. The enemy resolve showed itself most forcefully on 26 March when Laporte was amongst those who watched a mass of enemy soldiers issuing out from the gates in the stout crusader walls:

A mass of Turks threw themselves forward like wild animals, pouring out from the town and from some ditches; brandishing sabres in their hands or holding them in their teeth, or with muskets, they fell on our men in the forward trenches. Our picquets could not resist this shock and fell back and a bloody struggle commenced. Some brave Turks came and grabbed the barrels of the muskets of our men in the trenches but a quick death was the reward for their temerity.

Gerbaud provides a more detailed assessment of this first test of resolve:

> Between three and four that afternoon the enemy, numbering 500 or 600 men, issued forth from their defences under cover of intense firing from the castle and from the British sloop and gunboat. There was firing along the line but the shouting from those sailors could still be heard. From the tops of the towers to the curtain wall, everyone was firing. Our outposts replied. The enemy surged into our batteries and some of the 59th Line and the 2nd battalion of the 13th broke and ran. By six, however the enemy was beaten back. The firing had been intense for three hours with bombs, shells and roundshot crashing into our defences. We lost ten dead and thirty-six wounded in Lannes' division. We saw twenty-five enemy dead.

Detroye limited himself to recording that the sortie commenced at two and lasted for three hours, with the Turks 'contenting themselves with carrying eight French heads back to their pasha and wounding thirty of us'.

The French returned to work and Napoleon, worried that his artillery would soon lack ammunition or that relief might reach the city, drove them hard. His impatience was given spurs by the arrival of the Dutch courier Wynand Mourveau, who, having made it to Egypt on the *Osiris* under a Spanish flag, reached camp bearing a welcome case of Bordeaux wine and unwelcome news of defeats in Europe. Napoleon saw that taking Acre would secure Egypt, and thus perhaps allow him to leave for France. The city would have to fall, and the sooner the better.

The French infantry, seeing their gunners turning to suppressing the enemy's guns, sensed an assault was being readied. Even though many of the engineers and artillerymen cautioned it was too soon, that the gap they had opened in the ancient ramparts was just too narrow, Napoleon's impatience easily swept aside their technical objections. Richardot on the staff of the artillery felt that everyone was clamouring for victory:

> On the 28th the batteries were ready. We had four 12-pounders, four 8-pounders and four mortars. We opened up at dawn and had largely suppressed the enemy artillery by three in the afternoon and flushed their troops from the tower. The grenadiers were impatient to be allowed to launch the assault. They were told to wait but persisted, loudly, in their demands. There was, as yet, no practicable breach, and the artillery officers repeated their advice. It went unheeded following our success at Jaffa and the grenadiers seemed determined. They had fascines to throw into the ditch and ladders with which to scale the tower.

Miot had caught sight of the forlorn hope which would lead the attack: 'Captain [Minerve Claude de] Mailly had been ready in the trenches since dawn and now waited for the order to storm the breach. By three it seemed practicable and the signal was given.'

Richardot was there to observe the approach:

The grenadiers under Mailly threw themselves forward, dropping their fascines into the ditch, pushing across it and placing their ladders against the wall. They barely reached half way up. Mailly was shot as were many grenadiers and others were knocked down by a hail of stones thrown from the battlements.

Undeterred, Millet and his carabiniers swept forwards:

Djezzar was secure behind the walls with his troops and we began our trenches, making good progress as everyone lent a hand. The guns were placed in batteries on 27 April [*sic*, 28 March] and began to try to open a breach and we advanced towards the walls, using an aqueduct as cover as we waited for the breach to be practicable. An assault was ordered for four that afternoon. Our regiment was the first to go in, led by General Junot. The charge was sounded all along the line and we crawled forwards with fascines which were only 12 paces long in order to bridge the ditch protecting the battered tower. This ditch was 20 paces wide and 15 deep and when we were close enough we threw the fascines into the ditch and tried to cross, finding not only that they did not allow us to cross the ditch but also that the breach was not yet ready as it was only wide enough for one man to pass at a time.

That slim opening was a dangerous place, as Vaxelaire found to his cost:

As we reached the breach I was hit in the head by a stone or piece of shrapnel and fell backwards. As I fell I grabbed at the tails of an officer's coat and almost pulled him down with me. He shouted, 'Has he gone mad?' but saw what I was about when blood began to cover my head.[21]

Although the Turks had momentarily panicked they now saw that the French assault was faltering. The breach was too narrow, the ladders required to get to it too short. Miot then watched horrified as the French turned to run, leaving the wounded and the unfortunate Mailly to a cruel fate:

Mailly was wounded and could not walk and he begged a grenadier to carry him on his back. This latter soon saw that this deed would

---

21. He promptly fell ill in hospital where, for a revolutionary soldier, he had an unreasonable thought: 'We are in the Holy Land, perhaps I will be saved.'

cost him his life, and might not save the officer, and so dropped the unfortunate Mailly. The Turks came out to cut his head off, a fate all the more horrible because he was still conscious and could only watch as the butchers drew their knives.

'If only the grenadiers had been supported by other troops!' lamented François. He was forced to watch the Turks 'come down into the ditch to begin to cut the heads off those soldiers who had fallen there as well as those who were dead or wounded. That night the ferocious pasha exhibited those heads, fixing them on pikes and displaying them on the ramparts. We heard that he presented one to Sydney Smith but that he recoiled in horror. I don't believe a word of it as this Smith is English.'[22]

That evening the jackals kept Pelleport on edge, but the sight from the battlements was even more unsettling:

That evening, around nine, we heard some savage cries and a burst of barbaric music. We looked up at the ramparts and saw torches being carried as well as the heads of our comrades who had fallen in the moat being borne along on pikes.

The garrison seemed unshakeable, and, when not removing heads, kept busy cramming sacks of earth and bales of damp cotton into the gaps into the walls, and reinforcing them with beams. Napoleon's artillery tried to set the beams on fire with incendiaries whilst his engineers opted to dig galleries and place mines beneath the walls. This would conserve shot, for the French were short of ammunition and were soon reduced to recycling roundshot from the Royal Navy. Smith's French-named warships were in the habit of sweeping towards the shore in attempts to rake the French trenches. Richardot had survived much worse and shrugged his shoulders at these broadsides:

Their two ships, the *Tigre* and the *Thésée*, would approach and position themselves alongside our camp, which was 3 kilometres from the shore, and then send us five or six broadsides. It was quite

---

22. The writer adds, 'This barbarous custom of the Turks sickened us and we swore never again to take them prisoner. We kept our word.' The Europeans, however, treated each other a little better. Gerbaud recalled that 'the commander-in-chief treated the English prisoners magnificently, sending them wine and mutton'. Miot saw the twenty-six sailors and two officers who had been seized, remarking, 'Lambert had asked for a surgeon to treat the prisoners. They were still drunk when I arrived ... it seems that the English have the habit of serving large amounts of strong drink during a battle.'

a spectacle and generally took place between two and three in the afternoon.

But the British were also active on land, perhaps to better effect. The engineer Phelippeaux had done much to strengthen the walls and, on those same walls, Laporte caught sight of 'a good number of people on the ramparts and we could make out some English officers observing our position'. They seemed to be pointing out objectives for sorties, and indeed, at ten o'clock on 30 March, the garrison launched another attack. François was once again waiting for them:

> Around noon [on 30 March] the besieged came out under cover of a bombardment, issuing out on the right by the shore and followed by some English. They attacked in force and the initial clash was so violent that we found it hard to resist, falling back to the aqueduct ... their early success did not last long. General Vial, in charge of the trenches, rallied those soldiers who had recovered from their initial surprise and counter-attacked.[23]

The French counter-attacked by setting off a mine close under the walls on 1 April, but François Vigo-Roussillon, of the 32nd Line, then witnessed the failure of Napoleon's subsequent assault:

> We only had a 32-pound carronade and four 12-pounders and so General Caffarelli suggested using mines. The first attempt partially demolished a piece of the counterscarp. Galleries were pushed forwards in attempt to place another under a tower whilst our guns also shot at the walls in an attempt to open a breach. A gap, only the width of two men, was opened and a second assault was ordered but this met the same success as the first. We started to run out of ammunition and the soldiers were paid to bring in roundshot fired from the British ships or the fort.[24]

---

23. Casualties were heavy and included the engineer Detroye, author of some observant notes on the campaign to date.

24. Lacorre says that the soldiers received 12 paras for a 4- or 8-pound shot, 16 for a 12-pound shot and 30 for one which was 18 or 24 pounds. Laporte says they got 5 sous a roundshot, and Giraud, an officer, thought it 10. Bizarrely lead for bullets was later obtained from the roofs of the churches at Nazareth. The more republican-minded officers found this amusing. The reaction of the Supreme Being is not recorded. Paper for cartridges was also in short supply, and regiments were ordered to hand over non-essential records and registers.

According to François, another assault on 3 April cost the attackers forty-two dead and wounded, whilst still another on 6 April met with no greater success. Then on 7 April the Turks again attacked, this time led out by officers of the British marines. One witness noted, 'We saw five or six English at their head, recognisable from their round hats decorated with black plumes.' Peyrusse confirms this, observing how 'the English had placed a few companies under good officers to lead this sortie. We let them approach into the trenches and then went at them with bayonets. The English came off worst, they lost fifteen and an officer by the mine gallery.'[25]

The English casualties were heralded as a victory by their French rivals and Laporte reports that 'our men were invited to see the dead English, these men who had allied themselves to barbarians. ... We learned from the English wounded who had had been left for dead and abandoned, but then taken by us to the hospital, that they had on their side a talented engineer or artillery officer who had been at school with our general but who had then emigrated and found service with the English. He was called Philipeaux [*sic*].'

Herded back into the city, the besieged then seem to have vented their own frustration on the civilians trapped within, but soon there was a grisly twist to this already grim struggle. 'They brought in a spy,' noted Lacorre, 'and he told the commander-in-chief that it was certain that two days ago Djezzar had had massacred all of Acre's Christians and Europeans. This was soon confirmed when we saw a huge number of corpses washed up on the shore with their arms and feet bound.'[26]

The bitterness was reaching its height. François saw 'the besieged hurling threats at us in Turkish, Arabic, English and even French'. In response, Napoleon's beleaguered troops intensified the bombardment. The besiegers were starting to feel besieged themselves, with gunpowder running short, and food only available to those able to pay in gold. The infantryman Millet complained that 'the inhabitants from the mountains around Acre came down with wine, bread and other edibles so that those who could afford them did for nothing. But there were few who could do for wine was six francs a bottle and bread 20 sols a pound. These greedy people thought to return a second time even though they had taken all the money we had.' He was perhaps being uncharitable, for Doguereau marvelled at the 'figs

---

25. Niello-Sargy heard how the sortie came out in three columns 'with some English troops at their centre, and was repulsed with the loss of the English captain Thomas Aldfield'. Lavalette calls him Haldfield. He was, in fact, Major Thomas Oldfield and he was identified by the papers found on him after some grenadiers from the 9th Line harpooned the corpse and pulled it into the French lines.

26. Between 200 and 400 bodies were found bound in baskets along the beach, strangled by the Turks. One of them was Eugene de Mailly, brother of the captain, who had been captured earlier in the campaign.

and raisins, eggs, cheese, butter and nuts' they brought in.[27] Indeed, most saw reliable friends in Abbas-el-Dahir and his clan, and Sheikh Mustapha Bechir's Druze, who hated the pasha and hoped to take possession of this regional capital.[28] Lacorre, tasked with supplying the army, seemed particularly grateful for their help:

> The Druzes, upon hearing of the arrival of the French before Acre, hurried to greet the commander-in-chief. They offered us food and troops[29] with which we could attack the town. A few who had fled to Damascus made the same offer. These brave people seem honest and loyal and give the impression of being good soldiers. They are all Christians, of a kind. Many had been mutilated by Djezzar and bore the marks of his barbarity.

Word also soon came from those same men of the mountains that the Ottomans and their allies in Damascus had formed a relief army to break the siege. The French had first sent dashing Murat, and then duller Junot, to conduct a reconnaissance in force. The French pushed down the road to Damascus and, whilst there were no revelations to be had, Junot and his men at least enjoyed a warm welcome in Nazareth, where they also found the paper essential for the manufacture of cartridges.

Beyond there the first enemies Junot encountered were bands of fugitive Mamelukes, intermingled with Djezzar's Nablusian raiders, bad Samaritans who robbed caravans and assassinated French marauders, but, on 8 April, at Loubia, he fought a much bigger force to a halt, an encounter Napoleon rendered quite biblical by dubbing it the battle of Nazareth. Still, there were rumours that an even larger enemy army was heading to Acre and Kléber's division was rushed out to prevent Napoleon's men being crushed between the hammer of this army and the anvil of that city. On 16 April Kléber's men did indeed find themselves before this vast host under a commander Pierre Louis Cailleux called Abdullah of Damascus. The resulting battle of Mount Tabor would see 25,000 enemy cavalry flowing around a few

---

27. Gerbaud was delighted to see the food being brought in by 'women who do not wear the veil'. Peyrusse was more distracted by Napoleon's meeting with a Druze village elder, a man claimed to be 115 years old.

28. Abbas-el-Daher visited Napoleon. He was the son of a former governor of the province, and Napoleon dubbed him Sheikh of Tiberias with Beirut as his capital. He also promised him Acre by rather grandly informing him that the Book of Destiny decreed that this would be so. That book is currently unavailable on Amazon.

29. Some Syrian Janissaries under Yacoub Habaïby and Youssef Hamaouy were raised for service with the French.

French squares. François was surrounded, and much impressed, by these wild warriors:

> The general had us moved forwards onto the plain in squares one under his command, the other under Junot. ... In the eight years in which I had served as a soldier, and having lived through campaigns in Holland, Germany and Italy, I can say that I have never been attacked by so many cavalry. There were nine or ten times as many of them than us. We needed all of our heroism not to give way to our initial feeling of shock and fear. In addition to this mass of horsemen a large number of infantry also opened up against our skirmishers placed in front of our squares.

Millet was also amongst the isolated French infantry:

> That army of knaves was composed of men from all nations. The cavalry was composed of Mamelukes under Mourad Bey and Ibrahim Bey. There were North Africans, Syrians, Samaritans, Egyptians, Turks from Constantinople and the men of Djezzar as well as the hill tribes. There were so many of them that one could not see the end of them. ... Our division was of 2,500 men, formed in several squares, and we advanced to meet them. The general, not wanting us to proceed too far, had us halt. They charged us a number of times, but always without success. The grapeshot from our guns, plus our volleys, hurt them and forced them to retreat after each attempt, making off more quickly than when they had advanced.

Citizen Grapeshot did his bloody work so well that François was able to report that 'by two that afternoon our squares were being protected by a rampart of dead men and horses. In addition, there was also a large number of men, more or less badly wounded, screaming like wild beasts. I have never seen a battlefield covered with quite so many casualties. They began some 20 paces from our ranks.'

Even so, as Millet noted, 'we were stuck there from six in the morning until four that afternoon and our ammunition was running short'. Had the cartridges run out, defeat, and a massacre, would have been inevitable. Even so, the weary, sunburnt and thirsty soldiers were on the cusp of collapse when, at four that afternoon, 'we heard firing from behind the enemy lines. At first we thought that the enemy must be receiving reinforcements but then we saw them begin to fall back, making us think that it was our side which had been reinforced. And so it was, it was General Bonaparte who arrived to support us with General Bon. He had driven the enemy before him and seized 400 camels loaded with weapons, food and the baggage of Ibrahim Bey.'

Napoleon had hurried over from Acre with Bon's division, his Guides and some cavalry under Leturcq. The sight of relief lead to a final push and it was the French turn to surge forwards:

No sooner had General Kléber seen and had confirmed to him that the reinforcements were French than he sounded the charge. The drum beats began and the soldiers advanced. Think how happy we were to see ourselves saved in such a moment. The mere sound of the drums restored our courage as we pushed against the multitude of cowardly Orientals, and they just broke and fled like sheep before hungry wolves.

Élie Krettly of the Guides actually formed part of those reinforcements and he had charged into the fray only to be brought short by a determined but dismounted Mameluke:

He broke my sword when he hit it with his scimitar but I recovered quickly and threw myself at him, resolved to die fighting. Fortunately, I grabbed him by his beard and, swinging him around so that his head was against the chest of my horse, I hit him so hard with the butt of my pistol that I killed him.

The battle cost the French six killed and seventy-four wounded, whilst 6,000 enemy dead were piled up around the French position. Lucet felt it more important to record that 'we took forty camels laden with food and supplies'.[30] Few prisoners were taken, although François has it that 300 prisoners were captured but later executed at Acre.

Having destroyed the army hoping to relieve that city, Napoleon spent the night at the monastery of Nazareth, dining with the Italian-speaking Spanish abbot. Then, after seeing the wounded taken care of, and the final anointing of the dying Venture de Paradis, the general returned to his siege. Venture's colleague, Pierre-Amédée Jaubert, saw that the French infantry, tired and frustrated, would have welcomed the miracle of being able to turn water into wine just then, but, instead, took out their frustration on the villages of Soulyn and Genin. Millet had seen 'a dragoon of the 3rd Regiment' killed there, and he recorded their retribution as 'we pillaged the place and killed the people for what they had done'. The unit then made its way back to Nazareth and, from there, to the absolving waters of Galilee. Vaxelaire was also present but encountered more accommodating villagers who 'brought us food, whilst some of us made soup from the waters of the

---

30. Miot says that, following the capture of a convoy, 'the soldiers passed the night celebrating, dancing and praising the desserts from Damascus that they had gorged themselves on. They said that they could not remember having had such a good feast.'

Sea of Galilee, and others washed their feet in the waters where John the Baptist baptised our lord, whilst others undressed and bathed in the lake'.

It was a strange experience for those who had learned the catechism of the atheists in the years following the revolution, but it was a short-lived one, for the victorious men were soon obliged to return to a siege where success was proving more elusive. Still, the destruction of the relief army had, as François noted, 'restored our confidence and encouraged our zeal. We had food and, to add to our joy, we heard that Admiral Perée was before Jaffa with the siege artillery.' The little fleet had indeed reached Jaffa on 15 April, and Boyer brought the four 18-pounders and three 24-pounder siege guns to the camp the following week. They were soon hammering that 'blasted tower' which seemed to inspire peculiar loathing amongst the gunners. François was glad to be back so he could assist them in their work:

I helped man a 32-pounder [*sic*] and at each shot I saw stones fall from the ramparts in great quantity but the other guns only fired against that cursed tower even though it was almost demolished.

The state of the tower persuaded the generals that a fresh assault might now succeed and so, on 24 April, with batteries firing and mines going off, the newly returned infantry were fed into the slaughter. Millet and his comrades had barely had time to recover from their peregrinations before being launched against the walls:

Arriving back, we found that the only survivors were the wounded and they told us they had launched eleven assaults, and always been beaten back. We rested an hour and were then directed into the trenches. When we reached the spot where the commander-in-chief stood we were sent towards the breach which now seemed practicable and not so hard to reach. Our scouts went first and opened fire against the tower. But the English and the besieged took them in flank by issuing out of a passageway beneath it. The English also opened up with their sloops, bombarding the area in such a way that the ditches were soon full of the dead, the dying and those buried beneath the falling rubble.

Laporte had watched as 'the military bands began to play at nine precisely and the signal was given to detonate the mine. There was a delay, and we were all tensely waiting, but one of the three mines did go off ... but only brought down some of the wall of the tower opposite the trenches in our centre. A few Turks on the upper storeys were blown into the air and our grenadiers took advantage of the thick smoke and astonishment to attack.'

Vaxelaire was sent forward but did not make it as far as the walls:

We found ourselves at the foot of a huge pile of debris from a large wall our gunners had brought down whilst we were away in Nazareth.

As we stood looking at this mound our commanders shouted 'start climbing, start climbing'. I was amongst the first up towards the breach and found a general next to me. He pushed me forwards, saying 'go on' and, as I did so, I was hit by a ball in the arm and as I watched the blood flowing out another hit me in the neck and came out behind my ear. This one knocked me backwards and I was lucky for had I remained standing any longer I would have been covered in wounds.

Napoleon had indeed issued a dram of brandy to his grenadiers and sent them to take advantage of the surprise and, despite Ottoman grenades and sharpshooters, the foot of the tower was briefly occupied before the French were forced back. The exercise was repeated again on 25 April, this time with some grenadiers of the 18th Line establishing themselves in the edifice. However, the next day the Turks opened holes in the ceiling and dropped grenades and shells onto the French on the floor below, killing six grenadiers and wounding twelve out of the twenty who still held out.

News of another death followed when the chief engineer, General Caffarelli, who had been hit by a bullet 'fired by one of the capable Albanian marksmen' a fortnight earlier, died from gangrene.[31] Grief and humiliation merged with anger, but, still not reconciled to defeat, the French launched yet another attack on the afternoon of 1 May, this time sending the 85th Line and Napoleon's Guides to the slaughter. The defenders rained stones down upon them from the ramparts, opened fire to shouts of 'Allah, Allah' and drove the French elite back, taking the head of the colonel of the 85th as a trophy.

Now real desperation began to show. On 4 May, Napoleon decided to hazard a night attack in the hope of surprising his enemy. Laporte watched the French artillery soften up the defences in a nocturnal bombardment:

It was quite an impressive sight, especially as many of our soldiers had not seen a city under siege before, and this spectacle consisted of six luminous globes arcing majestically so as to fall on the Turks on the ramparts. They exploded, the horizontal blast slicing through moustaches, arms, bodies, legs and pipes ... our amusement at this sight was not, it seems, shared by Djezzar and his men because, a moment later, there was a sortie but, despite the darkness, they were well-received and many of them remained there on the ground.

Then as Rampon's assault was launched François found that the enemy was ready and waiting:

---

31. He was buried next to Napoleon's tent, and his heart later removed and taken to France.

The ramparts were lit up with lanterns and pots with resin were being thrown down to light the ditch. The harbour was as bright as daylight. The signal was given at ten and we leapt out of the trenches and some opened fire and others went forward with the bayonet. It was a success and we seized some positions and beat the enemy back. My company entered one of their batteries and fought with the Turks as we attempted to take three guns. However, the fire from the walls was so intense that, after fifteen minutes, we could barely hold out. Captain Sabattier was wounded by seventeen sabre cuts, our lieutenant was killed as well as sixty-three NCOs and soldiers. Only nine of us with the 2nd lieutenant made it back to our lines. ... We were furious over our bad fortune, cursing Acre, its governor and that Phelippeaux who had apparently even told the Turks that their custom of not fighting during the night was inimical.[32]

These repeated defeats reinforced the sense that Acre was impregnable and Napoleon was fallible. Bernoyer was hardly alone when he mused that 'the genius and good fortune which, like an enchantment, has hitherto carried Bonaparte to victory now seem to have stumbled before the walls of Acre'. He saw the soldiers grow mutinous to the point of turning renegade:

Whenever the commander-in-chief came out of his tent he was insulted or violently threatened. This discontent was openly shown by the soldiers but also by officers and generals who did not hide their views on the matter. General Murat, always frank, told Bonaparte that he was the executioner of his own soldiers.

A certain officer of engineers called Favier ranted in the hearing of Napoleon 'against those men hungry for conquest who sacrifice so many victims to their ambition' and Laporte, stuck in the trenches, saw 'rage and despair engraved on all faces'. Gerbaud, uncharacteristically, drifted into depression, merely listing those lost in this hopeless adventure: 'Since the start of the siege the division of Bon has 350 men *hors de combat*, Lannes' 166, Reynier's 169, the artillery 120, the engineers 139.'

His frustration was understandable, but had he known that Djezzar had just evacuated his wives and treasure, and was running out of ammunition, then he might have found some consolation. Napoleon's generals also sensed a change and tried another assault on the tower. However, their men had clearly had enough, with the 69th Line even refusing to advance. Gerbaud

---

32. The attack was launched by the scouts drawn from Bon's division. Peyrusse noted that each regiment had formed 'companies of scouts, with the intention of giving the grenadiers a rest' and Napoleon wanted them commanded by officers suitable for promotion.

then recorded that, once the fighting died down, 'the general reviewed the division and reproached the grenadiers of the 69th, threatening to have them dressed in women's clothing'.[33]

Then, after fifty days of siege, the decisive moment arrived. A breach by the tower had appeared and the besieged were struggling to repair it under intense French artillery fire. Lacorre was transfixed until he saw eighteen sail appear off the coast. Happy rumours soon spread that they were French transports bringing supplies, perhaps even Admiral Bruix's Toulon squadron with reinforcements,[34] but it was soon obvious that the ships were Turkish. Laporte heard that 'twenty-five sail had come from Constantinople' bringing Ottoman infantry from Rhodes. These relatively fresh troops included Sultan Selim's finest, soldiers ironically trained in modern tactics by those same French advisers Napoleon had once dreamed of joining.

Hoping to claim victory before the reinforcements could disembark, and exploit the breach that the siege guns were relentlessly widening, General Lannes sent in another reckless attack on 8 May, nominating General Rambeaud to place himself at the head of a column of grimly determined grenadiers. 'The troops were ordered to mount an assault,' noted Richardot. 'They arrived bursting with courage and enthusiasm; the grenadiers, led by General Rambaud [*sic*], were placed at their head and they were launched at the breach. ... The column ground to a halt, opened fire, pushed forwards and attempted to gain the breach. At this critical moment General Lannes pushed through the soldiers, reached the head of the column and saw at once that it was impossible to go further as the fire coming from the besieged was just too intense.'

Major Charles Nicolas d'Anthouard de Vraincourt also watched the attack:

The breach between the harbour and the main tower was deemed practicable. General Rambaud [*sic*] and 300 scouts led the way followed by Lannes' division in two columns with the 13th on the right, the 69th on the left and the 22nd Light in reserve. We could hear shooting so they had made it inside. The city looked like it would fall

---

33. D'Anthouard confirms this, writing that 'the grenadiers of the 69th refused to advance'. Only Sergeant Major Teris rushed forwards and, upon his return, he was promoted to second lieutenant.

34. Bruix had been sent into the Mediterranean to join forces with the Spanish and drive the English from that sea. It was then thought he could either reinforce Napoleon or, according to subsequent orders, bring him back to Italy. Unfortunately, the Spanish were not energetic allies and Bruix spent some fruitless weeks cruising off Italy before returning to Toulon. He actually carried orders to Napoleon from the government in Paris which requested the general's return to Europe.

and even the wounded encouraged those climbing the slope to hurry. Unfortunately, one of the idlers on the staff observed that the Turks were barricading themselves into the nearby houses and were firing from there. The commander-in-chief suggested that sappers be sent to break down the doors. The order 'let the sappers pass' rang out just as the two columns were on the cusp of entering the breach. There were no sappers but the Turks were pouring shot down on the head of our columns, who, hesitating as they were receiving no instructions to advance, then fell back to avoid the shot. The ends of the column thought we had been forced to retreat and fled back to the safety of the trenches.

Lieutenant Laval heard that the cry 'we have been cut off from the breach' was the real reason the attackers had retreated. Laporte actually saw the Turks launch an attack in the French flank, their men 'consisting of the newly disembarked coming out in formation rather like Europeans. We brought down the heads of the column but they returned three times.' The Ottoman reinforcements from Rhodes had made all the difference. Led up from the harbour by Sir Sidney Smith, they had burst through the gates and taken the French in flank. General Lannes was wounded in a counterattack and only dragged 200 metres to safety by his feet. General Rambeaud was not so fortunate and died in the fighting. Meanwhile some men of the 85th Line under Captain Jean-Joseph Tarayre found themselves stuck in the tower, hanging a flag from it to beckon for help. The French tried to oblige the following day but Lieutenant Laval found the already redoubtable redoubts stronger than ever:

The signal was given at eleven. We had crawled to within ten paces of the enemy and were lying down waiting for the signal. It was a mine going off. We then sprang up like lions and into a covered way. We killed, were killed, massacred and were massacred. Few Turks escaped, and we remained in possession until daylight. The grenades and firebombs the enemy dropped on us caused us serious loss. From our regiment alone there were 15 officers killed, including Boyer. The soldiers died in proportion. I was bruised by the stones they were throwing at us from the ramparts and my canteen of brandy was hit by a musket ball.

The Ottoman reinforcements not only bolstered the ramparts, they allowed the besieged to once again come out in force to disrupt the French siege works. François met them in the ditches as he and his exhausted comrades attempted to drive the Turks back into the city:

I jumped down into the midst of some Turks and a few of them attempted to grab me, some pulling me by my clothes, others seizing my musket. I could hardly defend myself in the confined space, my barbarous enemies being so close to me, but, fortunately, I had surprised them and they, perhaps unaware of what they were about to face, were content to try and drag me back into the city. Just then our men arrived, pushing forward, and jumping down after me, and the surprised Turks let go of me and ran for the city. I had been so caught up in the fighting that I had not thought of the danger I faced. My tunic was torn to shreds and I had to replace it by taking one off a corpse.[35]

There were plenty of Turkish corpses too, for Laporte saw that any enemy wounded left behind were quickly finished off:

The ground was covered with their dead and wounded, and we always took great care to finish these off with the bayonet as our experience showed, indeed we had seen for ourselves, how they cut the heads off our wounded and even our dead who fell into their power.

As Kléber's remaining detachments marched in from watching the Jordan, Napoleon prepared for one last desperate gamble. Kléber's men were fresh and enthusiastic, even dancing the farandole as they drank brandy in their camp the night before the attack. At dawn on 10 May a dance of quite a different kind began and General Verdier, still limping after a fall from his horse at Nazareth the month before, led the grenadiers of the 19th and 75th Line forwards with some sappers. François says he took part in an infantry attacking to the left as a diversion:

We reached the enemy and cut them down, I myself finishing a few off. We continued on bravely, this time thinking that we would get into the city but, unfortunately, the same obstacle brought us short: a second line of defence behind the breach.

Successive attacks were launched, and even General Murat, doyen of the cavalry, carried a standard towards the breach, exhorting the soldiers forward until, as Miot noted, 'he was shot, musket balls catching at his cravat and coat', forcing him back. General Verdier was also forced to abandon the breach, where the French had briefly held out, but General Bon was less fortunate, being fatally wounded with a bullet in the abdomen. François had also been hit and had had his arm broken, as had his friend, Noel, hit by a roundshot which 'killed three sergeant majors and quartermasters, and cut the legs off my friend Noel, the sergeant-major, and a quartermaster, and sending the brains of another sergeant-major, another of my friends, into my face'.

---

35. Doguereau's brother was mortally wounded during this sortie by the defenders.

These were hard losses to bear, and Acre, although wounded, had held out. Napoleon admitted defeat, although he was extremely bitter about it according to François Vigo-Roussillon: 'The commander-in-chief was extremely frustrated and his anger was primarily directed at Sir Sidney Smith and the English.'[36]

Peyrusse was also bitter, writing home to his mother that 'it has been decided that the town of Acre shall not fall to us; the good fortune of an adventurer and a brigand have triumphed over ours ... Given the manner in which the general had hitherto conducted the siege, we feared that he might wish to bury himself in the place, but he sacrificed his glory to the greater good and we prepared for our march back.' It began on 19 May. The men, grumbling that Napoleon's siege had had the same effect as 'lobbing a shell into a shitty puddle', were already in a foul mood. They were right to be, for the retreat, as Vigo-Roussillon noted, was going to be an ordeal:

We had more than 1,200 wounded to transport back, and we had to spike our artillery before Acre and threw our gunpowder into the sea. Then the army, or what was left of it, marched back into the desert it would have to retreat across for 240 miles. All the wounded were carried on stretchers exposed to the sun of Syria and consequently suffering a great deal. Those that carried them were tormented by fatigue, hunger and thirst.

Some effort had gone into transporting the wounded as the army retreated. Peyrusse, for example, saw how 'the wounded were loaded onto camels or donkeys but lots of the incurably sick were abandoned. They took care to have them poisoned and the hospital burnt down.' Millet noted that 'all the officers with horses were obliged to dismount and even the commander-in-chief gave up his horses so that the wounded could be carried'. The anonymous officer of the 32nd Line specified that the wounded were supposed to have been sent off by sea to Egypt: 'Two convoys were organised, each of 500 men, and set off; one via Damietta, using little boats from the port and sailing along the coast, the other via El-Arich, escorted by a battalion of the 69th Line.' The port of Tantourah was the collection point for the wounded but, in fact, it was there that Bonnefons saw the invalids 'laid out on the beach. We had the misfortune to have to abandon these people.' Peyrusse disagrees:

We arrived at three in the afternoon. We had hoped that everything would have been evacuated by now but we found 700 or 800 wounded

---

36. Napoleon had indeed earlier lambasted the British for having supported Djezzar and turned a blind eye to his atrocities, in a critique so cutting that Smith had told his officers that he would go out and challenge Napoleon to a duel.

or sick, twenty or so guns, 1,200 roundshot and a boat to ship all that out. We made a quick decision. We threw all the guns and shot into the sea and burnt the limbers. We took the horses and mules and we sent the wounded off leaving just a dozen behind us.

The wounded would have to make their way to Jaffa as best they could. Vaxelaire, injured at Acre but still capable of walking, acted as escort to less fortunate comrades:

We had collected as many horses, donkeys and camels as we could to carry the wounded and sick who could not march and we camped in the desert at night. The plaintive cries from these unfortunate men were relentless and made me shudder.

François's friend Noel, who had lost his legs at Acre, was at least carried across Palestine by 'twelve men on a stretcher even though seven of them died'. That retreat was a harsh one even for those in one piece. Bonnefons 'heard some shots and ran over from the convoy. What a horrible sight, for there were soldiers who, not being able to withstand the torments of thirst any more, had suicided [*sic*] themselves.'

Bitterness was universal and Vertray saw that 'orders were issued that each village or town we passed through was to be razed'. The walls of Caesarea [Keisarya] were blown up, as the walls of Jaffa would be the following week, and later the wells along the line of march were destroyed by sappers. Miot notes that 'we began to burn the villages and farms as the inhabitants had committed numerous murders and attacked our convoys; besides, more prudent than our enemies, we wanted to make it impossible for them to follow us by depriving them of the means to follow us to Egypt'. Moiret also wrote that 'in order to slow the enemy pursuit, the army took the precaution (a deplorable consequence of warfare) to blow up all the forts, set fire to all the villages and burn down all the fields of wheat along our route'. Merme of the dragoons agreed, stating that 'we set fire to everything as we fell back, pillaging and devastating the countryside to cover our retreat and to deprive the enemy of food'. Only the generous Doguereau felt sorry for the poor peasants:

We burnt down the olive grove, and, as we left, also destroyed the fields and the village. Wherever the locals had fled to, they must have seen the flames marking their ruin and the destruction of their homes. These unfortunates, who hated the tyrant who oppressed them as much as we ourselves did, were the same people we had told we were coming to make happy. They were ruined by our retreat as we laid their lands to waste with fire and sword.

Some of the Syrian refugees who had left with the army for fear of Djezzar's retribution[37] were also suffering, but the vagabond army, 'a curious sight, dressed as we were with whatever we could find, for we had cut up Turkish coats to make red, green, blue or yellow trousers',[38] was also pitiful to behold. It reached Jaffa on 24 May and, whilst a distribution of tobacco and brandy raised spirits, another tragedy also awaited. There were some 1,500 dying and wounded, not only those recently evacuated from Acre such as generals Lannes and Veaux, but also those who had been injured at the fall of Jaffa. But there were others there, too, for the town was full of plague victims, as François Vigo-Roussillon relates:

> A large hospital had been established where those suffering from the plague were kept. The fort was blown up and a decision was made to abandon the sick. They were certain to be killed as the Arabs following us would finish them off. Napoleon apparently ordered his chief medical officer, Desgenettes, to poison them with opium. Opinion among the troops was that they were then indeed poisoned. Nobody saw anything but what we did see was that a number of amputees and those with serious wounds were left behind as, according to the soldiers, they were no longer useful to the commander-in-chief.

Napoleon apparently visited the hospital to urge the sick to make efforts to leave with the retreating army. Some could not and Niello-Sargy heard that Napoleon had suggested poisoning those who were to be abandoned:

> Whilst we waited in Jaffa the commander-in-chief, who had already proposed administering a fatal dose of opium to those sick and beyond hope as we quit Acre, repeated this horrible suggestion. He met with the stubborn resistance of Doctor Desgenettes and, being unable to persuade him, turned instead to the army's chief pharmacist [Claude Royer]. Just as the sick and wounded were being evacuated, some by sea to Damietta, others by land to El-Arich, rumours began that

---

37. Jaubert had been the interpreter when Napoleon had promised those Christian Syrians and Druze who had supported him land and exile in Egypt. Napoleon had also promised to return 'in less than six months' to 'chase away the brigand who oppresses you'.

38. Laporte and his men were also by now in rags, and they were 'down to a cravat and a few shreds of clothing, having fought nine times since coming over from Italy with Bonaparte'.

400 or 500 of those sick with the plague, and so who could not be transported, would be poisoned for humane reasons.[39]

François, as ever, was present and jotted down some names and numbers:

> At Jaffa we came across the plague house and, in order to spare those soldiers who were suffering from that disease, Bonaparte ordered that a secret committee be formed to rule on the fate of these unfortunates. His idea was to poison them in order to prevent them from that horrible fate which awaited them should they fall into enemy hands alive. Some thirty were poisoned and eighteen of them survived, among them Gariot the son of our lieutenant.[40]

Good Dr Desgenettes was reluctant to poison patients but the pharmacist, Claude Royer, proved his conscience was biddable and obtained 6 litres of the poison known as the Laudanum of Sydenham from a certain Mustapha Hadji. This seems to have been administered to thirty plague patients who could not walk. Lieutenant Laval later met a soldier from his regiment who told him this remarkable tale:

> He told me he had escaped from the hospital at Jaffa. There they had given him a drink telling him it was to give him strength to cross the desert. As he was next to the pot he took a second dose and then sicked it all up. He saw that the others who had taken the drink had died so he left the hospital and marched along after the army.

The 200 plague victims who did try to follow the army faced a fate just as cruel. They could not keep up and were soon abandoned in the sand. Doguereau saw 'men with the plague who had collapsed by the roadside carrying what they had, and imploring everyone who passed by to give them something so that they could continue to follow the army and not be abandoned'. Millet was in the rearguard:

> As we began to leave Jaffa we saw some twenty-five men who were sick with the plague. Those who could still walk came to us to implore our

---

39. Laporte heard the rumours that 'they were poisoned whilst others had it that they were simply abandoned counting on the English to intercede with the Turks on behalf of these victims of war'.

40. The officer of the 32nd thought that 'fifty convalescents remained, reduced to misery by the disease. A few found the strength to follow the army and others, reduced to a desperate state, remained behind in the hospital. It is believed that they were given opium to poison them, put an end to their suffering and prevent them from falling into the hands of the cruel Turks.'

help, something which we could not do without exposing ourselves to this cruel disease. We did what we could for them, then camped in the gardens, quitting the place at dawn. Those of the sick who could follow us did so. General Kléber, who was with us, tried not to abandon them but the excessive heat, their thirst and the effects of the disease, soon took its toll as they were unable to support so many woes at once. We retreated slowly to help them but were soon obliged to leave them to the ferocious Bedouins who cut their heads off as we watched. We fired a few shots but we were too far off to do much harm.

General Kléber, commanding a rearguard which left Jaffa two hours after the main body, himself saw how 'a grenadier of the 19th afflicted by the plague begged one of his comrades to finish him off and his comrade, showing remarkable coolness and resolve, rendered him this service'.[41] Whilst Richardot saw 'some soldiers in the rearguard aim and threaten to fire at a few of their comrades who had come down from the [plague] hospital in order to attempt to rejoin the army'. Merme, riding along with his fellow dragoons, was astonished to see 'one of those suffering from the plague grab the tail of a horse belonging to one of our officers. The officer, seeing this, cut the tail off with his sword and it remained in the hands of the sick man.'

Miot shuddered that 'if you want to survive the army then try not to have need of anyone, but, above all, stay healthy'. The healthy had marked their passage with a trail of dead horses and camels, and the dying wounded left to their fate. Scalding winds and sand storms pursued the remains of Napoleon's expeditionary force during its flight into Egypt, but things would soon improve once the men left the horrors of the Promised Land behind. Egypt came as a relief. Moiret was just pleased to be back, noting sardonically that 'in order to tolerate mediocrity with patience, one has to have endured misery' whilst Laporte, catching sight of the palm trees of Salheyeh, went further and sounded positively joyful:

Two days' march from Cairo we received full rations for the first time since leaving for Syria, that is we had fresh bread, meat and vegetables. We had a good soup. We felt as if we had come home after enduring so much during that cursed campaign.

The drummer Durand was also glad to be returning to something resembling home. The shops and cafes of Damietta, 'that place we had experienced so many unimaginable pleasures before leaving for Palestine', allowed the

41. Kléber apparently told some of the plague patients, 'My children, I shall look after you and you shall share whatever it is that I have. However, do not get too close for I do not intend the plague to be the cause of my demise.'

troops to 'once again indulge ourselves. We had a great dinner which was well-cooked and washed down with that liquid which warms the heart. Then, after dinner, we began to go off to the right and to the left in search of our former acquaintances. I discovered my girl, they discovered theirs.' Laporte says that when they reached Selbes 'we went into the French bars and the Turkish cafes, and spent much of the night drinking and telling the story of our unfortunate adventures to those French who had remained in garrison here'. When asked about their friends 'we replied that such and such had been killed at Jaffa, killed in a sortie at Acre, killed in an assault on the same city, killed by the plague, killed at Mount Tabor, or killed by the Nablusians, and they were relieved when we said so and so was just wounded'.

The death toll, which stood at 2,200 of Napoleon's finest, with the same number of sick and wounded, shocked everyone, but so too did the appearance of those survivors who trickled back. Vaxelaire limped into his depot only to be met by his bemused comrades, who exclaimed, 'How ugly you all are, we hardly recognised you! How black you have become, you are like devils.'

It had been a bitter experience. Kléber was bold enough to set his frustration down on paper, telling General Dugua that these French devils 'had committed enormous sins in the Holy Land, and behaved foolishly, but we must let the curtain of the Tabernacle hide those and not be seen to be lifting it for fear that the Almighty One, in all his glory, will punish us for our temerity'.

The almighty General Bonaparte was indeed glad to draw a veil over the episode, but he now required his exhausted subordinates to make one final effort. Knowing that rumours of defeat would unsettle Egypt, and undermine his rule, he would have to frame his adventures in the Holy Land as a victory. So as he approached the capital of his colony he formed up his men, placing them into columns and ordering them to follow him into Cairo to take part in a stage-managed triumph.

9

Arrivals and Departures

On 14 June, after spending two hours 'baking under the sun', as Jean-Pierre Doguereau put it, the survivors of the defeated army entered Cairo through the Gate of Victories. There had been something a little biblical in the orders the officer of dragoons received to ensure that 'each man was to wear a sprig of palm leaves in his cap as a mark of victory', although he noted that the damned 'grenadiers of the 69th Line were forbidden from doing so as the commander-in-chief wished to single them out for punishment for having refused to attack'.

That commander first greeted the Divan as it came out to meet him. He chided this council for having seemingly believed rumours of his death, assuring its members that he would not die 'until he had trampled under his feet the last of the Mamelukes'. He was then offered a Mameluke by way of atonement, and given another gift, a superb charger, held by this exotic new valet. Lieutenant Vertray marvelled at the sight:

> Sheikh El-Bekri, the most revered of the descendants of Mohammed, presented Bonaparte with a superb black Arab horse, richly harnessed, as well as a Mameluke, Roustan [sic]. Bonaparte, mounted on the horse which had just been presented to him, entered the town in triumph.

François confirms the gift of the horse, predictably named Sultan, and the Armenian slave Roustam Raza. 'Bonaparte was given the present of a superb black Arabian horse which,' he noted, 'had a golden harness covered in pearls and precious stones and which was led by a young Mameluke called Roustam, a slave of the sheikh who presented the horse. The intendent of the Copts gave Bonaparte two camels.'

Roustam, who joined Napoleon's Chinese valet in the general's household, also left an account of the triumph and of his first, and disappointing, sight of his new master:

> Bonaparte returned to Cairo. I saw him for the first time as he was returning. El-Bekri had ridden on to greet him with his Mamelukes and with some dignitaries. We had a magnificent black horse with us, all caparisoned in the Mameluke style. This is what I thought when I first saw him. He was covered in dust and out of breath. He was wearing cavalry boots, white kerseymere breeches and a general's tunic. His skin was dark, he wore his hair long, powdered and tied in a queue. It wasn't a favourable impression.

Napoleon, quenching his thirst[1] and smartening up, then entered the capital in style, hoping to convince the population he was back from a successful mission to purge Egypt of its troublesome neighbours. His troops marched along behind. The French tried to make the occasion seem as much like a Roman triumph as they could, escorting sixteen captured officers and General Abdallah,[2] and bearing seventeen captured flags. The French then entered Azbakiyya Square where the happy phalanx was met by 'the curious sight of a mixed crowd of Europeans, Janissaries, Greeks, Copts, peasants, North Africans, Nubians, other Africans and Mamelukes on horseback and on foot. Our band and that of the Egyptians led our column which was led by a delegation of members of the council, the military and civilian administration of the Copts, some notable merchants and a few others distinguished by their birth or wealth.'

Laporte of the disgraced 69th Line nevertheless felt the welcome was a warm one:

> They were surprised to see us, a little army which they had believed to have been condemned to death when we left, little thinking that a handful of infantry like us could survive such a perilous expedition. ... They looked out for those they had known during our stay at Cairo before we left and when they spotted someone they knew they hailed him and shook him warmly by the hand or even embraced them. These good people asked us naively what had become of our fine grenadiers and carabineers who had been admired by the entire city, and they wanted to know whether they would soon be arriving. We replied sadly

---

1. Pierre-Amédée Jaubert recalled that 'the general, seeing among the crowd a water-carrier carrying his tank and a cup, asked to drink and, after refreshing himself, asked me to give the man 100 sequins or 1,000 francs'.
2. Abdallah was to be ransomed but, when no money was forthcoming, the French cut his throat in the citadel of Cairo on 8 July.

that, yes, perhaps they would come, but they guessed our meaning and expressed their sadness at our loss.

The bittersweet return at least found Cairo at peace. Egypt beyond was more restless. General Desaix was still pacifying the south, securing territory whilst his band of scholars conducted their archaeological campaign to survey the treasures along the Nile. In the northern provinces the skeletal French garrisons, stripped of troops by the war in Syria, were facing an insurrection stirred by the enigmatic Ahmet El-Mahdi, the Angel or the Chosen One. In March 1799 this messianic rabble-rouser, a former juggler from Morocco, had thrown together a band of fanatics, deserters and the disaffected which, according to Niello-Sargy, 'included 10,000 believers'. The Mahdi told them he had been sent to Earth to exterminate the French, and that by throwing sand in the air they were invulnerable to the infidels' bullets, before leading his credulous followers out from the oasis of Jupiter and against the isolated French outposts around Damanhour and the Nile delta. General Lanusse was eventually sent against this prophet and his Oulad-Ali [sons of Allah] but not before, as Bricard relates, 'several small detachments of the Legion Nautique and Legion Maltaise were murdered in their camp near Damanhour by a mass of locals who had united with the Arabs. Only one Frenchman escaped as he was hidden by an old woman. A body of 200 men on its way to reinforce these men saw with horror how they had been murdered.' Lanusse responded to this murder with murder of his own, burning down Damanhour on 9 May, and bluntly informing his superior, Dugua, that 'Damanhour ceases to exist and between 1,200 and 1,500 of its inhabitants have burnt to death or been shot'.[3]

That June the Mahdi was in flight, his followers drinking from the cup of death or fleeing into the desert, but northern Egypt soon saw the arrival of another and much more formidable enemy. On the afternoon of 11 July, a few weeks after Napoleon had entered Cairo in pretend triumph, François-Etienne Sanglé-Ferrière was on watch by the Alexandria lighthouse when he 'caught sight of the white sails of a fleet heading for the far side of the new harbour. As they approached we saw that the fleet was vast and that those in the van were initially heading to the lighthouse before some signals made them veer further east. In the course of that day we counted about 200 sail heading for Aboukir. It was a Turkish fleet and it was landing some 20,000 Janissaries.'

---

3. Lanusse was a rather brutal officer. On 20 October 1798 he had stormed Kafr-el-Chair, killing a rebel dubbed Abou-Chair, then telling Napoleon, 'I would have preferred to send him to you alive, but I am having his head carried through all the villages I pass through and then tomorrow I shall send it on to you at Cairo.' A week later he informed his commander that he would not be sending the head after all, as it had gone off.

This Ottoman expeditionary force then disembarked on this fatal shore and, on 17 July, stormed the French earthworks at Aboukir which were overcome like a ship battered by waves. Then the little fort under Major Vinache also fell and most of the garrison were massacred, although some were saved by the intervention of a mysterious officer serving with the Turks, Lieutenant Colonel John Bromley.[4] An understandably nervous Lieutenant Thurman was then sent out from Alexandria on reconnaissance, 'although I was suffering from a condition common amongst riders. I kept up, through clenched teeth.' Nothing worse befell him, and he was able to report back that 200 men in the fort had indeed had their heads cut off.[5] More intelligence came in, and the officer of the 14th Dragoons heard how 'a spy, disguised as a cucumber merchant, came over to inform us of the latest details'. He evidently had a talent for espionage for he informed the French that 'the troops consisted of Arnauts and troops from Candia, although there were no Christians amongst them other than an English Marine officer'.

Napoleon had been informed of the Ottoman invasion whilst dining in the shadow of the pyramids. Armed with vague estimates of the enemy's strength, the general then concentrated his dispersed army around Ramanieh before moving on to Berket. By 23 July he had 10,000 men gathered at the wells between Alexandria and Aboukir. There, according to Miot, Napoleon gave an exaggerated harangue to his staff in the style of Alexander, and one which perhaps hinted at his own plans should the battle prove victorious, proclaiming that 'this battle will decide the fate of the world'. The troops, waiting by a neglected caravanserai and beyond the ruins of Caesar's castle, were given a simpler talk and heard their general tell them that fate had brought them back to Aboukir to revenge the loss of their fleet. Whatever fate was at stake, preparations now began in earnest and scouts under the engineer Picot were sent out to probe the enemy position. François, newly enlisted in the Camel Corps, was among their number:

The Turkish army was on the peninsula and had two lines of trenches with some artillery to protect its neck. The first line extended a mile from the Aboukir fort whilst their right rested on the shore and some entrenchments by a sandy hill with 1,200 men. A hamlet [Aboukir village], a third of a mile from there, had a further 1,500 men and four

---

4. This was in fact the emigrant Jacques-Jean-Marie François Boudin, Count of Tromelin, who had helped Sidney Smith escape from Paris. He later returned to France and served in Napoleon's armies, commanding a brigade for the emperor.

5. Bricard was closer to the truth when he stated that Captain Vinache of the engineers was spared and thirty-two Frenchmen survived. After being mistreated by the Turks they were sent aboard a British ship and looked after. The troops in the redoubt had been the ones overrun and killed.

guns. The left was further forwards than the centre and a few gunships protected it from between the two lines. Then the [former French] redoubt protected their centre.

Giving just enough time for his largely shoeless infantry to down a swig of welcome brandy, Napoleon attacked at dawn on the 25th.[6] Murat's men and some Guides under a black captain called Captain Damingue were launched against the first line. They broke through as the bulk of the infantry, having caught up, struck the centre and pushed on to the second line where the 18th Line, led by Adjutant Leturcq, tried their luck close to the redoubt. Laval of that regiment says his men advanced but then fell back to lure the Turks out, although the less charitable had it that the regiment was repulsed by the Turks. Whatever the truth, Leturcq and a dozen others were killed but, as the Turks left their positions to deal with the French wounded, Murat, who had returned to help, burst in amongst them with his cavalry. Desvernois and his over-dressed hussars were to the fore:

> My horse was hit by canister and went down, bringing me down too and almost crushing me just as the Turkish infantry began to run forwards from their trenches in the hope of decapitating the wounded. I thought I was done for, but General Lannes with the 22nd Line and a battalion of the 69th, overran the enemy position.

Leaving Desvernois struggling in their wake, the rest of Murat's cavalry galloped on and overran the Turkish defences. François watched as 'our generals saw that there was some confusion as the Turks had climbed out and left their position almost defenceless so they took advantage by ordering a general assault on the redoubt whilst General Murat skirted around the flank. Those who broke into the position were soon assisted by troops launched from our right against the enemy's left.' Indeed, as Murat's men went on to sweep the field, the infantry dealt with the redoubt. Laporte, with the 69th Line fighting alongside the rallied 18th, described how 'we attacked the redoubt, entering it on the left side having swept into the ditch with the 22nd Line and climbed over the parapet. We tried to seize those who were there as they were trapped by the cavalry of Murat and Lannes' men ... these Ottoman fanatics were, however, entirely ignorant of the laws which govern war between civilised nations, or perhaps they did not even think to ask for quarter, and they were all killed or drowned.'

---

6. When General Berthier baulked at such haste and timorously asked which unit should be kept in reserve, he was roundly rebuked with a rather Napoleonic reply: 'Reserve – who do you think I am, General Moreau?' In fact, General Kléber's men were held in reserve.

Desvernois, recovering enough to watch the Turkish position collapse, adds that 'the Turks were forced from their lines and, seeing themselves outflanked, hastily turned to flee. Then the cavalry charged them, broke through their second line and sabred most of them as they fled towards the sea.'

François then saw that 'the Turks with the sea to their backs, turned to fight to the last man' in a final attempt to keep the French at bay. Murat was wounded, being shot in the mouth,[7] as François and his men waded in. He later confessed that 'we just had to cut them down and push them into the sea where our cavalry, along with our men of the Camel Corps, pursued them until they drowned. Those who remained on the shore were bayonetted or cut down and I, not being in the best of health, soon grew tired of sabring and using my weapon.'

Lavalette was a witness as to how the Turks tried to escape vengeful sabres:

> All the Turks could do was to throw themselves into the waves. We could only see the turbaned heads of nearly 10,000 men and it was a terrible sight, watching as they desperately tried to swim out to the English fleet one and a half miles away. Some 2,000 more were on the beach, sheltering under a cliff and we could not get them to understand that they could surrender and lay down their arms. We had to finish them off.

The slaughter on the shore ended just after noon, and Laporte, glancing out to sea, noted that it was 'a sad sight, but at the same time a grand one with thousands of coats and turbans of all colours bobbing on the water and being moved by the waves'. Meanwhile, the French turned to finishing off those few pockets of Turks who, along with their commander, Seid-Mustapha, the Seraskier of Roumelia, still held out. The officer of dragoons found some Janissaries in the village:

> The Turks slung their muskets and came at us with a pistol in one hand and a scimitar in the other. They came again and again. Our horses were covered in blood until, finally, the village was forced by the 22nd Light and the 69th Line.

François Vigo-Roussillon also saw how dangerous this enemy could be:

---

7. He was taken to François-Etienne Sanglé-Ferrière's barge on the Nile. 'The general was wounded quite seriously; a ball had passed through both cheeks.' Napoleon's immortal quip was that Murat had, for the first time in his life, opened his mouth to good purpose.

The soldiers we fought at Aboukir were not the miserable *fellahs* who served the Mamelukes as infantry; they were brave Janissaries who carried muskets without bayonets and who, having fired their gun, swung it behind them and threw themselves at their enemy with a sword and a pistol.

He insists that it was his 32nd Line, rather than the French dragoons, who took the village of Aboukir:

The Turks had established their camp in the village of Aboukir. Mustapha Pacha [*sic*], the commander of their expeditionary force, had fled there with his Janissaries and had taken shelter in one of the bigger houses. Our company of grenadiers attempted to break down the gate, keeping close to the walls so that the Turks could not easily fire at us, although they did manage to drop some heavy stones and pieces of furniture, including a trunk full of coins, on us. The gate was soon forced and we ran into the courtyard. I was first in. A furious Turk came at me sword in hand. I could have shot him but wanted to preserve my bullet for a more extreme situation and so I lowered my bayonet. As the Turk raised his sword arm to strike, I lunged. He tried to parry my blow with his left hand so I pulled back whilst his arm continued its movement. I then thrust again and caught him in the chest. He fell back. I put a foot on his stomach and took his sword. However, he took a dagger from his belt and tried to attack me, so I cut him down with his own sword and my blow almost split him in two. It was an excellent blade that would easily have beheaded me had the Turk parried my blow.

In one of those houses, the French infantry, led by Captain Sudrier, ran to ground the Ottoman general. He had been wounded in the fighting and had lost three of his fingers, so he now willingly surrendered to the equally relieved soldiers. This left just a final and increasingly desperate bastion, a little fort packed with 3,000 Turks under Osman, the son of Seid-Mustapha. Heavy artillery and mortars were consequently brought forward and Gunner Bricard helped man the guns tasked with battering the enemy position. However, on 28 July he was appalled to see 'the Turks launch a sortie ... they had the barbarity to gather fifty local women at the head of their column in the hope that the French would forget their duty and run after the women but the reception they met with proved that such a ruse could never work. Some of the women were amongst the first to fall and the rest we kept as slaves.' Laporte evidently had a better view and noted that, rather than being a ruse, the civilians were actually being ejected because 'food had been so short that they had pushed out many villagers who had taken refuge there, including the women and children'. He says nothing about them being kept as slaves.

The fort endured a horrible siege before, on the morning of 2 August, the starving and thirsty garrison sought terms from General Abdullah Menou. Doguereau then watched as 'a crowd of them appeared at the breach and they threw their weapons into the ditch, and then knelt down before our outposts begging for water and pardon. They were dying of thirst.' Sanglé-Ferrière was also on hand to observe 'the garrison of the fort come out. They threw down their weapons and raced for the wells. These unfortunates had not had anything to drink for three days. They were burned black and seemed more like demons racing out from hell. They say there are 300 dead in the fort and that 1,200 or 1,500, mostly wounded or half dead, have surrendered.'[8]

Defeat had been complete and frightful, but victory brought an awkward kind of glory. It secured Egypt but also rendered absurd any negotiation for an evacuation of the colony. The French were more stuck than ever, but the troops consoled themselves by combing through the bodies and wreckage for valuables. Laporte says they seized 'cooking pots as well as their standards' whilst Thurman watched as 'our soldiers search the dead, the houses, the sand and were even diving in the sea in an attempt to retrieve valuables. I have bought a few precious things from them: a vermillion damask, a fine cutlass, a pair of pistols and a magnificent oriental tent. All for small change.'

Greater prizes were still out of reach, however. Napoleon already knew from Wynand Mourveau and Hamelin that, whilst battles were being won in Egypt, the war was being lost at home.[9] Indeed, Napoleon's conquests in Italy had been lost to the Austrians and Russians that summer, whilst the Directory's armies were also being flushed from Holland and herded back towards the Rhine. The general knew better than most that the French Republic's European empire was crumbling and that France, as well as her republic, might soon be in danger of giving way.

Napoleon, who had wanted to leave Egypt as early as January 1799, saw that he might exploit his victory in Egypt to now leave and save France. The role of the saviour appealed to the general, as well as to a clique in Paris that

---

8. The officer of dragoons was less sympathetic: 'The prisoners we took there are in a pitiful condition. They are half-dead from hunger and they fell on the food that was issued to them. Many have been struck down by illness from only having had sea water to drink. Their bitter obstinacy has been the cause of their demise.' Some 400 of them apparently died following surrender.
9. On 9 February, Hamelin says it was at Boulaq that Napoleon bombarded him with questions on the state of France. 'As I described to him the political situation in Europe, which had been transformed since he had left it, the faults of the Directory, and subsequent French collapse, his indignation knew no bounds. He stormed about ranting, from which I made out the words "poor France ... wasted ... the wretches ... lawyers ... anarchy".'

was ready to save the republic by betraying the revolution, and whilst the first battle of Aboukir had slammed one door shut, the second had pushed another tantalisingly ajar. He made quick use of the opportunity. He had been keeping the fastest frigates available primed for just such an eventuality, although they could do little with Smith's ships hovering off the coast. But Commodore Smith, as well as the nervous mandarins of the admiralty and East India House, might be just as happy to have Napoleon whisked away from the east and from India. So, for once in agreement, the two sides would now nod and wink their way through a series of meetings supposedly about an exchange of prisoners, but with some clandestine undertones. Colonel Marmont, Napoleon's aide-de-camp Merlin and Lieutenant Descorches on the one side, and Bromley, Sidney Smith and his secretary on the other, were kept busy whispering and writing. Merlin makes the opening moves in this drama all sound rather accidental when he says he entered Menou's tent only to encounter

> the secretary [John Keith] to Commodore Sir Sidney Smith as he had been sent there as an envoy to treat for the exchange of prisoners. He said 'the commodore has just received a mailboat carrying newspapers from Europe; as you have been denied news from there for so long, he thought you might read them with pleasure and has sent this packet which he asks me to present to you'. I hastened to take leave of Menou and to leave for Alexandria so I could take these blasted but vital newspapers to General Bonaparte. It was six in the evening and I arrived at Alexandria at just after midnight and found that General Bonaparte had gone to bed and was deep asleep. 'General,' I said, waking him, 'I have bought you a packet of European newspapers (the *Gazette de Francfort* and the *Courrier Français de Londres*). You will see in them that we have suffered a series of disasters.

Merlin observed the effect and recalled that 'as the general sat on the end of his bed and began to read, and he continued to do so for the rest of the night. At every moment angry or indignant exclamations escaped from his lips especially when he read that they had lost in a month the country [Italy] he had conquered with so much glory. On the next day, 3 August, he called in Admiral Gantheaume for an interview which lasted two hours and, on the 4th [*sic*], he left for Cairo.'

Merlin could be forgiven for not knowing that a decision had already been made, but perhaps not for failing to inform us that John Keith had already met Napoleon before he left for Cairo on the 6th. The British had cleverly played on his fears and his ego by telling him the Directory wanted him back to lead their armies in the theatre of his first glories. This part was true, but the Directory had wanted him *and his army* back, and had instructed Admiral Bruix, cruising off Toulon at the end of May, to fetch them. British sea power had cowed Bruix into inaction, but Napoleon was ready to leave whether or not his men were rescued. Indeed, by the time Napoleon reached Cairo preparations were well underway and there Merlin noted the significance of 'twenty camels assembled in the courtyard at headquarters and awaiting their cargo. It confirmed me in my opinion. General Bonaparte was about to quit Egypt.'

Napoleon was aware that this news would trouble the Cairo elite, collaborators who knew what to expect from the Turks should the French abandon them, so he merely informed the Divan that he was embarking on another expedition, which was not quite a lie, and would soon return to build the biggest mosque ever seen, which most certainly was. Meanwhile, Napoleon began to gather up those fortunates who would be returning to Europe with him and, as soon as he received word that the Turkish fleet had gone, and that fate had nodded and winked at Smith to the extent that he had also sailed off to Cyprus, the general ordered his apostles to pack. Monge, one of the few scholars being included, began but rather foolishly raised suspicion by suddenly donating all his books to the Institute library and his wine to a grateful but astonished Conté. Then, on the evening of 17 August, a few hours after six o'clock when Napoleon had received word from Alexandria that the coast was literally clear, Redouté looked out of his window to see 'the commander-in-chief's coach furtively arrive to collect Monsieur Monge and Berthollet. It was presumed they were going on a journey beyond Menouf and most of us thought that they simply could not be abandoning us as they were the ones who had encouraged most of us to come on this expedition in the first place, promising to bring us back safely home.'

Napoleon hurried off, only finding time to bid farewell to Madame Fourès, daintily dressed as a hussar, and was soon at Boulaq where he and his lucky band of 200 Guides, generals and selected scholars climbed aboard some barges to sail down the Nile. Young Merlin was included in this band of brothers and noted that when they reached 'Bad-el-Bakara, we followed the branch of the Nile that leads to Rosetta rather than that one going to Damietta. Napoleon reached Menouf where General Lanusse was in command and he spent twenty-four hours with this officer. During dinner that general pointedly remarked, "They say, my general, that you are going to take ship at Alexandria and go to France; if so, I hope that, once you reach France, you will remember your army in Egypt."'

General Lanusse was already unpopular with Napoleon, having fought a duel with Colonel Junot after the general had apparently insulted the commander-in-chief, but, as François Vigo-Roussillon shows, Napoleon had other concerns just then:

I saw that the commander-in-chief seemed preoccupied as he reviewed us and that when he talked to Berthier it was in worried tones. This contrasted with his aides-de-camp, among them Eugene de Beauharnais and, above all, Marmont, who seemed delighted. Before long Berthier announced that a boat had come to take them up the western branch of the Nile. He resumed a calmer aspect and left. We learnt later that he went on to Alexandria and from there to Aboukir where, on the evening of the 22nd, he embarked on the *Muiron* frigate with Berthier, Lannes, Murat, Marmont, Andreossy, the scholars Monge and Berthollet and a detachment of his Guides.

Vigo-Roussillon had the benefit of hindsight, but it was only at Berket on the way to the coast that Merlin himself learned the true purpose of their expedition. He was delighted: 'One has to have been absent from one's country for more than eighteen months and been beset, throughout that time, by the tribulations and dangers of a barbaric country, to understand the joy we felt when we heard this news.'

The party avoided Alexandria, instead settling on the beach by the camp of the Romans whilst word was sent to the French flotilla to come and fetch them. That little fleet of frigates had been ready by 19 August, three days after Gunner Bricard had noted that 'couriers had arrived from headquarters with orders that two frigates and three brigs be prepared for a long voyage'. Then Captain Dumanoir-le-Pelley had told François-Etienne Sanglé-Ferrière that 'he, the captain, was to command the *Carrère* which was destined for France'. Sanglé-Ferrière must have looked disappointed for the captain quickly told him 'to console myself as I was to come too and that I was to bring ten sailors of my choice, who are all good men and shall be rewarded – but come quick for Bonaparte is already going onboard the *Muiron*'.[10]

On 22 August, Napoleon and his chosen entourage ate their last supper in Africa. 'After the meal,' recounts Roustam Raza, Napoleon's Mameluke bodyguard, 'everyone was really happy and very lively. The soldiers were throwing their knapsacks in the air, the cavalry were handing [180] horses over to those soldiers who were to remain in the country. I turned to ask Monsieur Jaubert, the French interpreter who interpreted for the general, "what does all this mean, I see everyone is so happy". He replied that "we are leaving for Paris, it is good there and it is a large city. Those two frigates that we can see there before us are to carry us to France."'

By now night had fallen and so the party burnt some wood to signal to the ships that they were ready, and waited for the longboats.

---

10. Lavalette says that the two forty-four-gun frigates, the *Muiron* (named after one of Napoleon's aides-de-camp who had died at Arcole) and the *Carrère* (under Captain Dumanoir), were poor sailors. Merlin agrees, saying that they would not survive a six-hour pursuit. However, both frigates had a surplus of sailors and were loaded with blunderbusses, extra sabres and axes in case the British attempted to board them.

Roustam was a little nervous about this first crossing of the sea:

There we climbed aboard some boats that were to take us out to the frigates. The sea was quite rough, with some of the waves breaking over our heads and filling the boats with water. Everyone was sick on the way out apart from me, in fact I was hungry and asking for something to eat.[11]

But Merlin remembered that this scramble to get away would not be frustrated by just a few rough waves or, indeed, anything else:

Everyone, without distinction of rank, threw themselves forward, and their impatience and fear that they would be left behind was such that they waded out up to their knees so they could be the first to climb into the boats. Those who managed did so in a jumbled mass and then showed little consideration. The result was that a few quarrels broke out between the staff officers, although these were promptly forgotten when we reached the frigates. The frigates the *Muiron* and *Carrère* were anchored beyond the roads of the new port, half a cannon shot from the Pharillon. General Bonaparte climbed onto the *Muiron* at nine [in the evening of 23 August].[12]

Then, with forty centuries now presumably looking the other way, Napoleon promptly set sail for France. There were good reasons for the rush, not only the British but also because 'we feared that the garrison at Alexandria might do something when they heard that General Bonaparte was leaving'. The sudden departure would indeed come as a shock to the garrison. Bricard was there and was perhaps the first to realise that they had been abandoned. 'That morning,' he confided, 'we were shocked to see the brigs and frigates

---

11. Lieutenant Paul Bertier of the Guides makes the departure seem quite straightforward: 'Three or four days [sic] after the battle [of Aboukir] General Bonaparte had us embarked for France. He could only take a few of his Guides as everything was done in a hurry. We only knew that we were leaving when we sat down in the longboat and we left behind everything, from linen to money, that would have been useful to us just then.'

12. The *Muiron* had Napoleon, Berthier, Monge, Berthollet, Bourienne, Eugene, Duroc, Merlin, Lavalette and Roustam as passengers. Lannes, Murat, Marmont, Denon (and his pet monkey), Jaubert and Parseval-Grandmaison were on the *Carrère*. The frigates were to be accompanied by the brigs the *Independent* and the *Foudre* (although the latter, carrying captured Turkish standards, only came out later), and the *Revanche*, a four-gun xebec. All carried three months' supplies.

making off. The consternation was great and the departure seemed more like flight in these critical circumstances.'

However, the flight proved anything but quick. A slight breeze set them on their way on the morning of 23 August, but Sanglé-Ferrière soon realised that the leather-clad Venetian-built 'frigates were poor sailors and the winds were often against us'. Even so, as they hugged the African shore, and as Egypt loosened its embrace, the passengers were in no mood to complain and spent their time happily playing cards, talking politics or discussing Plutarch and the rise and fall of Caesars. In September they celebrated the birthday of the republic but also spent days listening to Napoleon 'talk about the Directory with a severity which bordered on disdain'. All were in fine spirits and indeed Sanglé-Ferrière 'saw General Bonaparte on the *Muiron*. He was less severe than before, indeed he was almost laughing.'

He soon had reason to be glad. After seven weeks of boredom and anxiety, and a short stay in his native Corsica, Napoleon was able to disembark at Saint-Raphaël on 9 October 1799. He was welcomed back to France by smiling crowds and promptly broke the law by ignoring quarantine.[13] Napoleon, the fugitive, the criminal, had returned as the saviour. Besides, his criminality hardly mattered now, for, a month later, following a bold coup, Napoleon seized power, declaring himself First Consul and France's chief magistrate.

---

13. A merchant, Jourdan, watched how 'two frigates and two little xebecs, serving as flyboats, entered our gulf but were soon assailed by a northerly wind, which determined them to come and moor in our harbour. They anchored at nine. A rowing boat came ashore telling us what they were about. They had come from Alexandria and the brave Bonaparte was onboard; judge then the joy with which such agreeable news was greeted, and how quickly it spread. He came ashore at ten and one could only hear Long live the Republic, or Long Live Bonaparte!'

10

Stranded

As Napoleon pursued the mirage of destiny, perhaps even sensing the hazy outlines of his imperial crown in the distance, those he had suddenly abandoned in Egypt were left to make sense of his flight. He had, after all, deserted them and they were now abandoned in a distant outpost of a very indifferent empire. The dragoon Merme saw how quickly the army turned against a man they had so recently idolised:

> Bonaparte's departure caused much complaining in the army. They were saying out loud that he had saved himself whilst abandoning us to the mercy of the enemy. They were calling him Bon-a-depart.

Meanwhile, Peyrusse thought that 'the majority could not believe' their commander had abandoned them and stated that there were even rumours that 'Commodore Smith had given Bonaparte a safe conduct for passage back to France' in order for him to overthrow the French government and usher in one which owed favours to Britain.[1] Moiret also sensed treachery, but he was probably the only one to think that Bonaparte had left 'carrying a passport from the court of Berlin'. Over in Cairo, General Dugua, a man who really should have been told about the general's departure, was initially incredulous and thought the news was merely 'a rumour planted by the enemy to stir discontent, excite mutiny and demoralise the army'. Whatever the truth behind the sudden departure, Miot confirms that the ragged army was uniformly appalled by Napoleon's flight:

---

1. Smith's behaviour was certainly strange. He had told the French that he was going for supplies in Cyprus. Still, it seems Napoleon thought this might be a ruse to catch him. It is harder to explain why Smith later delayed sending the *Theseus* after Napoleon's flotilla.

We were at Cairo when we heard that the commander-in-chief had arrived at Alexandria, embarked and left. The news was met with universal consternation. We were used to seeing him as being favoured by good fortune, commanding, as it were, events and had placed our own fate in his hands. We could not see how we could now leave Egypt, our trust in him leading us to believe that our only choice was to now die in Africa. Anger gave way to despondency, and everyone felt the same.

A dejected François agreed:

We were accustomed to seeing Bonaparte as the arbiter of our destinies and now could only imagine that death awaited us in this alien land. The officers and soldiers were indignant, each for his own reasons. They were saying it was Bonaparte's duty to see we were saved.

The scholars were just as bereft. Saint-Hilaire briefly mused on his fate:

Having enjoyed a remarkable career am I now destined to live as a mercenary imprisoned in Constantinople? I am resigned to sharing the fate of the army and the artists and either the scholars shall be dragged with it into the sands of Arabia or we shall regain France only thanks to the generous indulgence of our enemies.

His dark sense of humour quickly gave way to a mounting sense of bitterness:

The poor scholars of Cairo have seemingly been brought here so that one can read a eulogy in the history of Bonaparte. Small people are always the playthings of the great. ... I cannot stand Egypt any longer. I cannot recall but with sadness that which I have left behind, I have abandoned true and good friends in order to come here and exist as though in a monastery or in a small provincial town where our ridiculous ways are all the amusement we have. I have been plagued by disease and my body is so used up that I fear I shall not see my dear parents again.

Meanwhile, Vertray had strategic concerns alongside similar fears:

We had pushed further into the interior of a country that no European army had invaded since the Crusades. We had no secure retreat, no supplies and our only connection to the outside world was a fleet menaced by an enemy more numerous and more capable. When would we return home? What was the point of coming here? It was not like before when we were fighting the enemies of the republic.

Thurman's morale, meanwhile, reached a new low:

> Are we to be exiled forever? And for what? I do not know what France is gaining from all this, aside from some prestige for academics. The idea that so much blood has been spilt and some much suffered for nothing affects each one of us. Our veterans tend to express it thus: 'What the fucking hell are we doing here.'

General Kléber couched his concerns in politer terms. He complained to General Menou that the bird had flown the nest, that the *hero* and his worthy companions had gone, but added, 'I approve of the reasons why Bonaparte has left but I still have much to say on the way he has gone about it.'

It is true that Kléber had more cause to complain than most. For he, the former architect from Alsace, was being left in charge of the disaffected army of Egypt. The painful burden of command lay on his shoulders, and it was all the more awkward because the Alsatian had been doggedly against the campaign from the beginning. Indeed, he had blamed Napoleon's ambition for having exiled them all to Egypt.[2] This was a sentiment the troops shared with their new commander, and this bond, aided by his soldierly reputation, meant that his appointment brought a measure of relief, and hope, to the troops. The officer of dragoons thought that whilst Napoleon's departure had 'stunned the army' the 'appointment of General Kléber as commander rallied the brave. Every soldier was aware of his qualities, his sense of justice, and his integrity. We were safe in his hands.'

Laporte also remarked how, that stifling summer, 'General Kléber's paternal words calmed the anger of the soldiers who were saying out loud that we had been abandoned.' Miot also calmed when he heard Kléber was in charge:

> Big and handsome and turned out like a soldier, Kléber was imposing, his face noble and proud, his eyes bright and piercing, all traits which inspire respect. His voice was deep and he was capable of violence but also reflection, his conversation was educated and he was a fine judge of people. If you heard him talk of Bonaparte you would see that his opinion was at variance with many others and he was far from being an enthusiast.

Vertray thought the Alsatian 'a true friend of the soldier, in the full sense of the term. He did not spare himself on the battlefield and always sought

---

2. Galland, the printer, thought that Kléber 'was the god Mars when at the head of an army, and he knew it and was proud, which made it difficult for him to accept the brilliant reputation Bonaparte had acquired'.

to guarantee the well-being and good humour of his men in cantonment.' Moiret felt justified in adding that 'Bonaparte only ever worked for his own benefit and only kept in view his own progress along the path of fortune, but Kléber was not like that as he dedicated himself to the care and wellbeing of the soldier'. Indeed, Vertray agreed that Kléber 'was more careful than Bonaparte when it came to caring for his troops and in safeguarding their lives'. Miot, however, saw that his popularity extended beyond the army, observing that 'the Turks revered him because he listened to them and I always thought that they had found Bonaparte too short as the Turks often judge a man by his appearance and size. It is not fair, but different people have different ways.'

In many ways he seemed just the man to replace Napoleon. However, the situation that general had left him in was unenviable. Kléber did not so much feel the hand of history on his shoulder as sense it around his throat, for he was assuming responsibility for an army which was trapped, bitter, steadily shrinking and surrounded by encroaching enemies. Hope was dwindling, although Charles Lasalle, a hussar who rode and wrote with panache, seems to have seen a way out: 'Opinions are divided here on the departure of our general. A few (and I think they are the stupid ones) look upon it as nothing but treason. The others, the majority, see it as an opportunity, for either reinforcements shall come or peace will be signed, enabling us to return to dear old France.'[3] Gunner Bricard summarised the more pessimistic view, noting that 'it seemed as though our end would be an unpleasant one and as we had lost all hope of being reinforced; defeat therefore seemed inevitable even if we were at first victorious'.

Bricard was right that relief coming from France was unlikely, but was wrong to exclude other options. There was a chance for an exit rather than sudden death, indeed there was still the tentative option of victory leading to a negotiated evacuation. Some thought the British might help there, although perfidious Albion was more likely to try to encourage desertion and sap French power soldier by soldier. Indeed, in the spring of 1799 Redouté had heard 'a rumour which had been circulating for a number of days that Sir Sidney Smith, the commander of the English troops at Acre, had proclaimed that, in the interests of humanity, he would make welcome any Frenchman who wished to return to France'. Gerbaud soon met a Briton urging his soldiers to turn coat: 'He seemed to be trying to

---

3. Sabretache, 1894, p. 340. Jean-Pierre Doguereau often thought of dear France, too. He wrote that February how 'our friend Chateauvieux found us some wine and made us a vast omelette, and we had a good supper. We talked of our return, and the pleasure we would soon have of seeing our family, and our friends, once again.'

encourage desertion, saying that they would welcome onboard and take to France any who came with them.'[4]

Few deserted but, even so, Kléber's little army continue to shrink. It was a force that had not only lost its commander-in-chief, but many of its key generals.[5] Some, including General Junot and Dumuy, along with the pianist Rigel and the economist Corancez,[6] both presumably needed urgently in France, would also soon get away.[7] Napoleon's flight had triggered a small exodus, leading to another spate of unrest that autumn, something augmented by the colonial government's acute lack of cash. Laval reported that soldiers were so frustrated at not being paid that they 'were even saying that if they fought the English then they would surrender rather than fight'. The 22nd Chasseurs were mutinous but it was the 2nd Light which downed weapons first when, according to Major Schramm, on 22 November the troops were stood in formation from ten in the morning to five in the evening 'waiting for food. At the command march, they began to protest, shouting that we shall not march until we are paid.' François-Michel Lucet was there and watched with concern:

---

4. François saw how some Frenchmen deserted but turned to brigandage rather than the English: 'Many deserters were caught who had organised themselves into gangs. They murdered, robbed, raped and poisoned the water. Those arrested denounced the others and these too were apprehended. They were all shot, including three Frenchmen.' Galland agreed, saying that the roads around Cairo were infested with brigands calling themselves the Company of the Moon.

5. Kléber's view was pragmatic: 'The departure of those ships filled with important men and their trollops has given rise to some murmuring but those men who left formed part of Bonaparte's court and had to follow him.'

6. They left on the *American* and were captured. The pianist and economist were set back on land, presumably as useless mouths, while the generals were kept prisoner. Generals Desaix and Davout, along with Miot, would leave on the *Santa Maria delle grazie* and the *Etoile* in March 1800 and arrive in France on 5 May. Dugua, Poussielgue and two copies of the Rosetta stone left on the *Vengeance* and reached France on 14 June.

7. Leaving was not easy for more junior officers. In order to receive permission to depart Godet was examined by a hospital board and a medical board, then was sent to General Berthier for a passport, but he sent him to General Belliard, who granted permission and so Godet returned to Berthier who examined him, as did Napoleon, who was also present at the meeting. Joseph Felix Łazowski was more fortunate for he had been sent home with despatches in November 1800. He was suffering from blindness and would need at least three months to recover. One officer, Major Jacques Grobert, tried to get home by pretending to have a fever. Napoleon, furious that the medics had issued a certificate of repatriation, refused permission and had the officer sent to Salheyeh where he was 'to be continuously employed in the vanguard'.

The demi-brigade refused to march for Qatiyah and the officers and non-commissioned officers went to the port at Castel-Nazara in order to cross Lake Menzaleh. The next day the officers returned to Damietta in order to restore order and have the soldiers leave. Frustrated efforts. At noon the troops were mustered and the obedient soldiers left and embarked. I was at Castel-Nazara when I received orders from General Verdier to return and remain at Damietta and he gave me the money (for the arrears in pay had been the pretext for this insubordination).[8]

Alexandria was also restless, and Gunner Bricard noted the anger in the streets there:

> There was a mutiny at Alexandria when news came that a number of generals had taken money aboard a merchantman and were preparing to sail. The soldiers were angry at not having been paid, and at the departure of these newly rich men, with their fat baggage, who would leave Egypt with their money and thus give the impression to those in France that the army here lived in a land of plenty.

Kléber made a methodical effort to instil some discipline, turning first on some repeat offenders: 'The 69th has been kicked out of its lethargy. One man has been shot and eight sent to the galleys and a few other less rigorous examples now ensure that order has been restored.' He then did what he could to force Egypt to pay for its occupation, confessing that he would have to 'squeeze Egypt like a man who makes lemonade has to squeeze lemons'.

Even as order was restored, and money began to trickle in, Kléber was still left with the inescapable fact that his army was too small to occupy such a vast territory. On 12 October 1799, General François Etienne Damas would report that 'we now have less than 22,000 men from which we must deduct 2,000 sick or wounded who are in no state to serve. Around another 4,000 would be in no state to embark on a campaign. The roughly 16,000 men from all branches of service we have available are stretched across a vast

---

8. Kleber responded at first by dissolving the regiment, then relented on hearing 'the genuine atonement of the majority'. Gunner Bricard confirms the incident: 'The soldiers, stirred up by a few wretches amongst them, seized their weapons and went to their officers in order to demand their arrears of pay. They were told that the general was ordering them to march and that then their demands would be met. They refused to leave before being paid, adding that if the enemy did appear then they would of course fight.'

triangle the base of which, from Marabout to El-Arich, is 600 miles wide. It is impossible to concentrate more than 7,000 men at one particular point.'[9]

Using the diminished army wisely was therefore of vital importance. Kléber formed a reserve in the Nile delta to counter any incursion from Syria, fortified Rosetta as a port for the Nile flotilla,[10] and sent some reinforcements to Alexandria. He then instructed General Menou to establish a system of defences along the coast, and told General Dumas to inform Menou that he did not wish for any more of his 'monographs on the state of commerce between France and various different colonies' as the time for fighting rather than writing a thesis was upon them.[11] Kléber also enticed Desaix to return northwards, promising him the opportunity to 'fight the vizier and his elephants'. Kléber himself secured the perimeter around the capital and then waited for his enemy to make the first move.

His enemies, rather, for they were many. 'Now,' wrote Kléber with a sarcastic nod towards the departed Bonaparte, 'it is not, as it once was, a question of taking on a few bands of discouraged Mamelukes; no, now we must resist the forces of three major powers: the Ottomans, the English and the Russians.' The first two of these were not quite ready to open their campaign, whilst the Russians sensibly showed little interest in being dragged into a war outside Italy and Greece. There was therefore a brief lull as generals, pashas and admirals tried negotiations. General Morand made contact with Smith, who said that he would be glad to treat with a frank and loyal French soldier rather than the 'village solicitors then governing France', a view Morand probably shared. Poussielgue and Desaix, with Peyrusse as secretary and Savary as witness, then boarded the *Tigre* to outline some terms. Desaix 'hoped to find the English friendly, but I don't expect to find them reasonable'. They were indeed 'perfectly received' by Smith,[12] but it was the Turks, sensing that so few Frenchmen would be unable to keep the Egyptians loyal, who proved unreasonable. Indeed, many Egyptians knew that the French occupation would not last forever and, as Poussielgue put it, the local elites 'are sure the French want to leave Egypt

---

9. On 23 September, Poussielgue estimated the number capable of bearing arms as only 11,000 men.

10. There Captain Pierre-François Xavier Bouchard had discovered the Rosetta stone back in July. A letter from Kléber to Reynier on 30 November notes, 'It was Captain Bouchard who laid hands on the so-called stone of Rosetta as he was excavating there in order to repair the old fort 450 metres to the north of Rosetta on the left bank of the Nile.'

11. Menou seems to have ignored him and set to drafting a set of long administrative circulars. However, he also sent letters to the emperor of Abyssinia and the king of Darfur to suggest alliances.

12. Peyrusse noted that the 'wine was not spared and we had to drink every time an Englishman proposed a toast'.

and each one of them wonders what they should do to obtain a pardon'. This sense that the occupation could not hold, combined with their reading of the French opting for negotiation as a sign of weakness, determined the Ottomans to hazard yet another invasion.

An Ottoman army, with Mamelukes and local warlords alongside, then advanced out of Syria with an imposing body of cavalry, some infantry and some French-trained artillery with guns incongruously bearing the device *Honi soit qui mal y pense*. Ibrahim Bey and his cavalry commander, Elfy Bey, swept around the fort at El-Arich, isolating the unlucky battalion of the French 13th Line under Major Cazals of the engineers. The one-eyed Grand Vizier appeared beneath the walls, and the Turks uncharacteristically agreed to send any surrendering enemy to France. Colonel John Douglas of the Marines and Lieutenant Colonel John Bromley, the French emigrant who had put in an appearance after Aboukir, communicated these generous terms to the garrison, and sent in a French prisoner loaded with money and promises to sweeten the capitulation. Whilst the garrison's officers were determined to hold out, some eighty of the soldiers, according to Captain Ferray, were unwilling to sacrifice their lives when the prospect of being shipped to France with full pockets was literally knocking at the gates. The Turks therefore continued their attack all that week whilst Cazals struggled to keep his men at their posts. However, on 30 December 1799, discontent within the garrison saw the French flag hauled down and the besiegers allowed to enter. Vigo-Roussillon heard what happened next:

> The garrison knew there was talk of a negotiation and two factions formed – the reliable ones who wished to defend their post, and the discontent who demanded surrender. Ferray says that many were drunk on brandy. Worse, these mutinous troops shamefully opened a gate to the Turks and these, once inside, cut off the heads of all the French and without distinction.[13]

Remarkably, there were survivors. Indeed Cazals, fourteen officers and 216 soldiers managed to hold out within the fort for an hour, which was enough time to agree a formal capitulation. Gunner Bricard adds that these men were then subjected to a barbaric display from the Turks, who 'collected a quantity of heads and showed them to the miserable survivors'.

Kléber, rushing north with his field army, was dismayed to see this key to Egypt in Ottoman hands, but the Turks, wary of the desert, hesitated to advance further. So, before pairing off in the macabre dance of war, both sides again attempted to reach a negotiated settlement. Meanwhile, Colonel

---

13. The faction for surrender consisted of eighty men who had written to Cazals saying, 'You must give up the fort you are commanding to the enemy within twelve hours.'

Marie-Charles Fay Latour-Maubourg arrived from France bringing news of Napoleon's November coup in Paris.[14] Kléber, who despaired that 'France could not have been taken over by a more miserable charlatan', saw that Napoleon would be too busy saving France to spare troops for Egypt and so was happy to discuss repatriation so long as his soldiers went freely and not as prisoners of war. Negotiations through the British went well, and a draft treaty of 22 Articles was drawn up. The sick and amputees were even sent to Boulaq for evacuation to France on a convoy escorted by HMS *Bison*, whilst, on 25 January, Bricard in Cairo's citadel noted that 'everything points to the likelihood that we would soon have peace and evacuate Egypt'. Meanwhile the convention of El-Arich was signed on 24 January 1800. It stated that Egypt had to be evacuated within three months, so the French began evacuating Lesbeh and Damietta, as well as the right bank of the Nile and distant Suez.[15] The scientific commission was also sent north, Jollois recording that they had reached Rosetta on 9 February 'where we heard news of the change of government in France'. Redouté, on the coast, was buoyed by word that the general had heard from the English commodore that 'the scholars of England are not at war with those of France and that these civilians can therefore leave freely for France'. They clambered aboard but found themselves trapped off Alexandria when Lord Keith refused them passage despite Sidney Smith's insistent but rash promises.

Kléber had been treating cautiously, and was right to have done so. For this refusal to carry out the agreed terms was just one breach of good faith on the part of London. Everything soon came to a head. That March, Bricard heard about 'the text of a letter the English admiral had sent to the commander of French troops in Egypt'. It brought news that the British would not ratify the treaty, and would not permit the evacuation. Admiral Keith informed the French they would have to surrender if they wished to see France again.[16] This was a slap in the face for every Frenchman, and Laporte, who renders the admiral's name as Keitz, indignantly copied out the admiral's letter to Kléber:

---

14. This news was set out in a detailed report in number 2233 of *The Sun* newspaper, which in those days could be relied upon for accurate reporting of international events.

15. Suez had enjoyed a French presence since late 1798, but it was seen as a kind of internal exile. General Kléber noted how 'Perceval, who did not want to edit the *Journal d'Egypte*, and who did not seem to be interested in penning poems and hymns in honour of the Hero, was sent to Suez as a customs official'.

16. Loudly supported by an unapologetic Nelson, who had already declared that, regarding the French, 'I own myself wicked enough to wish them to all die in that country they chose to invade,' later adding, 'I wish them to perish in Egypt, and give a great lesson to the world of the justice of the Almighty.'

I warn you that I have received precise orders from His Majesty not to countenance any treaty with armies you command in Egypt or Syria unless such stipulates that you lay down your weapons, surrender yourselves as prisoners of war and hand over all ships and munitions in the port of Alexandria.

Kléber was livid with perfidious Albion and resolved to act, telling his equally furious army, 'Soldiers, only victory serves as a reply to such an insult. Prepare to fight.' The troops from Upper Egypt[17] and Donzelot from the Red Sea reached Cairo on 18 March and, two days later, Kléber issued out to attack the closest Ottoman army, the 80,000 men[18] then occupying the heights by Matarieh, a village built on the ruins of Heliopolis and just 5 miles from Cairo.[19]

The officer of dragoons watched the French advance:

We could see the squares of General Reynier to our left, each corner having two guns whilst the scouts were thrown forward as skirmishers. The grenadiers and carabiniers formed his reserve. To the right General Friant had taken up a similar position. No sooner had the first shots been fired against the village of Matarieh than a mass of cavalry emerged and, along with some infantry and Mamelukes, made a wide sweep in an attempt to gain the road to Cairo.

These men, under Nessif Pasha and the indefatigable Ibrahim Bey, were according to Millet, discomforted by the French guns:

The army advanced at dawn, heading towards the enemy position in a forest of date trees. When they saw us coming they prepared to defend

---

17. Mourad Bey had taken over Upper Egypt, coming to terms with the French through an intermediary, a Hungarian Mameluke, and entering into an alliance with them on 5 April.
18. A British diplomat, John Philip Morier, comments on this number: 'Two circumstances render it very difficult to ascertain with accuracy the efficient force of a Turkish army: first, the incredible numbers who follow it for any purpose but that of fighting, and who are not easily distinguished from the soldiers: secondly, the practice, which is very common with the chiefs of detachments, of giving in a return of more men than they bring into the field in order to receive the rations allowed for them and their horses.'
19. The French broke the armistice. This was nearly fatal for the French envoy then in the Ottoman camp, as he was dragged across the desert tied to a horse's tail. It was actually fatal for the five hostages the Ottomans had taken from the French to ensure compliance. Their bodies were discovered in 1923. They had been immured and had starved to death.

themselves and they came out into the plain, but in some disorder. They seemed to be readying themselves to charge but our artillery hit them with an effective salvo and they fell back, a retreat most disorderly and poorly led.

Łazowski of the engineers then saw the French turn their attention to taking Matarieh:

Reynier began to attack the village and General Lagrange sent the grenadiers and carabiniers against it whilst a battalion of Friant's moved against the other side of the village in order to block the enemy retreat. Their camp fell to us and the grenadiers were soon in the village. The enemy had fired a few artillery salvoes against us but our squares were not hit. They then came against us, sabres in hand and whilst there was some hand-to-hand fighting it was our volleys which flung them back.

With Matarieh taken and Nessif Pasha's horsemen beaten and driven off to their left, from where they would eventually wheel around the French and head for Cairo, the French now faced the bulk of the Ottoman army gathered by the village of El-Mergh. The French advanced again, with Desvernois observing that 'the four squares of Reynier and Friant with artillery in the intervals and supported by cavalry in columns moved forward in silence in order to fall on the enemy all at once just as the signal was given'. The Ottoman cavalry naturally sought to halt the French advance, and prepared to bear down on the French infantry then lumbering across the open plain. Jean-Pierre Doguereau, sick with the fever, was strong enough to watch as the Ottoman 'standard bearers gathered before the lines, the usual signal that an attack was to take place'. Their charge was then indeed launched, the horsemen rushing forward to fall on Friant's men. Richardot the artilleryman saw them attack and preferred to think of his guns as the key factor in the subsequent massacre:

Numerous cavalry came on and threw themselves against our right-hand square. We followed the order not to fire until they were at close range and then the canister from our six guns brought down riders and horses. A few of them fired their carbines and pistols when a second came on, but these too were brought down by canister as was a third, which was less vigorous and which also failed.

Belliard saw how the Turks 'did not coordinate during their attacks. Each soldier did what he wanted, coming and going as he saw fit, brandishing a lance or a flag, whilst another waved his sabre, whilst another dashes forwards and, at extreme range, fires off a carbine or pistol.'

The French guns were then manhandled forwards and, with a final whiff of grapeshot, the French broke the Ottoman will and the Turks were dispersed like a flock of birds disturbed by a hunter. The vizier, warned by his British liaison officer, Captain Thomas Lacey of the Royal Engineers, that he might be captured, then signalled a general retreat and 'by three in the afternoon the enemy had completely disappeared and the ground that had been so agitated an hour before was now nothing but desert'. With the French now masters of this parched field, the Ottoman camp at El-Khanka and the vizier's coach and horses, the time was ripe to exploit the victory. Desvernois set off in pursuit:

I took a sabre from a wounded hussar and chased after the Turkish cavalry. One of them had just knocked our trumpeter, Poultier, off his horse and was reaching down to cut off his head when I rode up and stuck him in the back with the point of my sword. Poultier shook himself free from the body and he cut the man's head off. We lost thirteen killed and fifteen wounded. We were met with a horrible spectacle when we reached Salhahieh. There we saw the heads of forty-two Frenchmen who had served in the Turkish artillery. The Grand Vizier had had them executed for he said they had fired too high in order to spare their compatriots the French dogs.

The plain and the roads leading from it were also covered with Turkish bodies, and Laporte saw that as 'we continued our pursuit of the debris of the enemy army the road it had retreated along was covered with men and horses which were either dying or dead. Their wounded were calling out to our soldiers and, despite their suspicion of infidels, were begging for water in Arabic (mollie, mollie!). It carried on like this for two days.' Doguereau saw the remnants pursued as far as Belbeis, where the French forced the surrender of a garrison also dying of thirst.

Despite the defeat, and the fact that the bulk of the Ottomans had fled northwards, Nessif Pasha and Ibrahim Bey had escaped to lead their cavalry into a restless and defenceless Cairo. Belliard had seen how 'we had taken so few precautions to prevent them from coming in, or for ejecting them' and so 6,000 horsemen simply trotted in to lift the standard of revolt. As early as 20 March there was firing in the streets, and isolated Frenchmen sought shelter in the forts or the citadel or at Kléber's headquarters, where 200 men under Major Duranteau prepared for the worst. It was not long in coming for now a second revolt commenced and it set much of Cairo and Boulaq ablaze. Bricard saw the rebels secure entire districts, watching as 'barricades of masonry were put across the streets and the adjoining houses were barred and fortified to protect the rebels and help defend their positions'. Antoine Galland saw the revolt become a settling of scores:

The rising became general and they threatened to burn down the houses of those who would not join them. The white standard was raised and the minarets rang with curses directed against the infidels.

The Mamelukes and Janissaries swept the town whilst the mob screamed. There were 50,000 men armed with muskets and others had pikes or clubs. The women and children expressed their pleasure in ululations. They turned on the Greeks, Copts and Syrians and they killed those they could and, so that there were bodies left in the street to be mutilated by the crowd.

Mustapha Agha, the Armenian chief of police under the French, was caught and impaled, and the lakeside house of Sheikh El-Bekri was plundered and his wives raped. Bricard also saw how it was not just those in the French administration who were punished, but many ordinary people who had allied themselves to the French too: 'Most of the Greeks and Copts were pillaged and abused by the brigands and the Copts from Syria were butchered as were many who had sided with the French.'

Kléber sent General Friant to put down the revolt at Boulaq and he did so in the usual style. Millet watched as 'the troops pushed into this place despite resistance from the Ottomans and the populace, and, with fire and sword, inflicted all the horrors of war on this unhappy town. Men, women and children, nobody was spared. The carnage lasted four hours before the troops were pulled out and we set fire to Boulaq.' Moiret was moved to regret 'how that poor town paid for its rash revolt ... I saw most of the inhabitants bayonetted to death and many houses burnt down or given over to pillage.'[20]

Kléber himself arrived before Cairo on 27 March, leading a French army in no mood to forgive. Malus had seen on the advance to the capital how 'we passed through Cored and shot all the inhabitants as they had sided with the Turks during operations near their village'. Reaching the capital, the French swept the rebels from the tanneries and the abattoirs, whilst Adjutant Alméras and some hand-picked veterans then secured the Coptic quarter, trapping the masses of insurgents into a much smaller area where fires, artillery and mines then began to sap their morale. A gloating Millet rather enjoyed this protracted chronicle of revenge:

Desaix's [Reynier's] old headquarters was full of the enemy and we lay a mine under this beautiful house. We made ready to blow it and decided to do so that night, for the Turks had gathered together to

---

20. François had a strange encounter there: 'We found some English officers amongst the rebels and some French deserters amongst the dead. Any European taken prisoner was shot on the spot. I myself took a man prisoner who I recognised to be English on account of the way he spoke. To be sure, I asked him something in Arabic. He did not reply. So I asked him "Are you English?" and he answered in a kind of German with English words mixed in. This persuaded me he was really English and so I blew his brains out.'

dance and play their music and to amuse themselves in their usual vulgar manner. They were shouting and their exuberance sounded more like the cries of bears than the celebrations of human beings. Seeing them in such good humour, we maliciously plotted to spoil their party. We detonated the mine and it had just the effect we had hoped for, burying these Muslims in the ruins.

François also saw the mine detonate, signalling a general assault on the rebels:

The mine went off at six and was a complete success and all the Turks stuffed into that building were blown to bits with Ezbekieh square being covered with the limbs of enemy soldiers. At this signal we charged in and started setting fire to everything as we passed through. We killed Ottomans, Mamelukes, Turks, men, women and children.

Such a show of brutal force cowed Cairo into submission. By mid-April, with Mourad Bey acting as intermediary, a treaty of surrender, with lenient terms, was agreed upon. Mercy followed payment of a punitive fine, the scale of which was only agreed after the Divan was locked in a room without water for a day. With Cairo safe, and money in the coffers, Kléber paid his men (Laporte noting that 'Bonaparte would never bother himself with such details'), consolidated his position in the delta and restored the garrison in Suez on the Red Sea.

Peace had been restored. Indeed, by June, all seemed well. At eight on the morning of 14 June, François was marvelling at the general's energy as the victorious commander reviewed the newly raised Greek Legion under the sycamores on the island of Roudah. That afternoon, Kléber returned to Cairo and, after a convivial lunch with General Damas, went off to inspect the repair work on his former headquarters. It was there, as he strolled through the garden with the architect Jean Constantin Protain, that tragedy struck. Bricard recounts the drama:

It was one o'clock in the afternoon and he was walking in the garden with his architect, Protain. A hypocritical wretch presented himself saying he wished to kiss the general's hand and Kléber, being preoccupied, did not have him dismissed. So the wretch profited from the opportunity and plunged a dagger into his left side.

Bricard says that the assassin, a twenty-four-year-old fanatic from Aleppo called Soleiman El Alepi, was then found hiding in a well and was seized by the throat. Laporte says that he nearly got away, but 'one of the guides hit the assassin on his arm as he was trying to scale the wall, and he collapsed. ... He was about to be stabbed a thousand times by the guides but their officers restrained them, calming their anger.' Peyrusse has it that the general's aide, Cerouges, nearly beat the prisoner to death, and that it was only with difficulty that he was spared.

The assassin had been taken. Protain, stabbed six times, survived but the general, who received four blows, was killed. When word got round that their commander had been murdered, many of his soldiers took revenge on the locals and François says that 'we used our swords and daggers to strike down any men and children we encountered'. Laporte too saw how 'everyone was furious and on every face there was hopelessness, we took it out on the Turks who were trying to run home, as we thought it must be some kind of conspiracy or the signal for a general revolt.'

Once emotions had cooled, the French authorities determined on bringing the assassin to justice. Still, once he had been found guilty, the men of Reason elected to use local methods. Desvernois saw three co-conspirators beheaded and their bodies burnt, as well as the fanatic's hand thrust into a brazier. Then François, who was a few feet away, watched as the killer was impaled on a spike which, according to Bricard, was 30 feet long. Vertray was also watching and left a rather detailed account:

> The chief Mameluke [*sic*] had asked for and obtained permission to act as executioner. He made Soleiman lie on his stomach then pulled out his knife and made a cut to the man's backside. The spike was then hammered in with a mallet before being lifted up and secured in a hole in the ground. All present could not fail to be impressed by the horror but also by the courage of the fanatic who seemed insensible to the pain.

François adds that the criminal spent his time reciting verses from the Koran, only pausing once to ask for something to drink, a request refused by his executioner, Barthémély of Chios. He lasted five hours according to Desvernois, who was 'present at the execution and can vouch for the details'. Laporte agreed, saying, 'All the soldiers were under arms and marched silently past Soliman on his spike and he remained alive on it for five hours.' Desvernois was so intrigued that he even came back 'to see the corpse four months later and Soleiman was still on the stake. The point had pushed into his ribs, and was sticking out beyond his left shoulder. The corpse was dried out and had not rotted. None of the birds of prey had touched it.'[21]

Justice, of a brutal kind, had been served. But Kléber was dead, and the enemies of France were closing in. The British were marshalling troops in Europe and India whilst the Ottomans seemed to enjoy an endless supply

---

21. In 1903 the skeleton of the assassin was in a glass case and still on display at the Jardin des Plantes in Paris.

of warriors, gathering more in Palestine and Syria and sending agents into Egypt. In truth, Heliopolis had only bought a lull in the fighting and the leaderless and isolated French army was caught on the point of a dilemma just as sharp as Soleiman's spike. They now had to choose between surrendering and going home, or going down fighting in a final blaze of glory.

11

Final Days

The portly General Jean-François, or Abdullah, Menou, who would now assume command of the army, much preferred the wisdom of the Enlightenment to any blaze of glory, for he was more a scholar than a soldier. Still, this former noble convert to republicanism and Catholic turned Muslim was not so keen on going home. Indeed, he was in favour of staying and turning Egypt into a permanent colony. This filled the army with unease and the troops rather took against the general and his wife, Zobaidah.[1]

Even those who tolerated his choice of wife, or ignored the fact that he would name his son Suleiman, the same name as Kléber's assassin, thought Menou too portly to ride at the head of the army, or too bookish to want to bother.[2] Menou was additionally 'loathed by all the generals whom he in turn viewed as traitors'.[3] This would cause problems, and indeed it seems as though, by October, generals Damas, Friant and Reynier, along with Lanusse, Verdier and Belliard, had formed a faction against their new commander. This made it difficult to command an army that was already proving stubborn, and Peyrusse expressed the pervading doubt that Menou might not succeed:

---

1. She would later get a safe-conduct from General Hutchinson to travel to Alexandria and thence to Turin. She would die in Italy but his son, Suleiman Mourad Jacques Menou, survived her only to die aged ten. She remained a Muslim; Menou lapsed.
2. Menou was a keen writer of scholarly texts on politics and the economy. He also, in July 1800, turned the Institute's library in Cairo into a public library and opened a school for mathematics.
3. Lieutenant Laval says Menou was hated by the generals mostly because he put an end to them claiming expenses for entertaining at the table.

General Menou had some literary pretentions, the constitutional assembly had made him familiar with the ways of a bureaucracy and the different committees he had sat on had given him an exaggerated sense of his talents. As for his military skill, whilst he told everyone that he had once been a musketeer it has to be said that he had served in numerous units and at different ranks, even being commander of the army of the interior in the Vendée. Still, my view is that he is not a great soldier, perhaps would be better as a politician and might do as a diplomat.[4]

Still, diplomatic skills helped and the ordinary soldiers were also soon mollified by his abilities as an administrator. Menou improved the barracks in the citadel[5] and ensured that those soldiers who had lost a limb were collected and looked after in reformed hospitals with a semblance of sanitation. Such attention by the seven-times wounded general won over a number of the grumblers. Moiret had considered Menou a 'renegade, a man who had betrayed his country in order to embrace the laws of Mohammed' but was soon appreciating 'his excellent qualities, his love of order and management, his affection for the soldiers, his complete understanding of administration and his moral virtues'. Millet too was soon suggesting that Menou had 'rare talents and much wisdom, along with a cautious nature, such that he soon won the trust of the army which, to some extent, consoled us for the loss of the brave Kléber'. François, whilst noting that 'he gave key commands to his creatures in preference to those who had served Kléber', was pleasantly surprised to see Menou visit his quarters in Cairo and 'hand out a 1 franc bonus to each man and NCO'.

That September, with the strange sensation of having coins in their pockets, the men celebrated Year 9 of the Republic and Menou exhorted his men to make one final effort for the republic and for Egypt:

You who have seen your name and glory sweep across Europe have bought the standard of liberty to the East! The flags that you carry here amongst your battalions stand as a signal to begin the civilisation

---

4. Gunner Bricard would agree, remarking, 'Menou looked after the soldiers, was an excellent administrator, restored our finances an no doubt encouraged the arts and sciences in Egypt. But he was no soldier and the task of commanding the army here was beyond him.'

5. There was a hospital at the citadel where 150 Britons, including Captain Courtnay-Boyle and the British crew of the *Cormorant*, which had run aground at Aboukir, were being held. Desgenettes saw that they had scrawled 'Old England forever!' on the walls. The English were evacuated to Damietta in October 1800.

of a neglected land which, once famous, has been squeezed dry by despotism.

The reality was that most of his men and nearly all his officers no longer cared for their civilising mission, and were sure that France no longer cared for them. The officer of dragoons complained that 'weeks and months passed with depressing monotony and news of Europe grew ever rarer' whilst Peyrusse, lamenting the lack of convoys from the motherland, and his own mounting sense of neglect, took solace in philosophy, musing that 'governments are always ungrateful, their skill lies in tricking us'. The government, which was now the Consulate directed by Napoleon, had overcome its Russian and Austrian enemies and now remembered its stranded army but, on account of the British blockade, could do little by way of sending supplies and reinforcements. The *Justice* and the *Egyptienne* braved the British and brought in some supplies, whilst, on 3 March 1801 the *Régénérée* even brought in 230 reinforcements of the 51st Line. Such efforts were insufficient, indeed they only really drew attention to official neglect. 'Where is [Admiral] Gantheaume?' railed Menou. 'What is he doing? He left before the *Régénérée* and should have reached Alexandria before it. Egypt would have been saved, he would have been covered in glory.'

There had in fact been an ambitious plan[6] for Admiral Gantheaume to land General Meyer and his troops at Derna in Libya where the locals 'would rent out camels to bring them to Alexandria'. More pragmatic heads prevailed and the admiral resolved to try to reach Alexandria instead. His little fleet was actually off Candia in June 1801 before losing heart and returning to Toulon, abandoning Menou and his men to their fate.[7]

That fate was to be left to the mercy of enemies growing stronger by the day. There were signs the British were raising an army on Minorca to bring to Egypt, and that the twin scourge of plague and Turks was again

---

6. This followed on from an earlier scheme in which the First Consul had worked on sending an expedition in September 1800, and had even asked the Spanish to help. They refused, and another scheme in December saw 2,500 men of the Expeditionary Legion, including twenty-nine black officers from the colony of Saint-Domingue and hundreds of Austrian deserters, assigned to take ship on a little fleet which included the *Desaix*, the *Constitution*, the *Bravoure* and the aptly named *Creole*. This expedition did not, however, reach Egypt, merely sailing from Brest to Toulon before exhausting supplies and crews.

7. In the spring of 1801, two frigates had landed a motley collection of 600 conscripts in Egypt who, according to Bricard, 'must have come from the prisons of France for they were covered in misery and vermin. They had to be issued with new uniforms and were incorporated in all the different regiments.' He also added that 'some fifteen French women also arrived, intent on joining their lovers or husbands'.

advancing from Palestine. Meanwhile, across the Red Sea, the British were even marshalling armies of sepoys to land at Suez. Peyrusse put on a heroic face before such odds:

> Egypt is invaded from all sides with barbarian hordes being led in by one of Europe's most civilised peoples. I do not know what our fate shall be. Whatever, we shall attempt to brave the coming storm and hold ourselves true to the worthy opinion we have formed of ourselves. If ungrateful fortune deserts us then we shall resign ourselves to the worst, avoiding only dishonour for, otherwise, brave men are of little worth.

The coming storm arrived when there was yet another landing at Aboukir, this time overseen by that admirer of Frederick the Great, Sir Ralph Abercrombie. A large fleet, escorting British and Swiss troops gathered at Minorca, was sighted off the coast and, on 8 March, to the martial music of sixteen French guns opening up from the fort, some 135 transports began unloading an expeditionary force on those infamous sands. General Friant with the 61st and 75th Line and some dragoons hastened over from Alexandria and gamely tried to drive the British back into the surf. However, twenty minutes of heroism could not halt the invasion and Friant's men were given a bloody nose by Abercrombie's Corsican Rangers, and, as they withdrew, sent urgent appeals for reinforcements to Menou in Cairo.

Menou had in fact known about the invasion since three in the afternoon of 3 March when, looking up from his books, a courier had barged into his study to announce that the British were coming. Whilst Menou finished his chapter, General Lanusse rushed northwards to help General Friant keep the British at bay around the Roman camp of Mandara and Nicopolis. Lanusse was rather fond of the offensive so Lieutenant Laval in the 18th Line quickly found himself sent against the British lines:

> We advanced against them in column, only deploying when we were within range. Then the firing began and our field guns opened up at point-blank range. We killed a great many of them but they kept order as they advanced and we were forced back. We had many killed and wounded, perhaps one-sixth of us, or 500 or so.

The 69th Line, acting as the rearguard, bore the brunt of this French retreat under English fire, a worthy feat of arms according to Joseph Laporte:

> We reluctantly retreated and lost many as we quickly fell back. The 69th in which I served behaved with uncommon bravery during the retreat and won the admiration of the English officers and of the French generals.

He added that the 'English were astonished at the brilliant conduct of what they called the black regiment, for we were almost all clothed in cloth of this colour'.[8]

It was a heroic defeat and it won time for Menou. Laval had complained that 'it had taken him a week to put his breeches on' but the French commander was now lumbering up to face General Abercrombie's men. By now Abercrombie, transcribed as Heuberc-Cambise by a Laval unfamiliar with the British and their devious spelling, had moved towards Alexandria and so the two armies met on 21 March and fought a battle the French would call Canope. Menou had mustered his men an hour before dawn, placing Reynier and Damas on the right, Friant and Rampon in the centre and entrusting Lanusse with the left. He then launched a series of disjointed attacks, starting with a feint by the jaded Camel Corps. Poor Vaxelaire, in a column composed of Rampon's 32nd Line, the 2nd Light and the Greek Legion, was amongst the first of the infantry to advance against the entrenched British lines. At one point they blundered into their own 4th Light and then, after correcting their alignment, came into range of British muskets:

We advanced against the English trenches and both sides started firing volleys at each other. I can say truthfully that I have never seen anything like it in my entire life. On top of that the English gunboats drew close to the shore and mauled us too.[9]

The officer of dragoons then watched as the French left tried its luck:

We mounted at three in the morning and went forward to our assembly point. General Roize placed the 3rd and 14th Dragoons in the first line under General Boussard whilst he held the 15th, 18th and 20th Dragoons in reserve. Battle began at dawn when General Lanusse's division opened fire on the English right flank. Lanusse was hit by a roundshot which carried off his leg.

---

8. After the surrender a rather proud Laporte wrote that 'during the march the English officers having seen us amongst the French units, accosted our officers and expressed their admiration for the fine conduct of our regiment, which they called the black regiment, and for its brilliant retreat at the battle. ... Our colonel, Brun, was complimented and showered with kindness by the English officers.'

9. Vaxelaire was wounded and taken to Alexandria where a doctor with a poor bedside manner told him, 'Ah, unfortunate Frenchmen, so they have brought you to this land to kill you and are not even giving you anything to soothe your woes.'

Lanusse was mortally wounded but found the energy to send an unusual message to Menou: 'I am fucked and so is your colony.'[10] His loss had further discouraged an infantry being sent across an open plain to attack redcoats shooting from entrenchments, dooming French attempts to coax victory from despair. Still, Menou, with the tenacity of the slow, persisted in launching attacks. This frustrated the Norman, Millet, who was serving alongside Vaxelaire:

> We attacked the English in their trenches. Firing broke out from both sides and the musketry and salvoes from the artillery created such a din that it could be heard for many miles. We hit the enemy entrenchments whilst the cavalry broke through three of their lines and wrought chaos in their camp and reserve. The enemy was almost beaten but we were too few and they were too many so we failed to win especially as only our division was really committed whilst other generals, who I shall not name, behaved so badly that it will shame their family names and the honour of France. We should have beaten the English and either taken them or forced them to drink sea water.

Menou, sensing that he was destroying his infantry, had indeed rashly decided to help them by destroying his cavalry and he had General Roize prepare his men for the charge. The general was dumbfounded, as was the officer of dragoons, who, having been sent forwards in the first wave, could not believe that his men were riding against unbroken enemy lines:

> The 14th was brought up short by a deep ditch which seemed uncrossable and which forced the regiment to swerve to one side before the enemy. So, for a few moments we presented a living target for the enemy muskets as we rode by before we found a way into the enemy camp. The English were horrified by this move and many threw down their weapons and hid in their tents. It became chaotic, our horses stumbled over ropes and tent pegs[11] whilst enemy gunboats fired canister into us and the 42nd Foot, overcoming their shock, rallied and began to massacre us. Our dragoons turned to make for our lines but the English had reformed and we had to run the gauntlet of their fire a second time. Of the 180 men who took part in the attack 74 were killed or gravely wounded. What pointless carnage!

---

10. Another witness has it that the general told Menou, 'You are not fit to run the kitchens of the Republic.'
11. Laporte thinks that 'the English had covered ditches with branches and leaves, and the French cavalry fell into these traps'. British accounts say these were just foxholes which had been dug for tentless troops to sleep in.

Merme was also there:

> We broke into the English ranks but when I reached the midst of them
> I was wounded in the left knee by a bayonet and my horse was killed
> under me. A second charge allowed my comrade Vautrins to pull me
> from beneath my horse but as he did so he was wounded and we both
> had to go to the hospital.

In the midst of the carnage and the tent ropes Abercrombie was mortally
wounded, the French claiming from a dragoon's cut, the British from a
shot in the thigh. The poor Roize was also killed and, having failed to
take advantage of the chaos his cavalry had caused, and after an extensive
exchange of artillery fire in which the French came off worst thanks to
the Royal Navy, Menou finally elected to fall back to the safety of walled
Alexandria. There his men 'saw masses of wounded who were all cursing
the commander-in-chief and telling their unwounded comrades that they
could expect to meet the same fate'. Menou, having lost many dead and
prisoner,[12] shut himself up with these wounded and his embittered garrison
and pondered his next move as the British, reinforced by 6,000 Albanians,
besieged the port whilst also pushing down the Nile to Rosetta, menacing
communication between besieged Menou and his lieutenant, General
Belliard, similarly isolated in Cairo. The British also captured Jacques
Cavalier and his camel riders at Alqam,[13] and Allied victories were
persuading some of the smaller French garrisons to shift for themselves.[14]
Over at Suez that May, Tarayre withdrew when the Anglo-Indian force of
8,000 British troops and sepoys finally landed at Quasayr and marched out
towards Belbeis.

Of the two surviving French garrisons in Alexandria and Cairo, the
capital was perhaps in more trouble. 'The plague was making frightening
progress and in just one day some 900 Egyptians died and 150 of the French
fell sick,' observed Jollois. 'The streets of Cairo presented the most piteous
sight for one only encountered convoys of the dead escorted, one might

---

12. These were well treated. Laporte noted that 'the English make war like a
    civilised nation and we treat their prisoners the same way'.
13. Cavalier, with 225 infantry and 200 mounted troops, surrendered to the British
    who agreed to transport his men back to France as free men, i.e. without being
    considered prisoners of war.
14. A detachment of the 2nd Light and Pierre Louis Cailleux was stuck in Lesbeh,
    and attempted to break out to Ramanieh on 13 March. Two Greek ships took
    them up the Nile to the coast where, split between four boats, they bolted for
    Greece. Three were captured, and eighty-nine Italians amongst the prisoners
    took up service with the British, whilst one boat made it to Rhodes. Pierre Louis
    Cailleux was in this ship and reached Messina in Sicily on 24 June 1801.

say, by those about to die. Some had violent headaches, others collapsed, vomiting, in street corners, both of which announced the arrival of this fatal disease.' Peyrusse recorded that between twenty and twenty-five men were dying each day and so the scholars, considered by the military as useless mouths, were probably delighted to be sent away. The grand and decrepit Commission of Arts and Sciences sailed northwards up the Nile that April, Jollois sharing a barge with a certain Lerouge although 'he was struck down with the plague, and he died when we reached Alexandria. We were unaware of the nature of his illness throughout the course of our voyage as he tried to disguise it in the fear that, otherwise, he would be left behind.'

The Commission was keen to quit Egypt and quickly found themselves back at Ramanieh, nearly three years after that first epic crossing of the burning plains. There they found that the French soldiers were as indifferent to the arts as they had been in 1798:

> During the night a number of the soldiers, profiting from the disorder caused by preparations for departure, crept into the tents and helped themselves to what they could. Whilst Rozière was absent he had left trunks of minerals outside the tents, thinking that their weight would prevent them from being carried off. He returned to find that the trunks had been forced open and that the samples from Mont Sinai, Mount Bavam, Syene, Cosseir, etc, had been stolen and that the soldiers were hitting them against each other whilst joking that 'these scientists carry around trunks which weigh as though they are full of gold, but which are full of nothing but pebbles'.[15] Rozière and his friends did not have the means to put an end to such disorder and they would have been murdered had they picked a quarrel with the soldiers. Their officers kept quiet, some even smiled. However, it should be said that only a few of the soldiers participated in this crime and a few officers stepped forward to re-establish order although they could not silence the brigands who had broken into the cases.[16]

When the scholars finally reached Alexandria, Menou imposed quarantine on them for five days before loading them onboard Captain Hyacinthe Murat's *Oiseau*. The British, however, would not allow them to sail and Menou, out of principle or chagrin, would not allow them back. After weeks of uncertainty, Menou relented and the scholars returned to Alexandria to eat horses, make bread from rice and serve as sentries in the National Guard.

---

15. Redouté saw how the soldiers 'broke into the cases and found rocks wrapped in paper; they threw what they called these ridiculous objects away'.
16. Carnet de la Sabretache, 1936, p. 306.

They were now stranded in Alexandria with Menou and his increasingly fractious generals[17] and dispirited army. The British had blockaded the port and were slowly strangling the city. Although French honour demanded resistance, morale was so bad that surrender could not be far off. The British sought to exploit French woe, offering incentives to desert. Merme was on the receiving end of such honeyed words:

> I was once on sentry duty when an English officer inspecting his own lines came over and tried to talk to me. The Englishman, who knew we were reduced to the last extremity, complimented me on my horse and said that the Arab horses were the best. Then he began, 'We know how bad things are with you, dragoon, you will have to surrender and it will be bad for you. However, if you consent to follow me I shall give you a goodly sum of money and shall look after you when you reach England.' I replied that even if our situation was not good he could give me the whole of England and I still would not commit such a cowardly deed.[18]

In Cairo, Belliard, far superior to Menou in terms of energy and those soldierly qualities that earned the respect of the troops, was keeping his men active. That May he had made a show of advancing against the Turks before falling back to the prepared defences ringing the city. Then there were regular inspections, pointed rebukes and tireless preparations for the almost inevitable siege.

Thurman was at Gizah, still recording events in his journal as these tireless preparations deprived him and his men of rest:

> I was ordered to put the fortifications at Gizah into a state of repair. Not much to work with as we were short of men, artillery, munitions. We stooped behind hastily erected ramparts knowing that nobody would come to save us and that we could no longer show ourselves abroad. We were trapped in Cairo, Boulaq, Raouda and Gizah. There were 4,000 of

---

17. Reynier was actually arrested in May and sent back to France, as were Damas, Daure and Boyer. Damas and Daure, placed on the *Good Union*, were detained by the British whilst Reynier, on the *Lodi*, made it to France where he later challenged General Jacques Zacharie D'Estaing, the man who had sided against him with Menou, to a duel and killed him.

18. Not everyone was so principled. The officer of dragoons noted how 'on the night of 3 and 4 June the dragoons Campagne and Desbille passed over to the English camp. Everyone was furious with such rank deserters.' It is possible that the French deserters were assigned to the Chasseurs britanniques which arrived in Egypt on 3 August. The traffic was not always one-way; three Hompesch dragoons in British service had deserted to the French in April.

us Frenchmen stretched out over a perimeter of 18 miles.[19] We held a
city in which each inhabitant was an enemy, all whilst being decimated by
the plague, and limited to punitive rations, and we could see approaching
the Grand Vizier advance with an army of 60,000 men whilst, on the
left bank of the Nile, the Captain Pasha with 15,000 Janisseries and
12,000 English, as well as countless Bedouins and tribesmen, also
advanced. The enemy must have had a good opinion of our valour to send
120,000 men against our mere handful.

The British were indeed now advancing down the left bank of the Nile,
and the imperial and imperious Ottoman army down the right. They
were to be supported by the Anglo-Indian force under David Baird which
was marching over from Suez at a pace too leisurely for coordinated
strategy. Before such enemies, Belliard could do little other than ensure a
reasonable surrender. Following a council of war, on 22 June, the French
set out their terms for capitulation. A draft treaty was hammered out in a
tented encampment beneath the pyramids and the parties signed the final
document, dubbed the Convention of Gizah, before it was finally ratified
on 28 June by Belliard and Hutchinson and the one-eyed vizier, Hadgy
Youssouf Zia. It came as a relief and François recalled that 'many soldiers
burst out crying' at this news.[20]

On 9 July 1801, Belliard's ragged army came out. It was accompanied by a
number of Greeks, Syrians and Copts, and those Egyptians, including 'many
Muslim women who had married Frenchmen', who had the most to lose
from the return of the Turks. The French were treated well and there was a
little fraternising, at least with the British, and Galland was surprised to find
that their army contained 'many emigrants, but above all, Corsicans' in its
ranks. Miot saw how 'the English behave with considerable decency whilst

---

19. In fact, Belliard seems to have had just 2,500 effectives; the rest were employees,
civilians or sick.

20. François himself was sent off with a detachment carrying a white flag but it was
ambushed by some Turks and most of the detachment killed. 'A cavalryman
who had taken two heads from two of our comrades killed in the ambush had
slung them on his saddle but now he handed them to me so that I would be
obliged to carry them. A cord had been passed through their cheek and out of
the mouth and he slung them around my neck.' He was sent to Gaza, Damascus
and Aleppo where he took service with the emir. After a few years of service in
the Middle East he was brought, as part of the escort, to Smyrna and Athens in
1803. There he was able to drink a glass of red wine, his first in five years. He
was impressed by the women as 'they used blue eye-shadow and red nail polish,
and they liked to drink'. He was even more impressed with his next port of call,
Constantinople, and it was there, in August 1803, that he sought out the French
ambassador and received a passport for France.

the Turks less so, they just wanting to get hold of everything'. The Turks were also presented with a petition by the populace asking for permission to massacre the Christians and, although they refused, there was a brief pogrom against those who had collaborated with the infidels. Indeed, Sheikh El-Bekri's daughter, Zaynab, was beheaded for having behaved immorally with the French, or for her father having been their loyal ally. Then, on 14 July, the French bade farewell to Cairo for good. Pausing to collect some 800 British and French blind and load the body of General Kléber and the skeleton of his assassin into a barge, they set off for the coast and for home.

The march there was not entirely orderly. Galland was on one of the barges fighting a dose of dysentery with red wine, but he managed to see that some of the French who wanted to stay in the country deserted to serve the Mameluke escort.[21] A British eyewitness, however, recalled how 'the soldiers were quite open about their joy at quitting Egypt, and paid little heed to their officers'. But for Vertray the smouldering ruins of villages destroyed by the advancing Turks was a more significant sign, as was the lamentation of the local peasants who 'revealed their fears that they would once again fall under the Turkish yoke, and expressed the hope that we would return'. Peyrusse also remarked on how friendly the locals were now the French were leaving. 'It was pleasing for us to witness the evident affection the country people held for us as we passed by. We were leaving, so it was not self-interest which prompted then to behave this way.'

General Belliard's column of prisoners was soon at the Mediterranean shore and there Laporte calculated:

> The number of French there was 8,000 including 500 or 600 Copts and Greeks who had enlisted, then there were also 2,000 civilian administrators, and the sick, wounded and blind, such that there were around 6,000 men actually under arms.

Belliard then climbed aboard the *Duke of York* whilst his army settled down on the transports as the civilians, including many Syrians and Egyptians fearing retribution, also tried to find a place in the convoy. There were some sad scenes of farewell as according to one British sergeant, Daniel Nicol, the French were forced to leave their mistresses behind and take only their wives.

Belliard's men were first to leave for home but the Alexandria garrison soon followed. Menou's surrender there was inevitable, and the French, troubled by blindness and scurvy, and with 3,000 men in hospital, held a council of war on 22 August and opted for a negotiated capitulation. This

---

21. Mathieu de Lesseps, the French consul appointed to Cairo in 1803 and the father of the more famous Ferdinand, estimated that there were then 200 French deserters in Mameluke pay.

forced the final surrender of the fortress where the invasion had begun and, on 1 September 1801, just as General Belliard was reaching Marseilles, the garrison of Alexandria opened the city gates. The victorious British marched in and took over the town, some even celebrating by scaling Pompey's column to drink punch to the king and knock down the cap of liberty which the French had placed on top of the monument.

It was symbolism that was keenly felt by both sides. The defeated French were saddened by defeat but keen to return home. For some, such mixed feelings were soon surpassed by a growing sense of regret that they were leaving a country that had been their odd and uncomfortable home for so many years. Thurman was one to express it:

> I embarked on the *Peggy-Success* [the *Pecqwis* by Peyrusse], a 500-tonne ship, at Aboukir, just opposite the fort which had witnessed so much of our woe. It was not without some anguish that I said goodbye to Egypt, to the shoreline I had patrolled, to the forts I had helped build, even to the Arabs of the villages at Bourlos and Fouah, who had made me feel welcome. I felt I loved those places and that I was now saying goodbye to friends.

Moiret, embarking on the more impressive-sounding *Sacra Familia*, also felt some regret, although a sense of defeat crept into his final accounting:

> We quit with the most complete joy, a country fatal to both ancient and modern Frenchmen, a country desolated by all the scourges of humanity: plague, blindness, brigandage, poverty and, above all, oriental despotism. However, it was not without regret that we thought of the men lost, the amount of blood shed, the fatigue and want endured and the fact that we had not been able to establish a colony worthy of the name as there had been no time to transform it thus.

Miot, however, seemed untroubled by sadness. Indeed, he left unbowed and unbroken, and seemed to be almost shouting from the rigging:

> Goodbye Egypt! Goodbye Muslims! We are leaving your land and taking with us the lasting memory of the superb monuments scattered across it, the unhappy recollection of your deserts and your sad houses and memories, just as poignant, of what we suffered for having troubled your slumber and covered your shores in blood.

Many of the troops were too absorbed by the details of their voyage home to have much time for regret. Gunner Bricard was glad to be finally 'leaving Egypt where we had suffered so much from want and neglect' and had boarded the *Braakel* (a former Dutch fifty-four-gun ship) with the 4th Light.

There he was pleased to see that he and his comrades were 'well received, the English officers inviting us to dinner with them'. Laporte had also been kindly received. 'Arriving on board,' he wrote, 'the English did us the courtesy of inviting us to store our weapons in trunks but our officers were always wary and so told them that whether at war or peace our soldiers always slept with their guns.'

With the nations reconciled a little as they set out warily on their shared journey, the French inevitably turned to finding fault with the food. Galland could not find a berth and was being fed 'hardtack full of worms and bacon boiled in seawater' whilst Bricard was complaining that 'we received the same rations as the English troops but the food was so badly prepared that it was impossible for me to eat it'. Laporte, too, was unimpressed. 'They only gave us four ounces of bad biscuit, all old and rotten, six ounces of flour which was to be mixed with sea water and cooked ... a glass of water, a glass of wine, four ounces of bad salt meat or bacon. We told them that French rations were better, as we got 14 ounces of biscuit, and they replied "Godam, English soldiers don't get more than you!"'

In such circumstances, the voyage was going to be a hard one. Thurman found it so:

> We set sail on a voyage which would last three months and during which the sea seemed to conspire against us. More than once we thought that we might never see France again. Storms, fires onboard, scurvy, everything combined to render the voyage horrible.

Auguste Colbert told his mother that his voyage home 'calls to mind those unfortunate princes who tried to regain their homeland after the expedition to Troy'. Laporte's odyssey came to an end only when he caught sight of his beloved France:

> After a voyage of fifty-two days we caught sight of the coast of Provence and there were spontaneous and general cries of delight as we greeted the homeland from which we had been separated for so long and which we had doubted ever seeing again. Even the English could not help themselves from getting emotional and they told us they envied us (although they had not gone through a thousandth of our suffering).

Thurman also reached Marseilles where 'we dropped anchor that evening. Imagine our joy, we were drunk, mad, laughing and crying at the same time. Even so we were not yet permitted to embark. A sloop bearing the sanitary commission came to inspect us and see our declaration. We were sent to Pomegue and then, yesterday, were sent here to Clos-Neuf, for quarantine. I cannot describe our impatience.'

Quarantine was the final obstacle, and perhaps the most difficult. Colbert lamented, 'After two years of suffering, the idea that they might have come to an end left me speechless but the thought that I could not yet take advantage of this change of circumstances quite yet filled me with despair. Curse this blasted quarantine, I detest this last constraint which keeps me from my family!'

Release finally came and the soldiers were eventually let loose. Doguereau recalled that 'we were overjoyed to be at the end of this adventure. We refreshed ourselves at the Hotel de l'Europe, forgetting our troubles, and spending a delicious week in town, before me and three friends took the stagecoach for Paris, arriving in late February.' Little Faye, too, was soon heading back to Paris and his native Normandy, his bag full of green coffee beans, his head full of memories.

For Bricard the reunion with French wine and white bread[22] was more important than family, whilst Laporte was self-aware enough to wonder how these hungry new arrivals might be regarded by the locals:

We were sunburnt like Moors, some were missing limbs, we all had a wild look and were dressed in different colours, each unit having its own, in short not very flattering to look at but, nonetheless, with a military bearing which would intimidate even the most resolute.

The Savants, of course, were also coming home. Their departure had been delayed because, although Britain had been vindicated in the art of war, a war of the arts had nearly broken out back in Egypt. There the British were insisting that everything in the French baggage train relating to art and archaeology – whether a mummified cat or a mysterious slab of black stone – was public property, and therefore belonged, rightfully, to the *Allies*. 'An article of the surrender [Article 16] stipulated that the Commission of Arts and Sciences will not carry away any of the public artefacts, Arab manuscripts or collections of remains,' declared Jollois. 'And that these shall be left to the English. This caused a serious dispute. The commission members who had seen this clause wrote at once to General Menou, protesting at this harshness and that whilst terms concerning the army and the government were open to negotiation, it was not in the general's power to treat with their private and particular property. General Menou

---

22. Ladrix was luckier, having even managed to obtain wine in the lazaretto. Red wine and baguettes were missed by many. Lasalle had told Dugua that he dreamt of floating in Champagne and flushing out the waters of the Nile that were polluting their entrails. But other things featured in the soldiers' nostalgia. Miot and Desaix, putting in to a Greek port in March 1800, were greeted by the French consul 'who hastened over and offered General Desaix whatever he could wish. Desaix asked for a lettuce salad and we devoured it.'

therefore wrote to the English but they paid him no heed as he was not much respected by them.'

Indeed, Colonel Hilgrove Tomkyns Turner of the 3rd Foot Guards and the Society of Antiquaries had first confiscated the artefacts before establishing a commission to determine which Egyptian relics should remain French and which should be gifted to the English. Menou, who had claimed the Rosetta Stone for himself, had his hands prised off it[23] and Turner says he came into Alexandria with a devil cart and a body of artillerymen to collect it for his crown. It was then taken aboard the *Egyptienne* frigate and sent to London, as were twenty other valuable items from the list compiled by Jean-Baptiste Joseph Fourier, and, upon arrival, the British Museum generously found space for it and these other treasures. The French were glad to save their personal papers and some valuable acquisitions from British hands, and even managed to transport some significant finds to France. Saint-Hilaire describes this final battle of the Egyptian campaign:

> The English designed the capitulation of Alexandria in order to deprive us of the means to record our findings on Egypt. They sent a young writer [William Richard Hamilton] to seize our collections in the name of their general. We argued forcefully and he only managed to make off with some of what we had. Our collection consists of forty to fifty cases and we are unable to arrange for their transport given the expenses we have endured in the midst of war and more particularly during the blockade of Alexandria. We have been without salary for six months and obliged to buy supplies by paying their weight in gold.

Only when the squabbling was over could the scholars depart. It had been an exhausting ordeal and a jaded Saint-Hilaire wondered, 'Why had I not listened to those who gave me that wise advice to remain peacefully where I was and enjoy all the advantages I then enjoyed?' But there was more trouble ahead and the Greek sailors, who were notoriously superstitious, refused to cast off if there were any pagan statues or mummies onboard. The voyage itself was gruelling but there was a final surprise in store

---

23. Turner left this account of the prising: 'All the curiosities, natural and artificial, collected by the French Institute and others were to be delivered up to the captors. This was refused on the part of the French general to be fulfilled by saying they were all private property. Many letters passed ... but the artificial, which consisted of antiquities and Arabian manuscripts, among the former of which was the Rosetta Stone, was insisted upon by the noble general [Hutchinson] with his usual zeal for science. Upon which I had several conferences with the French General Menou who at length gave way, saying that the Rosetta Stone was his private property but, as he was forced, he must comply.'

for them when they reached Marseilles. There Saint-Hilaire saw those mummies he had so carefully smuggled onboard promptly fall foul of some overly zealous customs officials unused to such odd imports. The relics were impounded for fifteen days, as was Savigny's equally suspicious insect collection, whilst the director of the Marseilles customs was also entrusted with two civet cats and asked to send them on to the Museum of Natural History in Paris.

The scholars, too, had to endure the requisite formalities of those returning from the lands of the plague. Villiers du Terrage on the *Amico Sincero* was off Marseilles on 16 November. There he found quarantine an ordeal as 'we were lodged in roofless barracks, exposed to the rain and cold of this intemperate season, something to which we were not accustomed. We sheltered under bits of sail and slept in the hammocks from the ship but, even so, we were happy for we were on French soil and were once again in touch with our relatives and our friends.'

Villiers was only released in the middle of freezing December but warmed to the news that France was no longer at war. A general peace had been announced on 9 November and, buoyed by this good news, he then set off by stagecoach to Lyon and was safely back home at 1544 Rue Saint Dominique in Paris on 28 December 1801.

Most of the learned who had gone out with the army had been profoundly moved by their experience and many would later come together in the capital and, from 1802, start work on the fabulous *Description d'Egypte*. Conceived by the tireless Denon, this huge undertaking would form a lasting testament to their curiosity and hard work and one which captured how Egypt was to inspire in Europe a new wave of curiosity for the Egyptians and their lands.

With the scholars and the soldiers settling back into France, a few hundred curious Egyptians also came ashore. These refugees included the Copt Gabriel Sidarious, his wife Marie Chovel and their daughter Rachil; there was Adrien Barakar, a former slave from Sudan who would die in the retreat from Moscow; Gaspard Joseph Agoub, who would be wounded at Waterloo; the Habaïby family from Syria; and the Amonts from Bethlehem. Many of the menfolk would take up service with the French and muddle on until 1814 when, following Napoleon's abdication, fate brought still more difficult times. Still, when they first arrived in Marseilles they were looked after, with even their sick and traumatised being treated in the city's hospitals.

They were soon joined by the army's own sick and wounded. Menou's surrender covered the 1,400 sick, including 1,300 with scurvy, and 240 invalids in Alexandria. These had been the last to leave Egypt and they were loaded onto sixteen hospital ships before spending weeks caught between the British and French bureaucracies. One of those too badly wounded to travel was Vaxelaire, who was forced to remain behind in British hands, lodged in an ancient Greek temple in the care of Dr Frank, until he was ready for the voyage. He was therefore obliged to watch his comrades leave before him:

> When the embarkation was taking place we cried like children leaving their mothers and fathers, thinking that we would never see them again even though we were being left in the hands of French surgeons. I noticed that one of these, too, had tears in his eyes, probably because he had seen us crying so.

Only in December could their journey begin:

> They carried us down on stretchers in order to place us on sloops which then took us out to our assigned ships. When they started raising the anchor, we started to laugh but one of the four officers amongst us told us not to laugh now but to save it for when we were in the harbour of Toulon.

After a long and dangerous voyage they, too, found themselves in the purgatory of the lazaretto where, in a 'little building which resembled a chapel',

> I, along with the others who could not walk, were fumigated in our beds and so that we were not suffocated we were obliged to cover our faces with our sheets. We were twenty days in quarantine and if anyone had died we would have had to wait for fifty days.

Vaxelaire was then released, but only into a military hospital as his wound refused to heal. Indeed, it became necessary for him to lose a limb to the butchers of the army.[24] Resigned to life without a leg, he consoled himself that he had seen worse on the hospital ship that had quit Alexandria:

> I had seen some who had two wooden legs, others with their legs off up to the groin, others missing an arm and a leg, and even with two arms missing. There was even a man from Comté on the ship bringing us back from Egypt who was missing most of his face and had just a round hole instead of his mouth. This man had been so depressed that, on leaving Egypt, he had sought out a gun with which to blow his brains out. The surgeons stopped him and did what they could for him. I also knew that many had returned blind and that these were probably sent to the Invalides in Paris.

The Egyptian adventure had indeed cost the lives of many, and ruined those of many more. Even the able-bodied had been damaged by the rigours of

---

24. Vaxelaire did not have a good opinion of the surgeons, calling them 'the butchers of the army, for that's what I called the surgeons on account of their techniques being very similar'.

life on campaign in Egypt. Young Laporte had nearly been broken by his trials and tribulations:

In the nine years and several months I was in the forces, there were only two occasions upon which I was moved to tears. That on the day I embarked at Genoa and 26 September 1801, the day I landed at Marseilles. Satisfied with my adventure, I swore that I would take the first opportunity to quit the army and this came a few months later when the general peace was signed at Amiens. My health had been destroyed by the misery, the fatigue and the privations of all kinds that I had endured since leaving. I was too young to continue thus on campaign, in camp, badly paid and badly clothed and lacking even the bare necessities.

He was young enough to recover, and was soon busy at work recording his experiences:

I thank God and Divine Providence for having kept me safe and sound through such dangers and all thanks to the grace of God. And I must add that I shall until my dying breath continue to give thanks for this favour. I will now give a list of commonly used Arab words which I have managed to remember since leaving the places I have described.

Bonnefons too resigned after the campaign, quitting the artillery after ten years, three months and ten days of service, whilst General Vial was tempted to do so as well, 'desiring nothing but to sit by my fire, and to continue doing so. I have to restore my health after this, and to sort out my affairs. I must do so in order to support an elderly, infirm father and a mother respectable on account of her age and concern for her children, as well as a young wife who has, for too long, had her life destroyed by those forces which have also made me their plaything.' This mixture of physical exhaustion and being overwhelmed by waves of conflicting emotion about what had been endured, and why, were characteristic consequences of the campaign and of the homecoming. There was regret that the building of an empire in the sands had proved something of a mirage, relief that the test had not cost them their lives, but also, alongside that lingering sense of loss, some pride at having survived such an ordeal, and having participated in this modern crusade.

Peyrusse, reflecting on his campaign, kept his emotions in check, writing simply that 'after three and a half years of trouble and woe here we were, at last, back on our native soil'. Auguste Colbert of the chasseurs, however, summed up his experience with a sense of dignity, and of achievement, when writing to his mother:

I have travelled through the Holy Land, I was at Nazareth, and I saw the castle of Safed where the cruel and holy Jew [Judith] cut off the head of Holophernes. I have drunk from the river of regeneration where John the Baptist baptised his believers. I have seen Genezareth and the lake of Tiberias and that of Galilee where the possessed herd of swine rushed off the cliff. I have seen Mount Tabor, where the Transfiguration took place, and Mount Carmel. I shall stop now for fear of boring you with all my 'I have seens'. I wish I had brought something back from Egypt but they do not have much worth buying, the things that I liked, such as the scimitars from Damascus or Persia, the weapons of the Mamelukes, were hardly likely to please my nieces, and yet I rate them highly as souvenirs of our wars in Africa and Asia.

The officer of dragoons was equally philosophical about his years in the sand:

We embarked on the 7th no doubt biding this land of Egypt an eternal farewell, this land where we had found so much glory and suffered so many tribulations, where we had braved hunger and thirst and disease as well as Turkish scimitars so that we could present France with a colony worthy of it. Abandoned by our homeland we received nothing but empty promises but, even so, we defended our conquest stubbornly for three years. So goodbye, land of Egypt. Perhaps one day our sons will remember our exploits below your sun and, through their own deeds, bring back to life the spirit of the heroes who fell in your conquest.

For Vertray, too, there was sadness over comrades lost or forgotten. 'We recalled our comrades who had died on the field of battle, or in the hospitals of Jaffa or Cairo. Those who were absent at the roll-call were more numerous than those who presented themselves, indeed the battalion to which I had belonged had lost two-thirds of its strength.' Desvernois felt the pain and regret of loss, too, and, uncharacteristically, restricted himself to reporting the facts: 'The 7th Hussars had returned to France with 254 men, officers included, meaning we had lost 508 men in the four campaigns the French army had waged whilst in Egypt and Syria.' Vertray's regiment, the 9th Line, left behind 584 dead in Egypt whilst Laporte, too, remembered the fallen: 'We had 384 men who had been through the attack on Jaffa and Acre, the battles at Aboukir and 25 July 1799 against the Turks, and 13 and 21 March 1801 against the English, having lost 1,416 men as we counted 1,800 when we embarked at Genoa.'[25] Once all the survivors were disembarked, tallied and sent off into the interior of France it was found

---

25. Laporte himself was a broken man. Following a winter in quarters in Aix, where the regiment shivered in the snow, and with his health deteriorating, he began to ask for his discharge. After numerous attempts he got it on 2 May 1802 and headed home to Grenoble.

that this adventure, this fateful expedition, had cost the lives of just over 8,000 soldiers. Thousands of sailors, too, had died, and at least twenty-four scholars succumbed in the service of France and knowledge.

It was Pelleport, however, who perhaps summed up the experience the best, touching on the themes of loss, love and history. He ended his account of the glorious expedition to Egypt and Syria with a rather poignant appeal to be remembered:

As we drew away from Egypt, where I had lost relatives, close friends and good comrades, I felt heart-broken and utterly sad. And so this great expedition came to an end. Then, and indeed for some time afterwards, it was an event which engendered pride and satisfaction in those who had taken part. Of course, the material and political gain was nil. Still, perhaps our grandchildren will reflect on our achievements. That is the sincere wish of this last of the Egyptians.

Epilogue

Napoleon's campaign had come to a disappointing conclusion. Political and material gain was, as Pelleport put it, nil. The adventure had failed, and Egypt found itself the plaything of the Ottomans and the hated British. The Egyptians were left to deal with this rapid transformation of events and rulers, and to struggle with the consequences of a French invasion just as a new century looked like turning into a new age. They had been completely invaded in that the French had not only broken into their lands but inserted themselves violently into their culture and their minds.

French minds had been changed too, of course. The defeat in Egypt had, rather paradoxically, generated a surge of interest in the region and its culture. This would be of great artistic and cultural significance, but this embryonic foray into distant lands also seems to have planted a seed of imperial ambition which gestated whilst France was conquering Europe, and which would only see the light once peace on one continent drove the men of war to radical schemes on the others. France would quickly forget the surrender of 1801 but would spend much of the century that followed conquering the rest of Africa.

In part, the prolonged life of this colonial adventure was because Napoleon had done so well in making it central to his legacy. Whilst France's star had dimmed in Europe, he had been galloping through deserts, seizing caravans laden with treasure and sacking exotic cities. He had then quit Egypt before the years of defeat set in and, like a victorious Roman consul returning from distant provinces, had returned as saviour and overturned an unpopular and corrupt republic. He thus converted his rash and costly adventure into the most beautiful and exotic steppingstone on his path to power.

This would be the way he would have his invasion remembered. Napoleon could then fashion Egypt into another column on that pantheon he dedicated to his own glory. This impressive temple was constantly added to in his own lifetime and he would bequeath it to a nation which had paid dearly for it. Still, over time, that nation would grow to love it and honour it as its own.

Whilst that monument was vast and impressive, it was built on bones. For all its grandeur as an idea, the invasion of Egypt had alone cost the lives of tens of thousands. Beneath that monument lay the dead and its shadow: the forgotten, the wounded and the mutilated. There were thousands like young Coquebert de Montbret who had died of the plague, or Detroye and Gerbaud, killed at the siege of Acre. And there were thousands like Jean Claude Vaxelaire of the 2nd Light Infantry who had been hit by a British musket ball in the ruins of Canope and lost his leg to gangrene in the ruins of a Napoleonic hospital. Most of him would eventually return to an indifferent France to live the rest of his life as an amputee:

> As I sat on a bench in order to rest I watched the people walking past and I grew angry at them seeing them strolling there, thinking that I, too had once done that and that now I was a cripple for the rest of my days.

Survivors like Vaxelaire had trickled back to France over five years, some welcomed, some barely acknowledged, some completely ignored. They propped up Napoleon's monument and the legend Napoleon was so successful in telling about himself and which others were so partial to believing. Napoleon's version of his adventure formed part of that legend and the narrative he advanced whilst stories like those of Vaxelaire, and the memories of all the forgotten and the obscure, were largely excluded from the record. The modest tales of these ordinary men could not compete in a world which was and is too dazzled by heroes. Yet, in many ways, their little glories can be far greater. Glories that, for once, speak less of victory or of triumph, but, instead, of overcoming want and hardship, or of the conquest of fear and despair. Then, when those battles are done, and the struggle ebbs away, there comes at last that final triumph, the simplest and most underrated of them all: being able to return home once again.

ANNEX I

Key Eyewitnesses

Antoine-Mathias Bonnefons, sergeant, Artificers
Pierre-François Xavier Bouchard, officer of Engineers
Louis-Joseph Bricard, second lieutenant, 4th Artillery, Pontonniers, attached
    to 9th Line
Pierre Louis Cailleux, lieutenant, 2nd Light
Antoine François Ernest Coquebert de Montbret, botanist
Nicolas-Philibert Desvernois, lieutenant, 7th Hussars
Jean-François Detroye, major of Engineers
Jean-Pierre Doguereau, artillery, aide-de-camp to General Dommartin
Charles François, quartermaster, 9th Line
Pierre-François-Jean-Baptiste Gerbaud de Malgane, from Limousin, 11th
    Line, then staff officer under General Vial
Jean-Baptiste Giraud, lieutenant (captain from early 1799), 2nd battalion,
    69th Line
Maurice Godet, captain, 21st Light
Grandjean, commissary
Jean-Baptiste Guillot, 25th Line
Jean-Baptiste Prosper Jollois, engineer
Élie Krettly, trumpeter in the Guides
Alexandre Lacorre, commissary
Jean-Anne-Alexandre Ladrix, 7th Hussars
Joseph Laporte, 1st battalion, 69th Line
Laval, lieutenant, 2nd battalion, 18th Line
François-Michel Lucet, 2nd Light
Étienne Louis Malus, captain, Engineers
Jean-Marie Merme, 18th Dragoons
Pierre-Jean-Baptiste Millet, 2nd Light
Jacques-François Miot, commissary
Captain Joseph-Marie Moiret, captain, 75th Line

Jean-Gabriel de Niello-Sargy, staff officer
Pierre de Pelleport, captain, 18th Line
André Peyrusse, paymaster then secretary to General Kléber
Henri-Joseph Redouté, Belgian natural history painter
Charles Richardot, lieutenant, 1st Horse Artillery, staff officer attached to
  Dommartin
Etienne Geoffroy Saint-Hilaire, zoologist
François-Etienne Sanglé-Ferrière, midshipman of the *Dubois* then signalman
  on the *Muiron*
Horace Say, geometrist
Pierre-Laurent-Marie Théviôtte, Engineers
Lieutenant Louis Thurman, lieutenant, Engineers
Jean Claude Vaxelaire, 2nd Light Infantry
Jean-Baptiste Vertray, second lieutenant, 9th Line
François Vigo-Roussillon, 32nd Line
Edouard de Villiers du Terrage, engineer

Bibliography

Eyewitness accounts by French participants

Note that Clément de La Jonquière's five-volume history, *L'expédition d'Égypte, 1798-1801*, published in Paris between 1899 and 1907, contains a number of eyewitness accounts of considerable interest (Belliard, Detroye, Durand, Lasalle, Leturcq, Savary, Théviôtte, etc). The *Correspondance de l'armée française en Egypte, interceptée par l'escadre de Nelson* (1798) is also a valuable source.

Anon [Horace Say]. *Bonaparte au Caire, ou Mémoires sur l'expédition de ce Générale en Egypte ... par un des Savans*. Paris, 1799.

Beauchamp, Alphonse de. *Mémoires secrets et inédits, pour servir à l'histoire contemporaine*, containing Niello Sargy, Jean Gabrielle de, *Mémoires sur l'expédition dÉgypte*. Paris, 1825.

Bernoyer, François. *Avec Bonaparte en Egypte et en Syrie, 1798-1800: 19 lettres inédites*. Paris, 1981.

Besancenet, Alfred de. *Un officier royaliste au service de la République: d'après les lettres inédites du général de Dommartin, 1786 à 1799*. Paris, 1876.

Bouchard, Pierre François Xavier. *Journal historique: La chute d'El-Arich*. Cairo, 1945.

Cailleux, Pierre Louis, 'Campagne d'Égypte et de Syrie' in *Carnet de la Sabretache*, 1931 and 1932.

Chanut, J. (ed.). *Campagne de Bonaparte en Égypte et en Syrie par un officier de la 32e demi-brigade*. Paris, 1832.

Chatton, Jean et Nicolas Leclère (ed.). *Cahiers de Vieux Soldats de la Révolution et de l'Empire*. Paris, 1903.

Dejuine, Noel. *La Campagne d'Egypte, 1798-1801: d'après les dessins inédits de Noel Dejuine du 20e Régiment de Dragons*. Pont-de-Briques, 1983.

Denon, Dominique Vivant. *Voyage dans la Basse et la Haute Égypte*. Paris, 1802.

Desvernois, Nicolas-Philibert. *Souvenirs militaires du baron Desvernois rédigés d'après les documents authentiques*. Paris, 1858.

Doguereau, Jean-Pierre. *Journal de l'Expédition d'Égypte*. Paris, 1904.

Dufriche-Desgenettes, René Nicolas. *Souvenirs d'un médecin de l'expédition d'Égypte*. Paris, 1893.

François, Charles. *Journal du Capitaine François (dit le Dromadaire d'Egypte)*. Paris, 1903.

Galland, Antoine. *Tableau d'Egypte*. Paris, 1804.

Geoffroy Saint-Hilaire, Etienne. *Lettres écrites d'Egypte*. Paris, 1901.

Giraud, Jean-Baptiste. *Le carnet de campagne du commandant Giraud*. Paris, 1898.

Hamelin, A. R. 'Douze ans de ma vie' in *Revue de Paris*, 1926.

Godet, Maurice. *Mémoires inedits et integraux du Capitaine Godet*. Online at http://assosehri.chez.com/labibliothequesc/m-moires-int-grales-du-capitaine-godet.pdf [accessed 16.02.2011].

Jollois, Prosper. *Journal d'un ingenieur attaché à l'expédition d'Égypte*. Paris, 1904.

Krettly, Elie. *Souvenirs historiques du Capitaine Krettly*. Paris, 1839.

Lacorre, Alexandre. *Journal inédit d'un commis aux vivres pendant l'expédition d'Égypte, voyage à Malte et en Égypte, expédition de Syrie*. Paris, 1852.

Ladrix, Alexandre. 'Lettres d'Alexandre Ladrix, Volontaire de l'an II' in *Carnet de la Sabretache* no. 303, 1926.

Laporte, Joseph, *Mon voyage en Egypte et en Syrie: Carnets d'un jeune soldat de Bonaparte*. Paris, 2007.

Larchey, L. (ed.). *Journal du canonnier Bricard, 1792-1802*. Paris, 1891.

Malus, Étienne Louis. *L'Agenda de Malus: souvenirs de l'expédition d'Égypte, 1798-1801*. Paris, 1892.

Mangerel, Maxime. *Le capitaine Gerbaud, 1773-1799*. Paris, 1910.

Merme, Jean-Marie. *Des pyramides à Moscou: souvenirs d'un soldat de Napoléon premier*. Moûtiers-Tarentaise, 2011.

Merreau, Commandant (ed.). *Journal d'un dragon d'Égypte* [anonymous officer, 14th Dragoons]. Paris, 1899.

Millet, Pierre. *Le Chasseur Pierre Millet, Souvenirs de la Campagne d'Égypte 1798-1801*. Paris, 1903.

Miot, Jean-François. *Mémoires pour servir à l'histoire des expéditions en Égypte et en Syrie*. Paris, 1814.

Moiret, Joseph Marie. *Mémoires sur l'expédition d'Égypte*. Paris, 1984.

Monge, Gaspard. *La correspondance inédite du géomètre Gaspard Monge (1746-1818)*. Online at http://eman-archives.org/monge/collections/show/12 [accessed 25.04.2019].

Morand, Charles-Antoine. *Correspondance et carnet de route d'un franc-comtois, le général Charles-Antoine Morand*. Paris, 1998.

Pélissier L.-G. (ed.). 'Un soldat d'Italie et d'Égypte' [Antoine Bonnefons] in *Carnet de la Sabretache* no. 121, 1903.

Pelleport, Pierre de. *Souvenirs Militaires et Intimes du Général Vicomte de Pelleport*. Paris, 1857.

Peyrusse, André. *Expéditions de Malte, d'Égypte et de Syrie: correspondance, 1798-1801*. Paris, 2010.

Redouté, Henri-Joseph. 'L'Égypte en 1798' in *La Revue politique et littéraire*, 1895.

Richardot, Charles. *Relation de la campagne de Syrie, spécialement des sièges de Jaffa et de Saint-Jean-d'Acre, par un officier d'artillerie de l'armée d'Orient*. Paris, 1839.

Sangle-Ferriere, François-Etienne. *Souvenirs de l'expédition d'Égypte*. Paris, 1998.

Skalkowski, Adam. *Les Polonais en Egypte* [Sulkowski]. Krakow, 1910.

Thurman, Louis-George-Ignace. *Bonaparte en Égypte, souvenirs publiés avec préface et appendices par le comte Fleury*. Paris, 1902.

Vaxelaire, J. C. *Mémoires d'un vétéran de l'ancienne armée (1791-1800) siège de Mayence, pacification de la Vendée, campagne d'Égypte*. Paris, 1900.

Vertray, Jean-Baptiste. *L'armée française en Égypte, 1798-1801: journal d'un officier de l'Armée d'Égypte*. Paris, 1883.

Vigo-Roussillon, François. 'Fragmens des Mémoires militaires du colonel Vigo-Roussillon' in *Revue des Deux Mondes* no. 100, 1890.

Villiers-Terrage, Etienne. *Journal et souvenirs sur l'expédition d'Égypte*. Paris, 1899.

Wiet, Gaston (ed,). *Deux mémoires inédits sur l'expédition d'Egypte* [Lieutenant Laval and commissary Grandjean] in *Le Revue du Caire*, 1941.

Local accounts of the French occupation

Jabarti, Abd al-Rahman al. *Journal d'un notable du Caire durant l'expédition française: 1798-1801*. Paris, 1979.

Sayigh, Fathallah. *Le Désert et la gloire: les mémoires d'un agent syrien de Napoléon*. Paris, 1991.

El-Turk, Niqula. *Histoire de l'expédition française en Egypte*. Paris, 1839.

Further reading

Cole, Juan. *Napoleon's Egypt: Invading the Middle East*. London, 2007.

Collective. *La Campagne d'Egypte, 1798-1801: Mythes et réalités, actes du colloque*. Paris, 1998.

Fierro, Alfred. *Bibliographie critique des Mémoires sur la Révolution écrits ou traduits en Français*. Paris, 1988.

Laurens, Henry. *L'Expédition d'Egypte (1798-1801)*. Paris, 1997.

Martin, Yves. *The French Army of the Orient 1798-1801: Napoleon's beloved 'Egyptians'*. Warwick, 2017.

Meulenaere, Philippe de. *Bibliographie raisonnée des témoignages oculaires imprimés de l'expédition d'Egypte*. Paris, 1993.

Rigault, Georges. *L'inventaire des états de services des officiers de l'Armée d'Egypte*. Paris, 1911.

Index